TRENDS IN ATTENTION DEFICIT HYPERACTIVITY DISORDER RESEARCH

TRENDS IN ATTENTION DEFICIT HYPERACTIVITY DISORDER RESEARCH

MARVIN C. SHRINER
EDITOR

Nova Biomedical Books
New York

For permission to use material from this book please contact us:
Telephone 631-231-7269; Fax 631-231-8175
Web Site: http://www.novapublishers.com

LIBRARY OF CONGRESS CATALOGING-IN-PUBLICATION DATA

Trends in Attention deficit hyperactivity disorder / Marvin C. Shriner (editor).
p. ; cm.
Includes bibliographical references and index.
ISBN-1-60021-321-9
1. Attention-deficit hyperactivity disorder. I. Shriner, Marvin C.
[DNLM: 1. Trends in Attention Deficit Disorder with Hyperactivity.
WS 350.8.A8 A88303 2006]
RJ506.H9A925 2006
618.92'8589--dc22

2006020529

Published by Nova Science Publishers, Inc. ✢ New York

CONTENTS

PREFACE

ADHD is characterized by learning and behavioral problems including short attention span, impulsivity, hyperactivity and impairments in perceptual, language and motor skills. Between 4-10% of school-age children are believed to have it with boys outnumbering girls 2-3 to one. An adult form is now recognized. The symptoms of Attention Deficit Disorder are caused by a neurological dysfunction within the brain. The underlying physiological mechanism which causes Attention Deficit Disorder is still not thoroughly understood and remains under intense scientific study. It is presumed that brain chemistry is out of balance and that specific chemicals called neurotransmitters may be lacking in individuals with Attention Deficit Disorder. Leading-edge research from around the world is presented in this new book.

Chapter I - Adult ADHD is a condition that affects between 1-8% of the adult population. The disorder has gained wider recognition over the last few decades as a result of long-term studies that indicate the continuation of ADHD symptoms across the lifespan. This recognition has resulted in more adults requesting assessment and treatment. Consistent with ADHD management for children, medication is the primary intervention for adults, and psychological interventions have been neglected. The first section of this chapter will examine the reasons for the neglect of psychological approaches to adult ADHD. It will be argued that a cognitive remediation approach may be useful for the management of the cognitive impairments associated with adult ADHD. The second section of the chapter will describe two randomised-controlled studies that evaluated the efficacy of a cognitive remediation approach to treatment. Study one examined a cognitive remediation program delivered in an intensive format with eight weekly sessions. Study two examined the same program delivered in a minimal contact form. Both interventions resulted in significant and immediate improvements in ADHD symptom expression, organisational skills, self-esteem and anger management, when compared to controls. Following the intensive program, improvements in ADHD symptom expression, organisational skills, self-esteem and trait anger continued one year post-treatment. Finally, the implications of these findings for the management of adult ADHD are considered.

Chapter III - Since the initial demonstration of high heritability for attention deficit hyperactivity disorder (ADHD), a large number of genetic studies have been published. Quantitative genetic studies, such as twin studies, have moved beyond the simple estimation of heritability and address more complex multivariate questions, such as the etiology of co-occurrence between ADHD and other disorders and traits. Molecular genetic studies have obtained preliminary evidence for several genes that are likely to be implicated in the disorder.

The success of the genetic research opens many questions regarding the functionality of the genes that contribute to ADHD. A key level of functionality is that of psychological processes. Much progress has been made in cognitive-experimental research on ADHD, but a consensus is yet to emerge on the key underlying processes. Part of the difficulty in specifying the key processes relates to the inconsistency that often characterises the performance of children with ADHD on cognitive tasks. Within-task manipulations with variables such as incentives often influence whether or not a cognitive 'deficit' is observed. Such observations need to be incorporated within the theoretical frameworks.

An interdisciplinary approach, which combines cognitive, quantitative genetic and molecular genetic approaches, holds promise for progress in identifying causal pathways in ADHD. Quantitative genetic analyses can indicate which candidate endophenotypes are heritable and therefore candidates for molecular genetic analyses. Multivariate quantitative genetic analyses address whether the same or different sets of genes influence different candidate endophenotypes, helping further to define psychological theory, as well as informing molecular genetic analyses. Yet further methodological approaches, such as environmental measures that may help capture gene-environment interactions or electrophysiological measures, could be incorporated to provide more detailed information on the underlying processes.

Here we provide a selective review of recent studies that are particularly informative on these issues, as well as summarising our own recent research on these topics.

Chapter IV - It has been proposed that children with conduct problems who also show symptoms of hyperactivity, impulsivity, and inattention constitute a unique subgroup who may be considered "fledgling psychopaths". This study was designed to test the predictions implied by the fledgling psychopath hypothesis. In the study, levels of psychopathy and aggression were compared in four groups of adolescent males (n = 129): three clinical samples and one non-diagnosed community sample. The first clinical sample comprised boys with conduct disorder who had also been diagnosed with attention deficit/hyperactivity disorder. The second and third clinical samples comprised boys diagnosed either with attention deficit/hyperactivity disorder or conduct disorder only. In general, results of group comparison and multiple regression analyses did not support the predictions implied by the fledgling psychopath hypothesis. Implications for the status of the hypothesis and for the measurement of psychopathy in adolescent populations are discussed.

Chapter V – Background: Undetected attention deficit hyperactivity disorder (ADHD) can result in a range of behavioural disturbances which create a burden for mental health, social and educational services when it persists into adulthood. Afflicted individuals do not maximize their academic or indeed intellectual potential and are more likely to have mood disorders and substance use related disorders in adulthood. Early recognition and intervention is therefore very important and serves as a preventive strategy to diminish the risk of behavioural dysfunction in adulthood.

Methods: Children referred to the courts for being out of control were assessed for a range of psychopathological symptoms and investigated for the presence of ADHD symptoms. They were then compared with an age and gender matched group of healthy secondary school students. Differences in ADHD symptoms and course were then compared by gender. Statistical analysis was then undertaken using correlation and significance testing. Retrospective analysis was also undertaken on a cohort of adult ADHD patients to determine the trajectory of their lives through adolescence to determine the points at which intervention could have occurred

Results: The children referred to the courts were much more likely to have ADHD symptoms though none of them had been previously diagnosed. These symptoms had contributed to poor academic performance and behavioural symptoms at home. They were also more likely to come from disruptive family backgrounds. The females were more likely to have had sexual experience and they were more likely to have initiated substance use.

A family history of criminal justice system contact also differentiated those with ADHD symptoms. Adults with ADHD underperformed or were excluded from school and initiated substance use and excessive gambling as early signs of adolescent dysfunction.

Discussion/Conclusion: The presence of unrecognized ADHD symptoms does increase the risk of major behavioural problems in early adolescence which are likely to persist into adulthood if they remain untreated. There is some indication that the symptom course may be different in females compared to males. There are associations with a disruptive upbringing suggesting that this may also contribute to the evolution of the disorder or perhaps to its lack of recognition. ADHD is particularly associated with substance use and impulsivity.

In: Attention Deficit Hyperactivity Disorder
Editor: Marvin C. Shriner, pp. 1-45 ISBN: 1-60021 321-9

Chapter I

A Cognitive Remediation Approach to the Management of Attention Deficit Hyperactivity Disorder (ADHD) in Adulthood

Caroline S. Stevenson[1] *and Richard J. Stevenson**

NSW Institute of Psychiatry, Locked Bag 7118, Parramatta BC, NSW 2150, Australia

*Department of Psychology, Macquarie University, NSW2109, Australia

Abstract

Adult ADHD is a condition that affects between 1-8% of the adult population. The disorder has gained wider recognition over the last few decades as a result of long-term studies that indicate the continuation of ADHD symptoms across the lifespan. This recognition has resulted in more adults requesting assessment and treatment. Consistent with ADHD management for children, medication is the primary intervention for adults, and psychological interventions have been neglected. The first section of this chapter will examine the reasons for the neglect of psychological approaches to adult ADHD. It will be argued that a cognitive remediation approach maybe useful for the management of the cognitive impairments associated with adult ADHD. The second section of the chapter will describe two randomised-controlled studies that evaluated the efficacy of a cognitive remediation approach to treatment. Study one examined a cognitive remediation program delivered in an intensive format with eight weekly sessions. Study two examined the same program delivered in a minimal contact form. Both interventions resulted in significant and immediate improvements in ADHD symptom expression, organisational skills, self-esteem and anger management, when compared to controls. Following the

[1] Communicating author – NSW Institute of Psychiatry, Locked Bag 7118, Parramatta BC, NSW 2150, Australia (email:caroline.stevenson@nswiop.nsw.edu.au; Phone: 2-9840-3833)

intensive program, improvements in ADHD symptom expression, organisational skills, self-esteem and trait anger continued one year post-treatment. Finally, the implications of these findings for the management of adult ADHD are considered.

Part A: Approaches to the Management of Adult ADHD

Introduction

Attention Deficit Hyperactivity Disorder (ADHD) is considered to be a neurobiological condition characterised by symptoms of inattention, hyperactivity and impulsivity (Nadeau, 1995). It has long been recognised as a disorder of childhood with reports in the literature as early as 1902 (Still, 1902). The acceptance of ADHD continuing into adulthood has occurred as a result of several longitudinal studies, all of which demonstrate its continuity (e.g. Borland and Heckman. 1976; Gittelman, Mannuzza, Shenker and Bongura, 1985; Mannuzza, Gittelman-Klein and Addalli, 1991; Mannuzza, Klein, Bessler, Malloy and LaPadula, 1998; Mannuzza, Klein, Bonagura, Malloy, Giampino and Addalli, 1991; Weiss and Hechtman, 1986; Weiss, Hechtman and Perlman, 1978; Weiss, Hechtman, Perlman Hopkins and Wener, 1979; Weiss, Hechtman, Milroy and Perlman, 1985; Weiss, Minde, Werry, Douglas and Nemeth, 1971). It is estimated that somewhere between 4-66% of children diagnosed with ADHD continue to have lifelong symptoms (Barkley, Fischer, Smallish and Fletcher, 2004; Weiss and Hechtman, 1993).

Adults who present for assessment and treatment typically have the same symptoms as children but express their symptoms in different ways. For example, hyperactivity in adults is expressed as chronic restlessness and fidgeting, impulsiveness as impatience and 'not suffering fools gladly', and inattention as problems with staying focussed, and difficulties in planning and organising. Many adults who present for treatment complain of chronic job failure, difficulties maintaining relationships, low self esteem, poor frustration tolerance, difficulties coping with stress, poor organisational skills and poor time management (Weiss and Weiss, 2004). All of these ADHD related difficulties clearly impair an adult's ability to function effectively. Thus it is important to consider how to intervene to help adults overcome these debilitating symptoms and secondary problems.

When considering how to treat adult ADHD, the most appropriate place to start is to examine how children with the condition are treated. The rationale for this being that if adult ADHD is a continuation of the childhood condition, then the same treatments might be effective.

Stimulant Medication

The primary and most successful treatment for child ADHD has been stimulant medication. Stimulants (dexedrine, dexamphetamine, methylphenidate, adderall etc) have been demonstrated in randomised controlled trials to reduce primary symptoms of child

ADHD in approx. 85% of children (Spencer, Biederman, Wilens, Harding, O'Donnell and Griffin, 1996). The primary benefits being in improved concentration and reduced hyperactivity. Thus one would anticipate benefits from stimulant medication for adults with ADHD too.

Stimulant medication as an intervention for adult ADHD has been examined in a small number of clinical trials. A Meta-analysis of adult studies of methylphenidate suggests that about 75% of adults gain some benefit from stimulants (Farone, Spencer, Aleardi, Paganot and Biederman, 2004). While medication is helpful, there are a sub-group of non-responders, and many adults do not want to take medication and some adults want to build on the benefits of medication by learning new coping strategies. These considerations all point to the need for other interventions. Indeed the National Health and Medical Research Council (NHMRC, 1996) guidelines for the management of ADHD recommend that medication should not be used alone but in conjunction with psychological approaches. Inevitably, this leads to the question of what type of psychological intervention will assist adults in managing their symptoms. Yet again, the logical place to look for answers to this question is to consider what psychological interventions have been helpful for children with ADHD.

Psychological Interventions for Children with ADHD

Psychological interventions have been extensively explored for child ADHD. It is important to thoroughly review this literature because, as we noted above, child and adult ADHD both produce similar cognitive deficits, so it might be expected that similar strategies would be helpful for both groups. However, as we describe further below cognitive strategies have been of limited success for children and possible explanations for this need to be considered. This is especially so if a similar approach is to be trialled with adults. Two principal psychological approaches have been examined for child ADHD; cognitive training and social skills training. Both of these approaches have been tried with and without medication, and we review this literature first. We then examine why they have not been more successful.

Cognitive Training

Cognitive training (CT) is a term used to describe psychological strategies taught to children to remediate problems of inattention and impulsivity. The first CT strategy evaluated for child ADHD was self-instructional training (SIT). SIT is a procedure that teaches the use of internalised speech as a method of behaviour control. SIT was first developed to improve the self-control of impulsive children (Meichenbaum and Goodman, 1971) and was then later used with child ADHD. Despite initial success for child ADHD, SIT has had limited utility because it focuses on only one component of problematic ADHD behaviour. Consequently, 'multi-push' packages, which have included a range of cognitive strategies, were developed for child ADHD.

Douglas, Parry, Marton and Garson (1976) were among the first to evaluate a multi-push approach to child ADHD, which included self-verbalisation, modelling, self-monitoring and self-reinforcement. These authors recruited boys aged between six and ten years old who scored one and a half standard deviations above the mean on either the teacher or parent Conners Rating Scale (Conners, 1973) and who had a mean latency on the Matching Familiar Figure Test (MFFT) below 10 seconds. Eighteen boys were recruited for the Cognitive Training (CT) group and 11 boys for the control group. The CT group received 24, one-hour sessions of training over a three month period. To generalise the programme both parents and teachers were trained and taught how to encourage skills use. Outcome was measured using a battery of cognitive tests, behavioural rating scales and achievement tests. Compared with controls, the CT group improved on a range of measures including the MFFT, the Bender-Gestalt Test (Bender, 1938) and Listening Comprehension (Durrell, 1955). These improvements were maintained at a three-month follow-up. However, no noticeable improvements were found on behaviour rating scales. Consistent with Moore and Cole (1978) the authors explained their results by the intervention's focus on internal thought processes, rather than outwardly observable behaviour. Thus the authors suggest a change in behaviour rating scales would not necessarily be expected.

CT programmes were also evaluated for children with ADHD as an adjunct to medication. This was important for a number of reasons, all of which might suggest enhanced functioning if CT were combined with medication. First, CT might make it possible to reduce dosages of medication. Second, medication might increase the benefits of CT. Third, CT and medication might target different responses in the same situation (i.e., the medication might curb impulsiveness and the CT strategies improve the ability to focus attention).

One of the earliest studies to examine the efficacy of CT and medication was conducted by Brown (1980). In this study, children between the ages of nine and 13 years old were recruited from educational centres for children unable to cope in regular school placements. Children who scored two standard deviations above the mean on the Matching Familiar Figures Test (MFFT) were selected. The final sample included 120 children who were either medicated or non-medicated. Children were randomly assigned to one of three groups: a SIT group, a modelling group or a control group. The SIT group was taught a 'stop, look, listen, and think strategy' whereas the modelling group observed a seven-minute video on reflective behaviour. Outcome was assessed using the MFFT, the Coding subtest from the Weschler Intelligence Scale for Children and a copy task. For both training groups (SIT and modelling) only the medicated participants showed improvements. This result indicates either that a combination of CT and medication is the best intervention for hyperactive-impulsive children or that medication may have produced most of the therapeutic response. This result should be considered with some caution, as participants were not randomised and the medicated group demonstrated worse scores on pre-test measures.

The relative effectiveness of CT and medication were also evaluated for a younger age group. Cohen, Sullivan, Minde, Novack and Helwig (1981) recruited hyperactive kindergarten children (n=25) who had scores one and a half standard deviations above the mean on the Conners Abbreviated Teacher Rating Scale (Goyette, Conners and Ulrich, 1978). The children were randomly assigned to one of four groups: CT alone, medication alone, combined CT with medication, or a non-treatment group. The CT intervention was a multi-push programme along the lines of Douglas et al. (1976) and included 20, one-hour sessions. Generalisation was promoted by having both parents and teachers observe training sessions and thereafter reinforce the procedures at home and school. Outcome was assessed on a battery of measures including cognitive tests and two child-rating scales; one of self-concept and the other of locus of control. All groups including the non-treatment group showed significant improvements across the measures and these were maintained one year later. The authors readily acknowledge that maturational effect may have accounted for the improvements observed. In addition, the authors suggest that kindergarten children may not be at an appropriate developmental level to benefit from skills training.

Brown, Wynne and Medennis (1985) evaluated the efficacy of CT alone, medication alone (methylphenidate), a combination of CT and medication, and no treatment. Hyperactive boys (6-11 years old) were randomly assigned to the treatment groups but not to the non-treatment group for ethical reasons. CT groups received 24, one-hour individual sessions during which they were taught the strategies from the Douglas et al. (1976) study. Training was completed using educational tasks. Outcome was measured using a battery of tests including the Children's Checking Task (Keogh and Margolis, 1976), the concentration factor of the Weschler Intelligence Scale for Children-Revised, the Matching Familiar Figure Test and the Children's Embedded Figures Test (Karp and Konstadt, 1963), together with behaviour ratings and achievement tests. None of the children assigned to medication groups were medicated at the pre-treatment assessment, but at all subsequent assessments they were medicated. The medication only group significantly improved on the combined battery of measures when compared to CT or no treatment. Combined treatment also produced improvements on the complete battery with the exception of the academic measures. CT alone produced selected improvements on specific cognitive tests. CT was not as good as medication and the combination of CT with medication was found to be no better than medication alone. These results were disappointing as they suggest that medication may be the key ingredient for behaviour and cognitive change.

In a second study by the same group, initial findings were replicated (Brown, Borden, Wynne, Schleser and Clingerman, 1986). Thirty-five children (5 -13 years old) who met DSM III criteria for ADHD were recruited. Children were randomly assigned to one of four groups: a methylphenidate group, an attention control group, a CT group or a placebo group. The CT was a multi-push package administered in 22, one-hour sessions. The attention control also attended 22, one-hour sessions and were given equivalent exposure to a therapist and CT training material. The same cognitive battery was used as in the previous study (Brown et al., 1985); however for post-testing, children were not medicated. Findings suggested that CT provided no additional benefit over and above medication. Medication alone effects did not persist when medication was withdrawn and training with CT did not improve scores from pre-test levels when medication was withdrawn (possibly due to state dependent learning). Effects of CT alone were weak. The authors suggest cognitive immaturity may play a role in the poor efficacy of CT for these children. Moreover, the issue of whether children were able to acquire the skills, or acquired them but did not use them, was not addressed.

The efficacy of CT as an adjunct to medication has been further examined by Abikoff and Gittelman (1985). These authors recruited children (n=48) between six and 12 years old who were pervasively hyperactive, who had high scores on the Conners' Teacher Rating Scale (Conners, 1973) and who were on a maintenance dose of stimulant medication. Children were assigned to either a CT group, an attention control group, or a medication alone group for 16 weeks. The CT intervention was administered as described in Douglas et al. (1976). Asking parents to observe two of the training sessions and to thereafter praise reflective strategies when they observed their children using them ensured generalisation of the CT strategies. Outcome was assessed on a battery of measures including parent and teacher reports, achievement tests and cognitive tests. Combined CT and medication treatment was not found to significantly improve performance across the measures. Moreover, there was virtually no evidence for the efficacy of CT over and above that of medication. The authors suggest this finding may be explained by a ceiling effect produced by the medication so that CT effects were masked.

Social Skills Training

A general disillusionment with the CT approach lead to the investigation of alternative methods to manage the symptoms of child ADHD. Social skills training (SST) was the main approach examined because it targeted areas that were not so successfully treated by medication such as interpersonal skills and self-evaluation techniques.

One of the earliest studies to investigate a SST programme examined the efficacy of self-evaluation training (Hinshaw, Henker and Whalen, 1984a). Self-evaluation training intended to reduce impulsive responding by requiring children to stop periodically and evaluate their performance. Hinshaw et al. (1984a) examined the effects of self-reinforcement on the social behaviour of 24 ADHD boys (aged 8-13 years) participating in a summer school research project. All the boys had received a primary diagnosis of ADHD from a treating physician and had been on medication for at least three months. Boys were assigned to one of four conditions: first to a methylphenidate or placebo group; then these groups were sub-divided into groups receiving reinforced self-evaluation (RSE) or extrinsic reinforcement (ER) alone. Over a four-week period, boys in the RSE group were trained to monitor their behaviour, compare it to criterion and also to match their own behaviour ratings with an independent person who rated their behaviour. The ER group was on a token economy programme where they were awarded points that could be exchanged for privileges. Outcome was assessed by observation of the boys' positive and negative social behaviour over a two-day period. The combination of RSE and medication was found to be the most effective intervention. This combination reduced negative social behaviours to below the level of controls. Strengths of this study are that the children were taught RSE during the course of every day activities and that behaviour change was carefully monitored over the course of several days. There are nonetheless limitations to the study: information about maintenance and generalisation of the skills was not obtained.

In a separate study, Hinshaw, Henker and Whalen (1984b) examined the effects of SST and methylphenidate on anger control. In this study, 24 boys between the ages of eight and 13 years old with a primary diagnosis of ADHD and continuous use of medication for at least three months were recruited. All participants received two weeks training in SIT and problem solving. Then boys were assigned to either a medication or placebo group; these groups were further sub-divided so that half the boys in each condition (medication or placebo) were assigned to either a further cognitive component or a control condition. The further cognitive component emphasised interpersonal problem solving and stress inoculation procedures. Outcome was assessed by observation of behaviour. The groups (both medicated and non-medicated) that received further cognitive training demonstrated higher ratings of self-control and better coping skills. Generalisation across time and setting was not evaluated.

Hinshaw, Buhrmester and Heller (1989) investigated whether medication could enhance treatment response following an anger management programme. Twenty-four boys (6-12 years old) who had a primary diagnosis of ADHD confirmed by a diagnostic interview and rating scales and who were on maintenance doses of stimulant medication were recruited. All received cognitive training in anger management. At post-training assessment, boys were randomly assigned to a placebo condition or to a medication condition that received a 0.6mg/kg dose of methylphenidate. Outcome was assessed by observation of the boy's response to verbal provocation in role-play situations. A moderate dose of methylphenidate was shown to enhance self-control, reduce retaliation and increase coping with verbal provocation. Medication was only manipulated for the post treatment assessment and its role in actually learning the skills was not explored. Nonetheless, the medication appeared to improve participants' ability to use the trained skills when compared with the placebo group. This finding supports the idea that a combination of medication and skills training may produce benefits over that of medication alone.

Two studies have investigated the role of more general social skills training programme (Frankel, Myatt, Cantwell and Feinberg, 1997; Pffifner and McBurnett, 1997). Important aspects of these studies are the inclusion of methods to ensure the maintenance and generalisation of skills. Frankel et al. (1997) recruited 35 children with ADHD diagnosed using DSM IIIR criteria and who were receiving medication and 14 children without ADHD, to participate in a 12-week outpatient treatment programme. These participants were also compared with 12 ADHD and 12 Non-ADHD children on a waiting list. The SST was an eight-week programme with one session per week. It included components on conversational techniques, how to make friends, negotiation and persuasion techniques, and making fun of teasing and how to handle confrontation. Parents attended sessions at the same time as their children and were trained in how to reinforce the skills at home. Outcome was measured by the Social Skills Rating System (Gresham and Elliott, 1990) completed by parents and by the Pupil Evaluation Inventory (Pekarik, Prinz, Liebert, Weintraub and Neil, 1976) completed by teachers. Participants with ADHD showed improvements comparable with that of those children without ADHD on all teacher and parent measures of peer adjustment and social skills. The authors suggest that the combination of medication and SST with a parent generalisation component may be the best intervention for child ADHD. However, a follow-up was not included and the results have yet to be replicated so these preliminary results should be interpreted with some caution.

A second SST study (Pffifner and McBurnett, 1997) similar to the Frankel et al. (1997) included a follow up assessment. In this study, twenty-seven children (8-10 years old) who met DSM IIIR criteria for ADHD and had disturbed peer relationships were recruited. Parents were asked to maintain the children on their current medication regime (on or off medication). Children were randomised to one of three groups: an SST group with parent training (SST-PG), a SST alone group, or a waiting list group. The SST was conducted over the course of eight weeks and had six modules: development of sportsmanship, accepting consequences, assertiveness, ignoring provocation, problem solving and recognising feelings. In the SST-PG, parents attended eight sessions at the same time as their children. In these sessions, parents were taught how to reinforce the use of the social skills. Parents were also provided with social skills handouts for their sons/daughters class teacher. Outcome was assessed by evaluating social skills use and social skills knowledge by the child as well as by symptom change and satisfaction with the programme. Both SST groups (with and without parent training) improved their social skills knowledge and showed improvements in parent reports of their social interaction and home behaviour. These improvements were maintained four months post treatment. Parent training did not augment treatment effects. However, the non-PG group was kept informed about the SST by handouts so it is possible that they were able to reinforce the skills in the same ways as those parents who attended the group. An important factor for generalisation may thus be parent involvement.

One of the major problems with both CT and SST studies has been the attempt to answer long-term questions with short-term studies. To overcome this problem long term studies are required. One such study is reviewed here (and its follow-up). It examined the efficacy of an individualised multi-modal approach for child ADHD (Satterfield, Satterfield and Cantwell, 1980 and 1981). Individualised treatment plans were developed for over 100 children between the ages of six and 12. Components such as medication, family therapy, academic skills training and CT were included in the treatment packages.

Two years after recruitment, treatment effects were examined for 61 children who continued to be treated (Satterfield et al., 1980). These children had excellent outcomes: primary ADHD symptoms were significantly reduced, the children self reported improved peer relationships and they were not as far behind in their school work. These results were encouraging and implied that an individualised long-term approach may be important in producing good outcomes for child ADHD.

The effect of duration of treatment was later examined. Satterfield et al. (1981) followed-up all the children recruited in their initial study, three years after the children had enrolled. They compared children who had followed their individualised plan for nine months (n=44) with those who had continued for 34.7 months (n=56). There were no differences between the groups on initial measures. However at the three-year follow-up, the group who had more treatment showed the greatest improvements on parent and teacher ratings, school adjustment, achievement tests and global ratings. Obviously, one problem with the study is that it is difficult to know what the effective components of the package were. Nonetheless, it suggests that a comprehensive individualised treatment may produce good treatment outcomes. Caution is, however, required in interpreting this result, as the study was not controlled.

The National Institute of Mental Health study known as the Mutimodal treatment study for children (MTA) is considered the landmark study on treatment of childhood ADHD in the literature (Richters, Arnold, Jensen, Abikoff, Conners, Greenhill, Hechtman, Hinshaw, Pelham, and Swanson, 1995). The main purpose of this large trial was to compare the efficacy of behavioural treatment (BT), medication management (MM), combined behavioural and medication management (COM) and a community treatment by own choice comparison group (CC). Children between the age of 7-9 years of age were recruited from a large number of centres and randomly assigned to one of the treatment groups. After 14 months of intervention, it was found that all groups improved but the best outcomes were achieved by MM and COM (MTA, 1999). This study is one of the largest treatment outcome studies reported. Nonetheless, there are criticisms of the study. The first of these is that the BT was not tailored to the needs of the children (Green and Ablon, 2001). The second is that the BT program was very intensive and does not equate with how this type of intervention would be implemented in clinical practice.

Given these very mixed and inconclusive results is there an argument for trialling psychological based interventions with adults? Adults obviously differ from children in many ways, and the key differences likely to be relevant here are: (1) adults tend to self refer; (2) adults tend to be highly motivated and be ready for change; (3) adults have reached cognitive maturity; and (4) more adults do not respond to stimulant medication. So is there any support for trialling a psychological intervention on adults with cognitive impairments? To answer this question two further areas of the literature are explored. First, trials of psychological interventions for adults with mild brain injury, as many of the cognitive deficits of this group are similar to those that occur in ADHD. Second, the emerging literature on psychological interventions for adults with ADHD.

Psychological interventions for adults with mild brain injury

Two distinct types of cognitive techniques are described in the adult brain injury literature: re-stimulation approaches and compensatory approaches (Goodwin and Bolton, 1991). Re-stimulation approaches aim to promote recovery of function by repeated practice on specific tasks (Ben-Yishay and Diller, 1993), whereas compensatory approaches aim to circumvent deficits by capitalising on other, intact abilities. Only a small number of studies have reported using either of these approaches, probably reflecting the difficulties of recruiting brain-injured participants and controlling for natural recovery post-injury.

Studies evaluating the efficacy of attention remediation techniques have mainly appeared in the last two decades. The majority of these studies have examined the efficacy of computerised attention training programmes that aim to re-stimulate functioning. In addition, one study has examined the efficacy of self-instructional training (SIT); an approach previously used with child ADHD. These studies are reviewed first.

Computerised attention training programmes aim to re-train aspects of attention (sustained, divided, etc) by repeated practice on computer tasks. Typical attention tasks are REACT and SEARCH. REACT is a reaction time task where the user is required to detect visual stimuli appearing from the sides of the screen. To stop stimuli crossing the screen the space bar is pressed. Improved attention is indicated by reduced reaction time. SEARCH is a visual search task where users are required to search among an array of shapes for one that matches a target stimulus in the centre of the screen. Improved attention is indicated by reduced search time and reduced errors.

A number of studies have examined the efficacy of computerised attention training programmes for brain-injured adults. Sohlberg and Mateer (1987) were among the first to evaluate such an approach. They found brain-injured adults who received computerised attention training significantly improved post-intervention on cognitive testing. This finding has been replicated (Gray and Robertson, 1989). However, other authors have found that when recovery and practice are controlled for there is little additional benefit to be gained from computerised attention training (Nieman, Ruff and Baser, 1990; Ponsford and Kinsella, 1988). Moreover, there is no evidence that specific improvement following computerised attention training translate into improved day-to-day functioning. Consequently, it has been proposed that compensatory strategies may be more useful for overcoming attention deficits (Nieman, Ruff and Baser, 1990; Ponsford and Kinsella, 1988).

Only one case study has examined a compensatory approach to remediate attention deficits (Webster and Scott, 1983). In this study, the self-instructional technique (SIT) as developed by Meichenbaum was taught. HD a 24-year-old unemployed man who had a closed head injury was selected for the study. Neuropsychological evaluation showed evidence of both memory and attention impairments. Training involved 11 sessions of SIT, listening strategies and practice in asking for instruction repetition when attention had strayed. Outcome was assessed using the Story Memory Test (Heaton, Chelune, and Lehman, 1978). Scores on this measure significantly improved post-treatment. HD also reported that he had generalised the strategies himself to improve reading and his sexual enjoyment. At a 16-month follow-up, these improvements were maintained. This case study suggests efficacy for a cognitive remediation compensatory approach. However, the study needs to be replicated with a larger sample in a randomised-controlled trial.

There are a small number of studies that have examined the remediation of executive functions. An early case study evaluated the efficacy of a programme to reduce anger and impulsivity in a young head injured man (Lira, Carne and Marni, 1983). This intervention included twelve, 30-minute sessions of self-instructional training (SIT), challenging negative self talk and relaxation training. Following the intervention, anger outbursts reduced from a baseline level of over two outbursts per week to their elimination, post-treatment. This improvement was maintained at a five-month follow-up. While this case study shows promise of a very effective intervention, it has never been replicated.

A further case study has examined the role of compensatory strategies to remediate planning difficulties (Cicerone and Woods, 1987). A young man, who had sustained a closed head injury, was recruited for the study. The intervention involved 16, one-hour sessions of training in self-verbalisation starting with a talk aloud strategy and fading to a sub-vocal strategy together with problem solving techniques. Outcome was assessed by the Tinker Toy Test (Lezak, 1982), WISC-R Mazes, selected subtests from the Weschler Adult Intelligence Scale-Revised (WAIS-R: Weschler, 1981) and on ratings of 'off task' behaviour. Significant improvements were found on the Tinker Toy Test but changes were not found on the other cognitive measures. Training was later included to teach application of the strategies to real life situations. According to anecdotal reports obtained from family members improvements were evident in day-to-day functioning. Again, while this case study shows promise it has not been replicated.

Only one controlled study has examined the remediation of executive deficits (Freeman, Mittenberg, Dicowden and Bat Ami, 1992). These authors examined the efficacy of a combined memory and executive function programme. Twelve participants were assigned to either the intervention group (n=6) or a non-treatment control (n=6). Groups were matched on pre-test cognitive test scores. The intervention involved six hours of training weekly, over two and a half weeks. Training included: note taking, self monitoring, stop and think self verbalisations, restating events in one's own words and the use of imagery. Outcome was assessed on a paragraph memory task. When compared with the control group, significant improvements were observed in the treatment group. Generalisation and maintenance of skills were not examined so it is difficult to interpret the clinical meaningfulness of this result. However, the findings suggest that the general approach may warrant further investigation.

The majority of adult brain injury studies have examined short interventions and conducted follow-up evaluations after a brief period. However, one long-term comprehensive programme has been reported (Scherzer, 1986). This 30-week intervention aimed to remediate a broad range of cognitive deficits. It included components on cognitive and perceptual remediation, problem solving, counselling, exercise, relaxation, social skills and pre-vocational training. Over a three-year period, 32 adults with severe brain injury were recruited into the evaluation study. Outcome was assessed using a broad range of cognitive tests. The programme appeared most effective in improving attention, visual processing and memory. Improvements were maintained at follow-up and all participants were reported to become autonomous in daily living. This study implies that an extended intervention using multiple strategies may provide the most appropriate approach to remediate problems following head injury. However, the study was not controlled and it is difficult to assess how much natural recovery may account for treatment gains.

Few studies have examined either the remediation of attention or executive deficits. Computerised attention training programmes have received the most research attention. However, improvements following this intervention have never translated into functional improvements. Multi-strategy compensatory programmes for both attention and executive dysfunction (as described in case studies and one controlled study) have greater appeal because of their direct impact on day-to-day performance but they require evaluation in controlled trials. The efficacy of attention and executive remediation approaches for adults with brain injury remain promising but unproven (Levin, 1990). Further research is needed to examine the efficacy of compensatory strategies for adults with brain injury. As for adults with ADHD, there have been a few case studies detailing the compensatory approach.

Psychological Interventions for Adults with ADHD

Psychological interventions, especially cognitive techniques may provide an alternative management approach for adult ADHD. Trials of this approach have lagged behind medication trials, most probably because psychological interventions for child ADHD have generally produced disappointing results. However, a number of factors suggest that a psychological approach may have utility in the treatment of adult ADHD. First, it is recognised that many of the deficits in adult ADHD are cognitive in nature (i.e., related to attention, memory and organisation deficits; Goodwin and Corgiat, 1992) and adaptive cognitive techniques have been successfully employed for adults with brain injury who have similar impairments (Goodwin and Corgiat, 1992). Second, adults with ADHD, in contrast with many children, may be motivated and ready to learn adaptive methods of functioning (Weinstein, 1994). This is supported by clinicians that advocate a cognitive remediation approach for the management of adult ADHD (Bemporad and Zambenedetti, 1996; Goodwin and Corgiat, 1992; Kane, Mikalac, Benjamin and Barkley, 1990; Nadeau, 1995: Weinstein, 1994). The efficacy of this approach has not undergone systematic clinical trials, however, a number of adult ADHD case studies using the cognitive remediation approach have been reported (Goodwin and Corgiat, 1992; Weinstein; 1994) and one small study has been undertaken (Wiggins, 1999) and these are reviewed next.

The Case of TL

The first case study to report benefits of a cognitive remediation approach to adult ADHD was TL (Goodwin and Corgiat, 1992). TL was a 21-year-old male university freshman, who attended 26, one-hour cognitive remediation sessions over a period of two and a half months. On presenting at the clinic, TL had an erratic academic history. He was disorganised, distractible and had difficulties with interpersonal interaction.

Neuropsychological evaluation found that he had superior intellectual skills and abilities with an intelligence quotient (IQ) estimated to be 120 on the Weschler Adult Intelligence Scale-Revised (Weschler, 1981). However, he had impairments on a range of concentration tests including the Symbol Digits Modality Test (Smith 1982), the Stroop Test (Golden, 1978) and the Trail Making Test (from the Army Individual Battery, 1944). There was also evidence of memory impairments on the Weschler Memory Scale-Revised (WMS-R; Weschler, 1987). He met the Utah criteria for adult ADHD and was subsequently diagnosed with ADHD, childhood onset.

To address TL's deficits a cognitive remediation programme was devised including strategies for orientation; selective, alternating and divided attention; memory and learning; organising and sequences; reasoning and problems solving; and executive functioning. Traditional approaches used with brain-injured patients were selected.

Orientation was addressed by external compensatory strategies: a colour coded map of the university was designed so that TL could find his way around, a programmable watch was bought which displayed time, date and day. This watch was waterproof so that TL never had to take it off, avoiding the problem of it being misplaced. Attentional abilities were remediated using a variety of techniques; a timer was set at regular intervals to cue TL to focus, TL was encouraged to work in a quiet setting and to ask others to minimise their noise.

Memory and learning problems were addressed by a number of internal memory strategies. These strategies included repetition, association, visualisation, verbalisation and the use of mnemonics. TL was also encouraged to use a memory planner and to write things down. Reasoning and problems solving strategies were implemented to overcome severe indecision. A step-by-step problem solving approach together with self-verbalisations such as 'what needs to be done first?' were taught. Finally, teaching TL self-monitoring and time management techniques achieved remediation of executive functions.

In addition to these cognitive techniques, TL received social skills training and medication (methylphenidate and desipramine). The success of the programme was determined by improvements in TL's academic performance as well as by his ability to function independently. TL's ability to take lecture notes improved and he was able to independently find his way around the university campus. At the end of treatment, TL continued to use the strategies and was observed to be effective in his use of planners.

The strength of this case study is its co-ordinated approach to the day-to-day problems of adult ADHD. However, it is not possible to separate which components of the programme were effective. Medication may have produced the primary changes. The authors comment on several important factors about their intervention. First, they suggest one to one work with TL was limited because there was no peer feedback or acknowledgement from others of his behaviour change. Second, they suggest one to one treatment provided no opportunity for practice of new skills other than in the role-play situation and this may have slowed the generalisability of the skills to everyday situations. Nonetheless, the general approach shows promise and a group programme could easily the overcome problems of teaching cognitive strategies in a one to one situation.

Further Case Studies

Additional case studies using the cognitive remediation approach for adults with ADHD have appeared more recently. Weinstein (1994) describes five 'typical' adult ADHD case studies. In these case studies a multimodal treatment approach for adult ADHD combining psychotherapy, medication and cognitive remediation is described. The cognitive remediation strategies taught to each individual are discussed here. None of the case studies provided information about how diagnosis was made, nor was outcome systematically assessed.

Case LT was a 45-year-old divorced woman with a long-standing history of attention problems and learning difficulties. She had a good response to desipramine but needed additional strategies to be able to achieve educational goals. Cognitive remediation strategies taught were basic organisational skills such as rules for doing homework, a calendar to plan activities, problem solving and study skills. LT reported that these strategies were helpful both at school and at home.

Case CS was a 19-year-old woman who was referred for a neuropsychological evaluation. On testing, she showed impairments in sustaining auditory attention and she had mild learning difficulties. CS decided against the use of medication. Initially, she was taught adaptive strategies such as studying at times when she was maximally alert; working in quiet places and taking regular breaks. This was supplemented with a note taker for her lectures and being allowed un-timed tests, which included open-ended questions. CS was also encouraged to volunteer for hands on learning experiences, which did not rely so heavily on listening skills. CS reported that the cognitive strategies were helpful but decided to take methylphenidate when she was unable to keep up with her coursework.

Case KE was a 31-year-old single woman with a history of depression who complained of memory problems, excessive daydreaming and periods of getting lost while driving. On testing, KE had mild visuo-spatial problems and mild attentional problems; she was also highly impulsive. Her intervention programme involved desipramine as well as a range of cognitive strategies. The cognitive strategies included: moving to a quiet section of her office to work, using self talk, breaking tasks into a series of smaller tasks which did not require so much concentration and doing the most demanding work early in the day. KE reported that she found that the cognitive strategies were most helpful to her, but on reflection felt that the combined treatment, that is medication plus cognitive remediation, was most useful.

Case SL was a 42-year-old married woman with two teenage children. She reported that she could 'never get things done' and that her family complained that she 'never listened'. On testing she showed impairments in learning auditory-presented material and showed difficulties with divided attention. Treatment recommendations included medication, cognitive strategies and education for the family. SL was encouraged to use a memory notebook, ask for instructions to be repeated and was encouraged to re-read all written instructions. SL reported that the multimodal approach was helpful.

Finally, case JS was a 39 year old married man. He had poor organisational skills and was consistently late for all his appointments. The intervention designed for JS included methylphenidate, marriage counselling as well as relaxation for his mental hyperactivity. The cognitive strategies JS trialled were predominately methods to reduce disordered thinking; the therapist taught him to keep on one train of thought by verbal prompts. There was no report of whether JS found this intervention helpful.

A Brief Group Intervention

Wiggins (1999) describes a brief group intervention for adults with ADHD. In this study a small group of adults diagnosed with ADHD were recruited (n=9) and compared to a group (n=8) who did not receive the intervention. An adult ADHD checklist and a seven-item organisational skills checklist assessed outcome. The intervention was a brief four-session group program. In session one, the characteristics of ADHD were outlined as well as how to set realistic goals. In session two, goal setting was reviewed and strategies for time management were introduced. In session three, road blocks to task completion were discussed and participants learnt how to give themselves rewards after a difficult task. In the final session, participants were taught how to organise their physical environment and how to overcome procrastination. The main finding was in the improvement of organisational skills of participants in the treatment group. This study has, however, a number of limitations including: small sample size, no clear diagnosis of ADHD, reliance on checklists developed by the author, no follow up data and no randomisation to group. Nonetheless, it does indicate that the approach warrants further investigation.

Critique of Psychological Approaches for Adult ADHD

In this section, six case studies and one small intervention study were described outlining the use of cognitive remediation techniques. These studies suggest that cognitive remediation strategies taught within a multi-modal intervention are helpful in overcoming the day-to-day difficulties associated with ADHD. However, the case studies were all descriptive, diagnostic procedures were not clearly detailed and outcome following treatment was not formally assessed and the intervention study had a large number of weaknesses.

The diagnosis of adult ADHD was not clearly detailed in the majority of case studies and in the brief intervention study. This makes the generalisability of the reports to clinical practice problematic. Moreover, three of the case studies described by Weinstein (1994) had co-morbid conditions. These co-morbid conditions cloud the possible efficacy of the intervention for ADHD, as it is feasible that the therapeutic effect of the cognitive strategies was brought about via the remediation of the secondary condition. Clear diagnosis of adult ADHD is needed to assist in establishing the possible efficacy of cognitive remediation strategies.

A major problem in interpreting the efficacy of the cognitive remediation strategies is that they were taught within multi-modal packages (i.e. medication vs psychological treatments). Under these conditions, the active components of the treatment cannot be segregated from inactive components. In child ADHD studies, medication has been shown to be as effective on its own, as when combined with a psychological treatment (Abikoff, 1987). This suggests that that the active component of the treatment in the case studies presented here may be the medication. The efficacy of cognitive remediation strategies therefore needs to be evaluated in systematic, randomised, controlled clinical trials both as a sole intervention and in conjunction with medication so that it can be determined whether cognitive strategies do have a role in the treatment of adult ADHD.

A final issue, which warrants comment, is outcome measurement. None of the case studies systematically evaluated improvements following the intervention. The best indication of a response to treatment was shown in the case of TL (Goodwin and Corgiat, 1992) where actual changes in his note taking ability, use of diary and watch, and greater independence where observed. These changes are important as they indicate that the intervention had an impact on day-to-day functioning. Future studies need to evaluate both symptom change (as in the medication trials) and also improvements in day-to-day functioning. Impaired functioning (DSM IV) and the presence of specific primary symptoms are equally important in the definition of ADHD, and equally should be targets for effective treatment.

To conclude, both the case studies and small intervention study outlining the use of cognitive remediation strategies are limited in their generalisability. Nonetheless, these case studies and the intervention study are thought provoking as they describe cognitive techniques, which have practical application. Medication does not teach adults with ADHD how to overcome disorganised patterns of behaviour or remediate skills deficits.

Is The Cognitive Remediation Approach Helpful?

Conclusions about the efficacy of the cognitive remediation approach for child and adult ADHD, and for adult brain injury, are difficult to make. For child ADHD, studies have targeted different symptoms, used different techniques and different methods for evaluations. Not surprisingly, response to these interventions has been variable. Many factors may play a role in mediating the success of child ADHD cognitive programmes. These include; the age range of participants, cognitive maturity, medication, motivation, dosage of medication, inclusion of generalisation strategies and outcome measurement. Predictors of positive outcome to cognitive remediation need to be established.

The cognitive remediation approach for adult brain injury is relatively new. While it appears promising, it is essentially an unproven approach because of the limited number of studies and lack of controlled trials. Compensatory strategies, which have been used with child ADHD such as self-instructional training (SIT), have been applied to this neurologically impaired adult population with some success. Further research is needed into the benefits of compensatory strategies within this population.

Implications for adult ADHD

There is only weak support for a cognitive remediation approach. However in light of the design problems with many of these studies, a cognitive remediation approach could be efficacious for adult ADHD if some of these problems were overcome. This view is further supported when the cognitive maturity and the high degree of motivation of adults with ADHD to improve their functioning, are considered. In the final part of this section, factors which may be important in the success of a cognitive remediation, programme for adults with ADHD are discussed: 1) the need for a multi-strategy approach; and 2) recognition of the cognitive maturity of adults.

A Multi-Strategy Approach

Given that adults with ADHD can have a range of primary deficits and secondary impairments it is unlikely that any one strategy will be sufficient to remediate all the deficits. A multi-strategy approach including a range of compensatory techniques is likely to be needed to overcome many of the problems associated with ADHD. Such an intervention could be developed by selecting 'priority areas' and remediating these with strategies available in the literature, thus replicating the approach described in the adult ADHD case studies.

From the child ADHD literature, there are clear indications that generalisation strategies such as teaching parents to reinforce taught skills could increase their use. A similar approach has been proposed for adult ADHD by using coaches to prompt or cue the use of appropriate strategies (Hallowell and Ratey, 1994). The use of coaches to promote generalisation could be adopted for an adult ADHD intervention programme.

Critics of both the child ADHD and adult brain injury literature have pointed to the brevity of some of the interventions as a possible confound when null results have been obtained. The implication of this for an adult ADHD programme is that the length needs to be sufficient for skills acquisition and subsequent establishment of skills in an individuals coping repertoire. This could be achieved by ensuring that newly developed adult ADHD interventions are at least eight weeks in length, consistent with successful child ADHD skills training interventions.

Adult ADHD Variables

There is no doubt that the relationship between participant variables and outcome is complex. Adults with ADHD differ from their child counterparts in that they are cognitively mature and they differ from adults with brain injury in that their cognitive deficits are subtler and life-long. This might suggest that adults with ADHD are in a better position to acquire cognitive strategies. A further factor, which indicates that cognitive remediation may be effective for adults with ADHD, is that they self-select for treatment. This suggests a high degree of motivation to learn new skills. Together these factors imply that adults with ADHD may benefit from a cognitive remediation approach more than the other groups we have examined above.

Improvements to Research Design

Many important lessons about research design can be learned from studying the child ADHD and brain injury remediation studies. These lessons need to be applied when developing outcome evaluation studies for adult ADHD. Many of the child ADHD studies used selection criteria, which were vague and ill-defined. Given that there has been concern about the assessment of adult ADHD, it is important to clearly define entry criteria and provide appropriate details about any adult ADHD sample selected for study, for replication purposes.

Methods for outcome evaluation are also important. A general concern levelled against the use of cognitive tests is that they do not measure change at the level of day-to-day activities. They are too specific. This suggests that an alternative approach to measurement may need to be considered for an adult ADHD programme. The use of rating scales as used in adult ADHD medication trials (e.g. Spencer, Wilens, Biederman et al., 1995) may provide an alternative approach, which warrants consideration.

Finally, evaluation of the long-term benefits of interventions is important too. Most of the child ADHD and brain injury studies do not examine outcome beyond a few months post-intervention. The absence of long-term follow-up may mean that essential information about skills training is neglected. For example, skills use might even improve over time with practice or they may not be used at all without reinforcement.

Conclusions

This selective review of pertinent child and adult ADHD, and adult brain injury literature is valuable in highlighting factors that should assist in the development and evaluation of an adult ADHD programme. There are indications that adults with ADHD are an appropriate group who could benefit from cognitive techniques. First, they self-select so they are likely to be motivated to learn new skills. Second, they have attained cognitive maturity, which may help in skills acquisition. Third, cognitive deficits in adult ADHD can be similar to adults with brain injury and early indicators suggest that this group responds to cognitive remediation. Finally, there is considerable clinical support for the cognitive approach to the management of adult ADHD (Bemporad and Zambenedetti, 1996; Goodwin and Corgiat, 1992; Kane, Mikalac, Benjamin and Barkley, 1990; Nadeau, 1995; Weinstein, 1994; Weiss and Weiss, 2004), especially as some adults may not respond to medication or may not wish to take it.

Given current knowledge about the application of cognitive strategies to child ADHD and adult brain injury, it would seem possible to overcome many of the methodological problems identified above. The aim of any new intervention should be to reduce the day-to-day impact of ADHD rather than focus on specific skills acquisition. This could be achieved by teaching a range of compensatory skills to overcome skills deficits, reduce stress and promote awareness about environments, which are likely to exacerbate symptoms. The inclusion of generalisation strategies such as coaches and ensuring the intervention is of a sufficient length to allow strategies to become established in participant's skills repertoire, could all be adopted to enhance the likelihood of programme success.

Currently, there is little information to guide clinical management of adult ADHD. Given that ADHD is considered to be a neurobiologically based condition a cognitive remediation approach provides a theoretically based treatment method. The ability to adapt to cognitive deficits is seen to be an indicator of positive outcome of ADHD. Thus, a cognitive remediation programme that teaches compensatory strategies to overcome everyday problems may assist in a positive adjustment to adult ADHD. Given that only limited numbers benefit from medication (Weinstein, 1994) and others are not able to tolerate side effects (Kane et al., 1990), this cognitive remediation approach offers an interesting alternative. Consequently, a cognitive remediation programme for adult ADHD needs to be developed and evaluated, and this forms the basis for the content of the second part of this chapter.

Part B: Research Into the Efficacy of a Cognitive Remediation Approach

Introduction

This section will first describe a multi-strategy cognitive remediation program for adults with ADHD. This will be followed by the details of two research studies that have evaluated the approach.

A Cognitive Remediation Program for Adults with ADHD

A cognitive remediation programme (CRP) was developed specifically for adults with ADHD based upon the literature outlined in Part A. A three-pronged approach was taken to reduce the impact of cognitive impairments: (1) retraining cognitive functions; (2) teaching internal and external compensatory strategies; and (3) restructuring the physical environment to maximise functioning. To ensure acquisition, generalisation and maintenance of skills, three strategies were incorporated into the program design: (1) eight weekly therapist-led group sessions; (2) a participants' workbook with exercises and (3) support people who acted as coaches.

Therapist led sessions were held weekly. In these sessions a combination of cognitive remediation and cognitive restructuring techniques were taught. The format for each sessions was as follows: review of previous session and homework exercise, introduction of a new topic together with appropriate remediation techniques and finally, the presentation of a new homework exercise. A summary of each session together with a homework exercise was supplied in a participant's workbook.

Support people were recruited for the CRP to aid participants with the acquisition of skills by reminding and prompting them to use them. It was recommended to participants that they select a friend or relative, who was generally well organised and did not have ADHD themselves, to act as their support person. A substantial number of participants were unable to nominate their own support person. Psychology students (senior undergraduates and postgraduates) were recruited to act as support people for these participants. All support people were required to attend a short two-hour training workshop prior to the start of the programme. The specific tasks support people were asked to undertake were: (1) to remind their partner to attend the programme; (2) to attend every session with their partner; and (3) to telephone their ADHD partner and discuss problems with their homework exercises, between sessions.

The CRP Session by Session

Session one: Motivational training. This session was devoted to providing an overview of the programme and to introducing techniques for increasing motivation. First, a general overview was presented including the components (sessions, workbook, and support persons) and the content of the programme. A description of the workbook and the role of support people followed this. Motivation problems in ADHD were then explained. A variety of motivational techniques were presented including goal setting, use of rewards and identification of personally relevant motivating factors. The homework exercise was to identify a boring task and write a list of motivators that would help in task completion. Participants were also encouraged to try out their ideas for self-motivation.

Session two: Attention training. This session began with a review of the homework. Attention problems in ADHD were then explained. Methods for improving attention were brainstormed and discussed. Strategies included: self talk, writing things down, asking for information to be repeated, breaking tasks into sections, reducing distractions and doing one thing at a time. The homework exercise was to practice using self-talk together with written monitoring of distracting thoughts.

Session three: Listening skills. This session began with a discussion of the homework task. Listening as a problem associated with poor attention was then discussed. The characteristics of a good listener were brainstormed. The importance of attending to words, body language, and developing empathy, were considered. Reflective listening was then demonstrated followed by participant practice in pairs. The homework exercise was to observe the body language of a favourite television character. Participants were also encouraged to try out the reflective listening strategy.

Session four: Managing impulsivity. This session began with a discussion of the homework task. The topic of impulsivity was then introduced with a discussion of factors which reduce self-control. A self-verbalisation technique known as 'stop-think-do' was taught. Then a problem solving strategy was explained and exercises were given to be completed within the session. The homework exercise was to keep a daily problem-solving log.

Session five: Organisational skills. This session began with a review of the homework. Organisational problems in ADHD were then reviewed and the use of structure and routine to contain symptoms was explained. The use of aids such as watches, diaries, and planners was discussed. Different types of diary were considered. The remainder of the session was devoted to: writing lists, time management, routines and daily plans. The exercise of 'planning a holiday' was given to practice the techniques. The homework exercise was to write a 'To do' list, prioritise tasks on the list and then develop a 'day plan' to try out.

Session six: Anger management. This session began with a review of organisational skills and a discussion of the homework task. Anger was described within the context of ADHD. The association between thinking and anger was demonstrated. Cognitive distortions were then discussed. Participants were encouraged to identify some of their own faulty cognitions. Examples were worked through during the session. The homework exercise was to keep a log of situations and thoughts, which increased anger.

Session seven: Self-esteem. This session began with a homework review. ADHD and its effect on self-esteem was then discussed. Participants were then taught to evaluate relevant cognitive distortions about themselves. The idea of having clear goals for their personal life, for work and for relationships was taught. The homework was to finish the goal setting exercise.

Session eight: Relapse prevention. This session began with a review of the programme including the final homework exercise. The difference between a lapse and a relapse was discussed. Each participant was encouraged to develop a three-month plan to maintain the skills which they had found most useful. Other methods for managing ADHD were then reviewed including support groups, diet and medication. The homework was to implement the three-month plan for skills maintenance.

The evaluation of this CRP formed the basis for study one. It was anticipated that the CRP would: (1) reduce ADHD symptomatology; (2) improve organisational skills; (3) reduce anger; and (4) improve self-esteem.

A major limitation of the programme described above is that participants have to attend multiple therapy sessions at a fixed location. Thus the format of the program was not accessible or practical for a large number of adults with ADHD. Consequently, we also decided to examine whether the program would be effective in a predominately self-directed format. For this 'self-help' program, the original cognitive remediation program (Stevenson, Whitmont, Bornholt, Livesey and Stevenson, 2002) was substantially redesigned to reduce the need for therapist contact (see Stevenson, Stevenson and Whitmont, 2003). A self-help book was written (available from the authors on request), that covered the following topics; education on ADHD, how to overcome attention and motivational difficulties, listening skills, organisational skills, impulse control techniques and cognitive strategies for anger management, and cognitive strategies for improving self-esteem. Three therapist-led sessions were included in the intervention, at the start, middle and end of the program. These sessions were primarily used as review sessions, but also had the function of monitoring progress and providing motivation to complete the program. In addition, participants were paired with a support person whose role was to telephone and remind them to complete readings and exercises on a weekly basis. The evaluation of the self-help programme forms the basis for study two.

Study One

Method

Overview

The study design was a randomised, controlled trial of the CRP with two groups: treatment and control. Adults with ADHD were recruited to the study from ADHD Support Groups and via referral from psychiatrists who specialise in adult ADHD. Outcome measures were taken before (Time 1; T1) and after treatment (Time 2; T2) for the treatment group and at equivalent time intervals for participants in the control group. To examine whether there was maintenance of any treatment gains, the treatment group was followed up at 2 months (T3) and one year post-treatment (T4).

Recruitment Procedure

Following ethics approval, applicants to the Cognitive Remediation Programme were sought from ADHD Support Groups in Sydney and via referral from Sydney based psychiatrists who specialise in the treatment of adult ADHD. Admission to the study was completed in three stages: (1) a telephone screen; (2) a mail-out; and (3) a clinic assessment. Applicants were eliminated at each stage if they did not meet requirements for study entry.

On receipt of a referral, applicants were telephoned and screened using an informal telephone interview. During the interview, demographic information (name, address, telephone number, gender, date of birth) as well as more specific information (diagnosis of ADHD, medication prescribed, drug and alcohol problems and learning difficulties) was obtained. If an exclusion criterion was endorsed, applicants were immediately eliminated and referred to an appropriate public service. *Exclusion criteria* were: (1) not having ADHD-like symptoms; (2) being under 21; (3) a current drug or alcohol problem; (4) history of psychosis; (5) current involvement in criminal activities or anti-social behaviour; and (6) mental retardation. Those who passed the telephone screen were sent an information package about the study.

The information package was mailed out within 24 hours of the telephone screen. It included a letter thanking applicants for their interest in the programme, an information sheet about the study and two standardised questionnaires: the Wender Utah Rating Scale (WURS; Ward, Wender and Reimherr, 1993) and the Parent Rating Scale (PRS; Ward, Wender and Reimherr, 1993). The WURS and PRS are both retrospective measures of childhood ADHD. Both have established psychometric properties (Stein, Sandoval, Szumoski, Roizen, Reinecke et al, 1995; Rosini and O'Connor, 1995).

The WURS is a 25-item checklist of childhood behaviours associated with ADHD concerning; concentration problems, acting without thinking, trouble-seeing things from others' point of view, etc. Each item is rated on a five point scale ranging from "not at all/very slightly" to "very much". The WURS was administered to assess for childhood ADHD symptoms. A score of 36 or higher on this measure correctly identifies 96 percent of adults with ADHD and a score lower than 36 identifies 96 percent of normals (Ward, Wender and Reimherr, 1993). Applicants who returned the WURS, with a score of 36 or higher (one person with a score of 34 was included in study one), were invited to the clinic for further assessment.

The PRS (a modified version of the Conners Rating Scale) is a 10 item checklist of childhood behaviours. This measure needs to be completed by a significant other that knew the applicant as a child. The measure was administered to assess consistency between self and others ratings of applicants childhood behaviour. Example items on the PRS are; restless, fidgets, fails to finish things started, etc. Each item is rated on a four-point scale from "not at all" to "very much". The PRS was not used as an entry measure for the study so that applicants unable to have the measure completed remained eligible.

The clinic assessment was conducted by the first author at the Badham Clinic, University of Sydney. It lasted between one and a half and two hours. Two further measures were administered at this assessment, the Semi-Structured Interview for Adult ADHD (Barkley, 1991) and a DSM IIIR symptoms checklist (American Psychiatric Association [APA], 1989). The Semi-Structured Interview for Adult ADHD provides a thorough evaluation of both medical and psychological factors, which can produce ADHD symptoms and was selected to assist in making a differential diagnosis. The DSM IIIR checklist was used to establish that applicants currently met full criteria for ADHD and that the symptoms were impairing ability to function. Applicants were asked whether they had a problem with each DSM IIIR ADHD symptom. When a symptom was indicated as problematic, the applicant was asked to give specific examples of their difficulties. *Inclusion criteria* were: (1) evidence of ADHD symptoms from childhood (i.e., a score of 36 or over on the Wender Utah Rating Scale); (2) current endorsement of eight out of the 14 symptoms of the DSM IIIR criteria for ADHD (APA, 1989); (3) a life long history consistent with ADHD; (4) evidence that ADHD symptoms were causing impairment in day to day functioning; and (5) a willingness to participate in a study and give informed consent. Following the clinic assessment, applicants were verbally informed of their eligibility. Those that did not meet the entry criteria (n=12) were referred to appropriate public services.

It is noteworthy that over 75 percent (n=33) of actual participants (n=44) had been diagnosed with ADHD prior to entry into the study. There were four applicants where disagreement occurred with previous ADHD diagnoses. Of these, two were ineligible due to a lack of childhood symptoms, one had symptoms more commonly associated with a borderline personality disorder and the fourth did not meet criteria for a current diagnosis. These applicants were excluded together with other applicants who did not meet the entry requirements.

Participants

In total, 69 applicants completed all three phases of the assessment. Of these, 57 met entry criteria for the study. Subsequent to drop out for other reasons (i.e., lack of baby sitter n=1, work/college on night of the programme n=5, moving overseas/interstate before programme commenced n=3, other n=4), 44 applicants participated. Participants diagnosed with ADHD by independent clinicians and prescribed medication stabilised at an optimum dose, were assigned to the pre-medicated group. Non-medicated participants were assigned to the non-medicated group. Participants were asked to maintain their medication status throughout the study and up until the two-month follow-up. Finally, within each group (pre-medicated and non-medicated), participants were randomly assigned to either a treatment group or a waiting list control group.

Outcome Measures

The CRP aimed to teach techniques to improve ADHD symptom management and day to day functioning. The following self-report measures were selected to evaluate whether this goal was achieved.

DSM IIIR ADHD Checklist. The main purpose of this measure was to assess improvements in ADHD management as demonstrated by symptom reduction. DSM IIIR diagnostic criteria for ADHD (DSM IIIR, American Psychiatric Association, 1989) together with three items from a questionnaire by Gittelman (1985) were combined to produce a 17-item checklist. A scale between one "not a problem" to ten "an extreme problem" was used for each symptom. The range on the checklist is from 17 "no problems with ADHD symptoms" to 170 "extreme problems with ADHD symptoms".

Adult Organisation Scale. This measure was adapted from the Child Organisation Scale (Zentall, Harper and Stormont-Spurgen, 1993). The purpose of this measure was to assess day to day improvements in organisational skills. Example items include, I arrive to appointments on time and I use a diary and write things down that I have to do. The measure has 26 items, which are rated on a five point category scale from one "never" to five "always". The range on this scale is from 26 "completely organised" to 130 "completely disorganised".

*Davidson and Lang Self Esteem Measure (*Davidson and Lang, 1960). The main purpose of this measure was to examine whether the CRP led to improvements in self-evaluation. In this measure, 30 polarised adjectives are presented (e.g., good-bad, happy-sad, popular-unpopular) and participants indicate how they see themselves on a five point scale. The range on this measure is from 30 "low self esteem" to 150 "high self esteem".

State-Trait Anger Expression Inventory (STAXI, Speilberger, 1991). The main purpose of administering the STAXI was to assess whether anger management improved following the CRP. Two subscales of the STAXI were administered, the State and Trait Anger Scales. State and Trait Anger Scales are both 10-item measures, scored on four point category scales. The range for each scale on this inventory is from 10 "normal anger control" to 40 "extreme anger dysregulation".

Outcome measures were administered to the treatment group on four occasions: pre-treatment, eight weeks later at post-treatment and at both a two-month and a one-year follow-up. The control group completed the measures on two occasions at an interval of eight weeks to equate with the pre- and post-treatment measurements. After eight weeks, people in the waiting list group were offered treatment, consistent with best ethical practice which suggests that treatment should be offered to control groups as soon as possible after a waiting period. Where an abbreviation is found in the following text, T1 refers to the first administration of the measures *(pre-treatment and first control measure; week 1),* T2 to the second administration *(post-treatment and second control measure; week 8*) and for the treatment group only T3 to the 2 month follow-up *(week sixteen)* and T4 to the one year follow-up.

Programme Evaluation

The CRP was evaluated to assess face validity and to elicit participant's suggestions for programme improvement. Following treatment at T2, all participants in the treatment group were asked to complete a self-report evaluation form. The form asked participants to rate the usefulness of (1) meeting others with ADHD; (2) topics discussed; (3) the workbook; (4) homework exercises and; (5) the sessions. Each item (i.e., meeting with others with ADHD etc) was rated on a category scale from 1 "not at all useful" to 10 "extremely useful". Participants were also encouraged to add their own comments about the programme.

Analyses

Descriptive statistics (mean, median, variance, standard deviation, range, skewness and kurtosis) were calculated for the participants' demographic data, assessment questionnaires and for the outcome measures at each time interval (i.e., T1 [week one], T2 [week eight], T3 [week sixteen] and T4 [one year]). For descriptive purposes, participants WURS scores were compared with a standardised sample (Ward, Wender and Reimherr, 1993).

Outcome scores on the measures at T1 (week one) and T2 (week eight) (the control group were offered treatment after eight weeks so T3 [week sixteen] and T4 [one year] scores were not available for this group) were initially analysed by three-way repeated measures analysis of variance (ANOVA) with group *(Control vs. Treatment)* and medication status (*Pre-medicated vs. Non-medicated*) as between subject factors and time *(T1 [week one] vs. T2 [week eight])* as a within subject factor. However, as we note below, medication status had no detectable effect, and so medication status was dropped from the ANOVA's reported in the results section and on the tables.

To assess whether patterns of improvement were different between Medication Groups across the four test times, a two-way ANOVA with Medication Group (*Pre-medicated vs Non-medicated*) as a between-participant factor and Time (*T1 [week one] vs T2 [week eight] vs T3 [week sixteen] vs T4 [one year]*) as a within-participant factor was conducted. As above, there was no effect of medication status. Consequently, we only report planned dependent t-tests, conducted to assess whether there was a significant improvement from pre-treatment levels to later follow up intervals in the treatment group (collapsed across medication status). As multiple t-tests were used a Bonferroni correction was applied.

RESULTS

Sample Characteristics

Participants pre-prescribed medication, were randomly assigned to a control (n=11) or a treatment (n=13) group. One pre-medicated participant withdrew from the treatment group after five sessions and was eliminated from the study, leaving n=12 and one pre-medicated participant withdrew from the control group, leaving n=10. Most pre-medicated participants were taking only stimulants (n=19), two were taking only antidepressants and two both medications. Non-medicated participants were randomly assigned to treatment (n=10) and control groups (n=11).

Pre-treatment status. Pre-medicated and non-medicated participants were compared for age and retrospective childhood ADHD as reported on the WURS and PRS and no differences were found between groups using independent t-tests. Pre-medicated and non-medicated participants scores on all the T1 outcome measures did not significantly differ. This was surprising as it was anticipated that medication might have led to reduced scores on these measures. As no differences were found between pre-medicated and non-medicated participants on either assessment or pre-treatment measures, groups were combined (pre-medicated and non-medicated) for all of the analyses reported in this section.

Comparison of treatment and control groups. Group (treatment and control) characteristics related to age, gender, WURS and PRS are illustrated in Table 1. There was no age difference between the groups. Gender distribution was also similar in both groups. On the WURS, the treatment group scores were significantly worse than the control groups (t=2.60, df=41, p<0.05). However, PRS scores were not different.

Table 1: Participant details pre-treatment/week 1 of the wait-list control, for Study 1.

Variable	Treatment group Mean (SD)	Control group Mean (SD)
Number (n =)	22	21
Gender (M/F)	16/6	13/8
Medicated (Y/N)	12/10	11/10
Age	36.4 (10.0)	35.3 (8.8)
PRS*	16.2 (17.9)	14.8 (7.1)
WURS	65.3 (13.8)	55.6 (10.6)

*PRS was obtained for n = 20 in the Treatment group and n = 18 in the Control group.

Table 2: Means (and standard deviations) for Treatment and Control groups across the course of Study 1.

Variable*	T1 Week 1	T2 Week 8	T3 Week 16	T4 Week 52
Treatment group	n = 22	n = 22	n = 22	n = 19
Symptoms	111.9 (19.0)**	73.7 (26.7)	67.2 (26.7)	72.6 (27.6)***
Organisation	84.1 (12.1)	71.5 (10.8)	66.1 (12.2)	68.5 (10.1)
Self-esteem	102.5 (12.3)	109.8 (12.4)	111.4 (16.6)	112.6 (18.5)
State-anger	13.5 (5.8)	10.7 (1.2)	11.2 (2.3)	12.6 (4.6)
Trait-anger	23.1 (5.3)	20.5 (5.6)	18.8 (3.8)	19.9 (5.5)
Control group	n = 21	n = 21		
Symptoms	112.5 (19.4)	112.9 (18.0)		
Organisation	86.4 (13.5)	86.1 (13.1)		
Self-esteem	100.7 (12.8)	97.4 (13.8)		
State-anger	12.2 (3.1)	14.0 (5.3)		
Trait-anger	23.9 (6.7)	24.3 (7.1)		

*Score reductions indicate improvement, excepting self-esteem where the reverse applies.
**1 participant had missing data.
***20 participants completed this measure.

Outcome measures scores at T1 can be found in Table 2 (this table also provides outcome data at T2 for treatment and control groups, and T3 and T4 outcome data for the treatment group only). There was no statistically significant differences between treatment and control groups using independent t-tests for any T1 outcome measures.

Comparison of ADHD sample with normative data. For descriptive purposes ADHD participants WURS scores (n=43) collected during assessment were compared with the mean standardised sample score for the WURS (Ward, Wender and Reimherr, 1993). WURS scores were not significantly different from the American adult ADHD standardised sample (mean for standardised sample=62.2, SD=14.6; mean for participants=60.6, SD=13.1; z=0.7; see Howell [1992], p162 for method). The correlation between WURS and PRS (significant other rating) was calculated, for those participants who had both measures completed. A moderate positive correlation was found between the PRS and WURS (r=0.39, n=38, p<0.025). This indicates some consistency between the recollection of childhood behaviour on self report and reports from a significant other.

TREATMENT OUTCOME

Outcome Measures

In Table 2, group means for each outcome measure by group (treatment and control) at each time interval (T1, T2, T3 and T4) can be found. (Note there is no outcome data at T3 and T4 for the control group as they were offered treatment after 8 weeks on the waiting list). All of the results (and analyses) were conducted on combined treatment and control groups (i.e. collapsing across medication status), as this variable had no significant effect on any of the analyses that are reported here.

Table 3: Significant treatment effects (p < 0.05) observed for Study 1

Variable	Control vs. Treatment & T1 vs. T2 (ANOVA)			Treatment alone	
	Time	Group	Group x Time	T1 vs. T3	T1 vs. T4
	$F_{1,38}$ =	$F_{1,38}$ =	$F_{1,38}$ =	t_{20} =	t_{20} =
Symptoms	25.46	15.61	26.48	6.84	6.17
Organisation*	16.78	6.40	16.78	6.40	5.36
Self-esteem*	NS	4.87	6.18	2.71	2.56
State-anger*	NS	NS	10.17	NS	NS
Trait-anger**	NS	NS	NS	3.75	2.55

* Degrees of freedom for these analyses $F_{1,39}$ and t_{21} respectively

** Degrees of freedom for these analyses $F_{1,39}$ and t_{20} at T1 vs. T3 and t_{19} at T1 vs. T4

In the treatment group (CRP) all outcome measures showed improvement after treatment, when contrasted with controls. This was largely confirmed by the ANOVA (see Table 3), as Time (T1 vs. T2) by Group (Treatment vs. Controls) interactions were significant for all measures, excepting trait anger. That is the improvement, pre- to post-treatment, in the Treatment group, significantly exceeded any reported change in the Control group. Thus, treatment significantly improved reported ADHD symptoms, organisational skills and self-esteem (note improvements here are indicated by an increase in scores in contrast to the other measures). State anger was also significantly reduced. A number of significant main effects are also evident on Table 3, however the significant interactions described above render these of little interest.

Maintenance of Treatment Gains

Analysis of outcomes in the treatment groups (pre-medicated vs non-medicated) revealed no significant differences between these groups in terms of outcome on any measure, so data were again collapsed across medication status. Examination of the mean outcome measure scores at 12 months (see Table 2) revealed a similar picture to the 2-month follow-up, with gains apparently preserved. This was confirmed in the analysis (see Table 3), in that all treatment measures significant at the 2 month follow up, were still significant at 12 months (the paired t-test compared pre-treatment scores (T1) with the 12 month follow-up (T4) scores). It should be noted that participants were not asked to maintain their medication status to follow up.

Clinical Significance of Symptom Changes

The clinical significance of symptom reduction was examined using criteria published in recent adult ADHD medication trials, i.e., that of a 33 percent reduction in symptoms (Findling et al., 1996; Spencer et al., 1995). There were no apparent differences in response rates between pre-medicated and non-medicated participants and so the data were collapsed again. Using the 33 percent reduction criterion, at T2 (week 8) 36 percent of the participants (n=8) were responders to treatment in terms of ADHD symptom reduction. This increased to 55 percent (n=12) when T3 (week 16) was examined and dropped to 50 percent at T4 (Week 52; n=11). This degree of improvement is comparable with medication trials where response rates fall between 25-78 percent (Wilens, Spencer and Biederman, 1995). Using the 33 percent reduction criterion to examine improvement in organisational skills, at T2 (week 8) 9 percent (n=2) of the participants were responders in terms of improved organisational skills. This increased to 22 percent (n=5) at T3 (week 16) and dropped back down to 17 percent (n=4) at T4 (one year). A 33 percent reduction in symptoms was not examined for the Davidson and Lang Self Esteem Measure and the STAXI as change scores were uniformly small.

Programme Evaluation

Following the last session, the usefulness of: (1) meeting others with ADHD; (2) topics discussed; (3) the workbook; (4) homework exercises; and (5) the sessions were evaluated. All aspects of the programme were reported to have scores of 8 or above (maximum score was 10) suggesting all the components of the treatment programme were judged useful by participants.

Examination of the Role of Support People in Skills Acquisition

A post hoc analysis was conducted to examine whether support person type (Student vs. Relative/friend) influenced outcome on the DSM IIIR ADHD Checklist score. A two-way ANOVA with Support Person Type (*Student vs. Relative/friend*) as a between participant factor and Time (*T1 [week one] vs T2 [week eight] vs T3 [week sixteen] vs T4 [one year]*) as a within-participant factor was conducted. The analysis revealed a main effect of Time ($F(3, 51)=17.28$, $p<0.01$), but no effect of Support Person Type and no interaction between Support Person Type and Time. This implies that type of support person did not influence outcome. As with all previous analyses, medication status had no impact upon these results.

Conclusions

The results from study one indicate positive outcomes for adults with ADHD following a multi-strategy cognitive remediation programme, with detectable effects evident one-year post-treatment. The magnitude of the treatment effect was in the same range as for drug treatment of ADHD. An intriguing finding was that the participants medication status appeared to have no detectable effect on either treatment outcomes or upon symptoms when measured at baseline. Obviously the intensive nature of the treatment program used in study one would not be practicable for many prospective clients. Consequently, we attempted to determine whether a conceptually similar program but utilising a 'self-help' approach with reduced therapist contact, would be effective too. This formed the basis for study two.

Study Two

Method

Overview

The study design was a randomised, controlled trial of a Minimal Contact Cognitive Remediation Program (MCRP) with two groups: treatment and control. As in study one, adults with ADHD were recruited to the study from ADHD Support Groups and via referral from psychiatrists who specialise in adult ADHD. Outcome measures were taken before (Time 1; T1) and after treatment (Time 2; T2) for the treatment group and at equivalent time intervals for participants in the control group. To examine whether there was maintenance of any treatment gains, the treatment group was followed up at 2 months (T3). The effect of medication status was also explored as in study one.

Recruitment Procedure

As in study one, admission to the MCRP was completed in three stages; (1) a telephone screen; (2) a mail-out; and (3) a clinic assessment. Applicants were eliminated at each stage if they did not meet requirements for entry to the study. Details of the telephone screen and mail out are identical to those in study one and will not be repeated here. However, the clinic assessment was altered to include measures of IQ, academic ability and depression, anxiety and stress. These measures were included to assess whether they might have any impact on outcome.

The clinic assessment lasted approximately two and a half-hours and was completed by the first author, at the Badham Clinic, University of Sydney. The Semi-Structured Interview for Adult ADHD (previously described in study one; Barkley, 1991) together with a DSM IV ADHD Checklist were administered. The DSM IV ADHD Checklist was used to establish that participants currently met full criteria for one of the three subtypes of ADHD and that these symptoms were impairing functioning. Participants were asked to indicate whether they had a problem with each symptom. When a symptom was indicated as problematic, the applicant was asked to give specific examples of their difficulties. In addition, the measures described below (Depression Anxiety Stress Scale, vocabulary subtest and Wide Range Achievement Test-Third Edition) were administered to provide a comprehensive description of the characteristics of adults with ADHD in this study.

Depression Anxiety Stress Scale (DASS; Lovibond and Lovibond, 1995*)*. This measure was selected to examine co-morbidity of ADHD with depression, anxiety and stress and to assess whether severity of these problems influenced outcome. The DASS is a set of three self-report scales designed to measure the negative emotional states of depression, anxiety and stress. Each of the three DASS scales contains 14 items, which are rated on a four-point severity scale. It has good psychometric properties and has the advantage of local normative data.

Vocabulary (Weschler, 1981). This test was selected to estimate intellectual ability and to assess the relationship between intellectual ability and treatment outcome. Vocabulary has been recognised as an excellent guide to general mental ability (Lezak, 1995). It also has a high loading on 'g', an estimate of intelligence, in factor analytic studies (Weschler, 1981). The test consists of 35 words arranged in order of difficulty, the examiner asks the meaning of the words on the list until five consecutive errors are made or the list is completed. It has good psychometric properties and normative data is available in the Weschler Adult Intelligence Scale Manual (Weschler, 1981).

Wide Range Achievement Test -Third Edition (WRAT-3; Jastak and Wilkinson, 1994*)*. This test was selected to assess the numeracy and literacy skills of the sample and to examine whether poor literacy skills impaired ability to benefit from the MCRP. The WRAT-3 measures achievement in Spelling, Arithmetic and Reading. The WRAT-3 is normed by age and produces standard scores and percentiles to compare an individual's performance with others of the same age. It has good psychometric properties.

Inclusion criteria were: (1) evidence of ADHD symptoms from childhood (i.e., a score of 36 or over on the Wender Utah Rating Scale); (2) current endorsement of the DSM IV criteria for ADHD; (3) a life long history consistent with ADHD; (4) evidence that ADHD symptoms are causing impairment in day to day functioning; and (5) willingness to participate in a study and sign a consent form. Exclusion criteria were the same as for study one.

It is noteworthy that over 95 percent of actual participants (n=33) had been diagnosed with ADHD by other health professionals prior to entry to the study. There were only five applicants where disagreement occurred with prior diagnoses. Four of these cases were ineligible for the study due to a lack of childhood symptoms. The fifth case had a Pervasive Developmental Disorder. These applicants were excluded together with other applicants who did not meet the entry criteria.

Participants

In total 57 applicants completed all three phases of the assessment; of these 42 met criteria for the study. Subsequent to drop out for other reasons (i.e., too far to travel n=2, other commitments n=3, other n=2) 35 applicants participated. Participants were accepted either on pre-prescribed medication or non-medicated and were asked to maintain their medication status (on or off) throughout the study and up until the two month follow up. Finally, participants were randomly assigned to either a treatment (n=17) or control group (n=18).

Outcome Measures

The MCRP aimed to teach skills to improve ADHD symptom management and day to day functioning. Thus the same outcome measures were used as in study one with the exception that the DSM IIIR ADHD Checklist was updated to use DSM IV criteria. The DSM IV ADHD Checklist is described below, for details of all other measures refer to study one.

DSM IV ADHD Checklist. The main purpose of this measure was to assess improvements in ADHD management as demonstrated by symptom reduction. DSM IV ADHD diagnostic symptoms for inattention, impulsivity and hyperactivity were turned into a checklist (APA, 1994). A scale between 1 "not a problem" to 10 "an extreme problem" was used for each symptom. The potential range on this measure is from 17 to 170. Scaling of DSM IV criteria has been used in one adult ADHD medication trial (Findling et al., 1996).

Outcome measures were administered to the treatment group on three occasions; pre-treatment, eight weeks later at post-treatment and at a two month follow up. The waiting list control group completed the measures on two occasions at an interval of eight weeks to equate with the pre- and post- treatment measurements. After eight weeks, people in the waiting list group were offered treatment, consistent with best ethical practice which considers that treatment should be offered to control groups as soon as possible after a waiting period. Where an abbreviation is found in the following text, T1 refers to the first administration of the measures *(pre-treatment and first control measure; week 1),* T2 to the second administration *(post-treatment and second control measure; week 8*) and T3 to the two-month follow-up, in the treatment group only.

Compliance

To assess whether participants complied with the intervention, support people were asked to keep a log of their telephone contacts. Each week, over the eight week programme, support people were asked to record: (1) if their partner had completed the set reading; (2) if their partner had completed the set homework exercise; and (3) if their partner had been using the skills. Reading and exercise completion were scored on a 3 point scale, from 0 "not completed" to 2 "fully completed". Use of skills was scored on a 2-point scale "yes" or "no". To further check compliance, the author examined participant's self help books at weeks four and eight and photocopied completed exercises.

Programme Evaluation

The minimal contact Cognitive Remediation Programme was evaluated to assess face validity and to elicit comments about how the programme could be improved. Following treatment at T2 (week 8), participants in the treatment group were asked to complete a rating scale to evaluate the usefulness of: (1) meeting others with ADHD; (2) topics discussed; (3) the workbook; (4) homework exercises; (5) attending sessions; and (6) help from support person. Each of these items (i.e., meeting others with ADHD etc) was rated on category scales from 1 "Not at all useful" to 10 "Extremely useful". Participants were also encouraged to add their own comments about the programme.

ANALYSES

Descriptive statistics (mean, median, variance, standard deviation, range, skewness and kurtosis) were calculated for the participants' demographic data, assessment measures and for the outcome measures at each time interval (i.e., T1 [week one], T2 [week eight] and T3 [week sixteen]). For descriptive purposes participant's Wender Utah Rating Scale scores were compared to the standardised sample (Ward, Wender and Reimherr, 1993).

As in study one an initial analysis was conducted, in which medication status was included as a between-participant variable. Medication status exerted no detectable effect. Consequently, for each outcome measure, T1 (week one) and T2 (week eight) outcome data (note T3 data [week sixteen] was only collected for the treatment group) were analysed by two-way repeated measures analysis of variance (ANOVA) with Group *(Control vs. Treatment)* as a between subject factor and Time *(T1 [week one] vs. T2 [week eight])* as a within subject factor.

Again for each measure, a dependent t-test was conducted to assess whether there was a significant improvement from pre-treatment at week one (T1) to the follow at week sixteen (T3). As before, medication status was found to exert no significant effect on maintenance and so is not reported.

Finally, compliance was examined using Spearman's Rho, by correlating treatment groups difference score on the DSM IV ADHD Checklist (calculated by subtracting T1 [week one] from T2 [week eight] scores) with a compliance score (calculated by adding scores for task completion during the programme [i.e., reading the self help book, completing exercises and using the skills]).

Table 4: Participant details pre-treatment/week 1 of the wait-list control, for Study 2

Variable	Treatment group Mean (SD)	Control group Mean (SD)
Number (n =)	17	18
Gender (M/F)	10/7	12/6
Medicated (Y/N)	11/6	12/6
Age	39.4 (7.7)	38.4 (12.1)
PRS*	12.0 (6.6)	15.3 (6.2)
WURS	54.9 (13.8)	64.9 (17.2)

*PRS was obtained for n = 13 in the Treatment group and n = 15 in the Control group.

RESULTS

Sample Characteristics

Pre-treatment status. Participant's age, medication status, WURS and PRS scores for treatment and control groups can be found in Table 4. On independent t-tests no difference was found between treatment and control groups for age, WURS or PRS scores (medication status had no effect on these scores either). Gender distribution was also similar in each group. Using independent t-tests no difference was found between the treatment and control groups on any T1 measure (likewise for medication status). Mean group scores for each measure on T1 can be seen in Table 5. Outcome on additional measures administered during the clinic assessment including the vocabulary subtest of the WAIS-R, the three subtests on the WRAT-3, the DASS can be seen on Table 6. There was no difference between the groups (treatment and control) on any specific characteristic, nor by medication status.

Table 5: Means (and standard deviations) for Treatment and Control groups across the course of Study 2

Variable*	T1 Week 1	T2 Week 8	T3 Week 16
Treatment group	n = 17**	n = 17***	n = 16***
Symptoms	100.5 (28.6)	77.8 (21.6)	73.3 (20.5)
Organisation	78.3 (17.2)	67.1 (13.4)	69.8 (13.0)
Self-esteem	102.5 (13.3)	109.9 (14.7)	106.6 (14.5)
State-anger	13.1 (4.1)	11.2 (1.7)	11.5 (2.0)

Table 5: Continued

Trait-anger	23.8 (4.7)	19.1 (3.5)	20.1 (3.1)
Control group	n = 18	n = 18	
Symptoms	109.9 (25.8)	106.9 (21.8)	
Organisation	82.2 (10.1)	86.0 (8.0)	
Self-esteem	105.0 (9.7)	97.5 (14.1)	
State-anger	12.9 (5.2)	15.7 (9.4)	
Trait-anger	27.0 (6.3)	25.9 (6.4)	

* Score reductions indicate improvement, excepting self-esteem where the reverse applies.
** n = 16 for organisation
*** n = 16 for symptoms
**** n = 15 for state and trait anger

Table 6: Means (and standard deviations) for the assessment measures used in Study 2.

Variable	Treatment group	Control group
Vocabulary (SS*)	WAIS-R	
	11.7 (2.3)	11.0 (2.7)
Spelling (SS)	WRAT-3	
	95.6 (14.5)	95.2 (12.5)
Reading (SS)	106.0 (8.5)	101.9 (11.8)
Arithmetic (SS)	93.8 (11.2)	92.3 (16.3)
Depression (RS**)	DASS	
	12.5 (9.3)	18.0 (9.8)
Anxiety (RS)	9.4 (7.4)	10.9 (7.7)
Stress (RS)	17.6 (9.8)	23.6 (9.9)

*Standardised score
**Raw score

Comparison of ADHD sample with control/normative data. For descriptive purposes the ADHD samples (n=35) scores on the WURS were first compared with mean standardised sample score for the WURS (Ward, Wender and Reimherr, 1993). The ADHD participants WURS scores were no different to the standardised sample (Ward et al., 1993; standardised sample mean=62.2, SD=14.6, participants mean=60.09, SD=16.2; z=0.85, see Howell, 1992; p162). Next, participant's scores on the PRS were correlated against their respective WURS scores. A moderate positive correlation was found between the PRS and WURS (r=0.49, n=28, p<0.01). This indicates consistency between participants and significant other reports of childhood ADHD behaviour.

Table 7: Significant treatment effects ($p < 0.05$) observed for Study 2.

Variable	Control vs. Treatment & T1 vs. T2 (ANOVA)			Treatment alone
	Time	Group	Time x Group	T1 vs. T3
	$F_{1,32}$ =	$F_{1,32}$ =	$F_{1,32}$ =	t_{15} =
Symptoms	13.00	6.05	7.68	4.13
Organisation *	8.80	9.28	31.37	3.13
Self-esteem**	NS	NS	15.61	NS
State-anger**	NS	NS	6.73	NS
Trait-anger**	14.50	9.06	5.54	3.00

* Degrees of freedom for t-test are t_{14}

** Degrees of freedom for ANOVA are $F_{1,33}$ and for t_{14}

Treatment Outcome

Outcome Measures

Table 5 illustrates mean scores, by group, for each dependent variable prior to treatment (T1), immediately after treatment (T2) and at the 2 month follow up (T3; for the treatment group only). In the treatment group, all outcome measures showed improvements after treatment, when contrasted with controls. This was confirmed by the ANOVAs, as the interaction between Time (*T1 vs. T2*) and Group (*Treatment vs. Control*) was significant for all measures (See Table 7), indicating improvements in the treatment group between T1 and T2, when compared to the control group. In addition to these interaction effects, a number of main effects are also noted in Table 7. These, however, are of little interest because of the significant interactions. Note that medication status exerted no significant effect on these results, nor at follow-up.

The treatment group was reassessed 2 months post treatment. As evident in Table 5, treatment gains were maintained for ADHD symptoms, organisational skills and trait anger. This was confirmed using paired t-tests (see Table 7), which indicate significant improvements when the T3 score (at 2 months) was compared to the pre-treatment score, T1.

Compliance

All the support people completed and returned the Logbooks. Compliance with treatment was calculated by combining Logbook scores for reading each chapter, homework completion and skills use. The treatment group compliance score was M=25.4, SD=8.23 (maximum possible score was 42). This suggests that participants generally complied with the intervention. The number of telephone calls made by the support people was also calculated (M=8.5, SD=1.63) indicating that nearly everyone received a telephone call on average once per week. A reliability check was made by comparing self-reports of homework completion with actual completed exercises from the Self-Help Books. Self report and completed exercises were completely consistent.

The non-parametric Spearman's correlation test was used to assess whether compliance correlated with improved ADHD symptomatology. A compliance score was calculated by adding reading scores, exercise completion scores and skills use score. This compliance score was correlated against a respective DSM IV ADHD Checklist score (calculated by subtracting T2 [week eight] scores from T1 [week one] scores). A moderate positive correlation was found (*rho*=0.54, n=16, $p<0.05$), suggesting greater compliance with the MCRP is associated with greater improvement in ADHD symptoms.

Clinical Significance of Symptom Changes

The clinical significance of the reduction in ADHD symptomatology was examined using the criterion from recent medication trials i.e., that of a 33 percent reduction in ADHD symptomatology (Findling et al., 1996; Spencer et al., 1995). Using this criterion, at T2 (week 8), 41 percent (n=7) of the participants were observed to be responders to treatment in terms of ADHD symptom reduction, at T3 (week 16) this decreased to 35 percent (n=6). On all other measures (organisational skills, self esteem and state and trait anger) changes were uniformly much smaller than 33 percent. Medication status exerted no influence here either.

The Effect of Cognitive and Behavioural Variables on Outcome

A further question addressed by this study was whether any of the following variables influenced treatment outcome: depression, anxiety, stress, reading and spelling ability and intellectual ability. To examine this question, participants in the treatment group had their T1-T2 difference score on the DSM IV ADHD rating scale calculated (the main dependent variable). This was then correlated with their score on each of the variables listed above. Outcome was not significantly associated with any of these variables (Pearson's r), suggesting no major influence of these variables on treatment efficacy.

Conclusion

The findings from study two are strikingly similar to study one. The program significantly improved performance on all measures, with most gains maintained to the 16 week follow-up. As before medication status exerted no detectable impact.

General Discussion

Study one evaluated a cognitive remediation programme (CRP) for adults with ADHD (some already medicated, some not). Following the treatment programme, participants reported that their ADHD symptoms were less problematic, that their organisational abilities improved, their self-esteem increased and that their anger management improved. Medication was not necessary to benefit from the treatment programme. At the two-month follow up, all therapeutic gains were either maintained or had continued to improve. Furthermore, at one-year post-treatment, statistically significant improvements in ADHD symptomatology, organisational skills, self esteem and trait anger remained apparent. Study two demonstrated similar results when the program had been converted into a predominately self help mode. These findings add weight to the argument that cognitive remediation techniques should be taught to adults with ADHD to assist with symptom management.

The sample selected for these studies can be considered representative of adults with ADHD. A clear set of diagnostic criteria and appropriate measures for clinical assessment were used. Diagnoses made by psychiatrists who specialise in treating adult ADHD were confirmed in the majority of cases. Furthermore, the clinical and demographic characteristics of this sample were similar to the findings of overseas studies (Sheikem, Asarnow, Hess, Zaucha and Wheeler, 1990; Ward, Wender and Reimherr, 1993). Participants with commonly co-occurring conditions such as anxiety, depression and learning disabilities were included, reflecting the reality that the majority of adults with ADHD have co-morbid conditions (Biederman, Faraone, Spencer, Wilens, Norman, Lapey, Mick, Krifcher-Lehman and Doyle, 1993). Outcomes from these studies can therefore be expected to generalise to typical clinical samples (albeit those who do not have substance abuse problems or anti-social behaviour).

In study one, the improvement in ADHD symptomatology was substantial following the CRP. Whilst direct comparison with medication trials is difficult because of differing entry criteria across studies, it is suitable to use the criterion of a 33% reduction in ADHD symptoms as an indication of satisfactory response to treatment. This criterion has been used in two adult ADHD medication trials (Findling, Schwartz, Flannery and Manos, 1996; Spencer, Biederman, Wilens et al, 1996). Using this criterion, a 50 percent improvement rate was observed between ratings at T1 and one- year post treatment. This outcome compares favourably with medication trials where the response rate varies between 25-78%. Furthermore, the CRP may have the advantage of being used as either an adjunct to existing medication treatment or as an alternative to medication.

Moreover, study two demonstrated that the programme could be used in a minimal contact form. Overall, the degree of improvement in ADHD symptoms shown by participants was very good for a self-directed program. It is possible to compare this program with other self-directed programs in the literature by comparing effect sizes. The effect size for the DSM IV ADHD Rating Scale (the main dependent variable) was $d = 1.4$. In a recent review of self help studies effect sizes varied from $d = 1.3$ for programs targeting sexual dysfunction to $d = 0.2$ for programs targeting substance abuse (Marrs, 1995). Thus the results from this program are clearly comparable, if not better, than others in the literature.

The success of the CRP in reducing symptom expression may be explained in a number of ways. First, strategies may act to partially circumvent the primary deficits associated with

ADHD. Similar findings have been observed in the brain injury literature, where adults who have been taught to use skills, such as self-instructional training and problem solving to compensate for organic deficits (Craine, 1992; Sohlberg and Mateer, 1989). Second, improvements in self esteem and anger management may contribute to the perception of improvement in primary symptoms. Third, the use of compensatory strategies may place less demands on attention and memory systems thus decreasing the impact of ADHD symptoms overall. In all probability, these mechanisms combine to improve symptomatology, suggesting that a multi-modal, multi-strategy skill approach is useful for adults with ADHD. Interestingly, many adults with ADHD who attended the program held the belief that they should be able to function without the use of everyday organisational tools and cognitive aids. Following the program, participants frequently expressed surprise at how simple strategies such as use of a diary, time management and reflective listening had improved their everyday functioning.

Disappointingly, there were not more substantial gains in self-esteem and state and trait anger. There is no doubt that both self-esteem and anger management are important issues for adults with ADHD. However, separate interventions may be required to obtain more substantial improvements in these domains.

The therapeutic effects of stimulant medication are known to enhance concentration and reduce hyperactivity (Spencer, Biederman, Wilens et al, 1996). These improvements in symptomatology could be expected to make learning new skills easier for those on medication. It might therefore be hypothesised that outcomes would be maximised if medication were used in conjunction with the CRP. However, in both studies non-medicated participants responded to the treatment as well as medicated participants. This may be an indication that those in the medicated group were non-responders or tolerant to their medication. An alternative explanation is that medicated participants had more severe symptoms prior to medication. However, this argument is weakened when childhood measures of ADHD symptomatology (WURS and PRS) are considered, as no difference was found between groups in the severity of childhood symptoms (in either study) suggesting that they were not more severely affected by ADHD. It is therefore probable that the medicated group were somewhat unusual, representing either a group who had become tolerant to medication or who had not responded.

During the skill acquisition phase, participants reported that the coaches/support people were helpful in enabling them to keep on track of the programme. In study one, improvements on all rating scales were found to be maintained or continued to improve, at two months post treatment, suggesting the strategies taught were used after the withdrawal of the support person. Furthermore, improvements in ADHD symptomatology and organisational skills were maintained one year later. The multi-modal approach ensured the programme was useful for all participants (and this was confirmed by the programme evaluation), as it enabled participants to individualise the programme by selecting strategies appropriate for their personal needs. In addition, participants had the continuing use of a workbook to review the programme. Thus maintenance of improvements is best explained by on-going skills use. Indeed, in study two it was demonstrated that compliance with the intervention was important for treatment outcome.

A secondary issue examined in study two was the influence of co-morbid factors on treatment outcome. This issue is considered important because of the childhood ADHD MTA study, that found children with different co-morbid patterns responded differently to the same intervention (Jensen, Hinshaw, Kraemer et al., 2001). In particular, children with co-morbid anxiety did better on behavioural treatments. In this study co-morbidity was not found to effect treatment outcome, although the relatively small sample size here might obscure any minor effect. This suggests that the program is suitable for adults with ADHD who have co-morbid learning problems and clinically significant levels of anxiety and depression.

Finally, it is worth commenting that the design (i.e sessions, workbooks, support people etc.) of the two programmes also was evaluated. All components of the programme were rated very highly suggesting that the programme structure was acceptable to the majority of participants.

Whilst these results are very encouraging, some caveats are necessary. First, outcome was restricted to self-report ratings that may be influenced by participant expectation. It was not possible to include independent clinical assessments in these preliminary studies, due to resource constraints. However, a less objective but equally important means of assessing treatment is to elicit anecdotal information from family or friends about a clients performance on day to day tasks (Wilens, Spencer and Biederman, 1995). Where possible the first author informally discussed progress with a relative or friend of each participant. In most cases, improvements were apparent to the significant other. In addition, feedback was obtained from psychologists and psychiatrists involved with the participants. This was equally encouraging in terms of observed improvements. While this information is anecdotal, it suggests that improvement ratings are reliable. This is consistent with the findings of other authors where adults with ADHD are reported as appropriate reporters of their own condition (Sheikem, Asarnow, Hess, Zaucha and Wheeler, 1990). A second caveat is that there are limitations to the interpretation of findings when a waiting list group is used, in that contact time with the mental health service is not controlled for. However, the use of an attention placebo group (i.e. 'a tea and sympathy group') is controversial both ethically and from a research perspective (Kendal and Norton-Ford, 1982).

As ADHD in adults becomes increasingly recognised, it is important that safe, effective treatments are trialled. Teaching cognitive remediation strategies provides one method of assisting adults in making a successful adjustment. Whilst these studies are only preliminary, the findings suggest that a cognitive remediation approach is an effective way of intervening to reduce the impact of ADHD on daily functioning and also that the approach warrants further investigation.

REFERENCES

Abikoff, H. (1987). An evaluation of cognitive behaviour therapy for hyperactive children. In (Eds.) Lahey, B. B., and Kazden, A. E. *Advances in Clinical Child Psychology, 10,* 171-216.

Abikoff, H., and Gittelman, R. (1985). Hyperactive children treated with stimulants. Is cognitive training a useful adjunct? *Archives of General Psychiatry, 42,* 953-961.

American Psychiatric Association. (1989). *Diagnostic and Statistical Manual of Mental Disorder. Revised Third Edition (DSM IIIR).* Washington. DC: American Psychiatric Association.

American Psychiatric Association. (1994). *Diagnostic and Statistical Manual of Mental Disorder. Fourth Edition (DSM IV).* Washington. DC: American Psychiatric Association.

Barkley, R. A. (1991). *Attention Deficit Hyperactivity Disorder. Clinical Workbook.* New York: Guildford Press.

Barkley, R.A, Fischer, M., Smallish, L., and Fletcher, K. (2004). Young adult followup of hyperactive children: Antisocial activities and drug use. *Journal of Child Psychology and Psychiatry, 45,* 195-211.

Ben-Yishay, Y., and Diller, L. (1993). Cognitive remediation in traumatic brain injury: Update and issues. *Archives of Physical Medicine and Rehabilitation, 74,* 204-213.

Bender, A. (1938). *A Visual Motor Gestalt and It's Clinical Use.* New York: American Psychiatric Association.

Bemporad, J., and Zambenedetti, M. (1996). Psychotherapy of adults with attention-deficit disorder. *Journal of Psychotherapy Practice and Research, 5,* 228-237.

Biederman, J., Faraone, S.,Spencer, T., Wilens, T., Norman, D., Lapey, K., Mick, E., Krifcher-Lehman, B. and Doyle, A. (1993). Patterns of psychiatric comorbidity, cognition and psychosocial functioning in adults with attenion deficit hyperactivity disorder. *American Journal of Psychiatry, 150,* 1792-1798.

Borland, B., and Heckman, H. (1976). Hyperactive boys and their brothers: A 25 year follow-up study. *Archives of General Psychiatry, 33,* 669-675.

Brown, R. T. (1980). Impulsivity and psychoeducational Intervention in hyperactive children. *Journal of Learning Disabilities, 13,* 19-24.

Brown, R. T., Borden, K. A., Wynne, M. E., Schleser, R. and Clingerman, S. R. (1986). Methylphenidate and cognitive therapy with ADD children: A methodological reconsideration. *Journal of Abnormal Child Psychology, 14*, 481-497.

Brown, R. T., Wynne, M. E., and Medenis, R. (1985). Methylphenidate and cognitive therapy: A comparison of treatment approaches with hyperactive boys. *Journal of Abnormal Child Psychology, 13*, 69-87.

Cicerone, K. D., and Wood, J. C. (1987). Planning disorder after closed head injury: A case study. *Archives of Physical Medicine and Rehabilitation, 68,* 111-115.

Cohen, J. N., Sullivan, J., Minde, K., Novak, C., and Helwig, C. (1981). Evaluation of the relative effectiveness of methylphenidate and cognitive behaviour modification in the treatment of kindergarten-aged hyperactive children. *Journal of Abnormal Child Psychology, 9*, 43-54.

Conners, C. K. (1973). Rating scales for use in drug studies with children. *Psychophamacology Bulletin*, (Special Issue-Pharmacotherapy with children), 24-84.

Craine, J. F. (1982). The retraining of frontal lobe dysfunction. In Trexler, L. E. (Ed). *Cognitive Rehabilitation. Conceptualisation and Intervention.* New York: Plenum Press.

Davidson, H. H., and Lang, G. (1960). Children's perceptions of their teachers feelings towards them related to self perception, school achievement and behaviour. *Journal of Experimental Education, 29*, 107-118.

Douglas, V. I., Parry, P., Marton, P., and Garson, C. (1976). Assessment of a cognitive training program for hyperactive children. *Journal of Abnormal Child Psychology, 4,* 389-409.

Durrell, D. D. (1955). *Durrell Analysis of Reading Difficulty.* New York: Harcourt, Brace and World.

Farone, S,. Spencer, T., Aleardi, M., Pagano, C., and Biederman, J. (2004). Meta-analysis of the efficacy of methylphenidate for treating adult attention-deficit-hyperactivity disorder. *Journal of Clinical Psychopharmacology, 24,* 24-29.

Findling, R., Schwartz, M., Flannery, D., and Manos, M. (1996). Venlafaxine in adults with attention-deficit/hyperactivity disorder: An open clinical trial. *Journal of Clinical Psychiatry, 57,* 184-189.

Frankel, F., Myatt, R., Cantwell, D. P., and Feinberg, D. T. (1997). Parent assisted transfer of children's social skills training: Effects on children with and without attention-deficit hyperactivity disorder. *Journal of the American Academy of Child and Adolescent Psychiatry, 36,* 1056-1064.

Freeman, M. R., Dicowden, M., and Bat Ami, M. (1992). Executive and compensatory memory retraining in traumatic brain injury, *Brain Injury, 6,* 65-70.

Gittelman, R. (1985). Self evaluation (teenager's) self report. *Psychopharmacology Bulletin, 21,* 925-926.

Gittelman, R., Manuzza, S., Shenker, R., and Bonagura, N. (1985). Hyperactive boys almost grown up. I. Psychiatric status. *Archives of General Psychiatry, 42,* 937-47.

Golden, J. C. (1978). *Stroop Color Word Test.* Chicago: Stoeltering.

Goodwin, R. E., and Bolton, D. P. (1991). Decision-making in cognitive rehabilitation: A clinical model. *Cognitive Rehabilitation, July/August,* 12-19.

Goodwin, E. R., and Corgiat, M. D. (1992). Cognitive rehabilitation of adult attention deficit disorder: A case study. *The Journal of Cognitive Rehabilitation, Sept/Oct,* 28-35.

Goyette, C. H., Conners, C. K., and Ulrich, R. F. (1978). Normative data on revised conners parent and teacher rating scales. *Journal of Abnormal Child Psychology, 6,* 221-236.

Gray, J. M., and Robertson, I. (1989). Remediation of attentional difficulties following brain injury: Three experimental single case studies. *Brain Injury, 3,* 163-170.

Green, R.W., and Ablon, J.S. (2001). What does the MTA study tell us about effective psychosocial treatment for ADHD? *Journal of Clinical Child and Adolescent Psychology, 30,* 114-121.

Gresham, F. M., and Elliott, S. N. (1990). *Social Skills Rating System.* Circle Pines, MN: Assistance Service.

Hallowell, E., and Ratey, J. (1994). *Driven to Distraction. Recognising and Coping with Attention Deficit Disorder from Childhood through Adulthood.* New York: Simon and Schuster.

Heaton, R. K., Chelune, G. J., and Lehman, R. A .W. (1978). Using neuropsychological and personality tests to assess the likelihood of patient employment, *Journal of Nervous and Mental Diseases, 166,* 408-416.

Hinshaw, S. P., Buhrmester, D., and Heller, T. (1989). Anger control in response to verbal provocation: Effects of stimulant medication for boys with AD/HD. *Journal of Abnormal Child Psychology, 17,* 393-407.

Hinshaw, S. P., Henker, B., and Whalen, C. K. (1984a). Self-control in hyperactive boys in anger-inducing situations: Effects of cognitive-behavioural training and of methylphenidate. *Journal of Abnormal Child Psychology, 12,* 55-77.

Hinshaw, S. P., Henker, B., and Whalen, C. K. (1984b). Cognitive-Behavioural and pharmacologic interventions for hyperactive boys: Comparative and combined effects. *Journal of Consulting and Clinical Psychology, 52,* 739-749.

Howell, D. C. (1992). *Statistical Methods for Psychology-Third Edition.* USA: Duxbury Press.

Jastak, S., and Wilkinson, G. (1994). *Wide Range Achievement Test-Third Edition.* USA: Psychological Corporation Ltd.

Jensen, P.S., Hinshaw, S.P., Kraemer, H.C., Leonora, N., Newcorn, J.H., Abikoff, H.B., March, J.S., Arnold, L.G., Catwell, D.P., Connors, K., Elliott, G.R., Greenhill, L.L., Hechtman, L., Hoza, B., Pelham, W., Severe, J.B., Swanson, J.M., Wells, K.C., Wigal, T., and Vitello, B. (2001). ADHD comorbdity findings from the MTA study: Comparing co-morbid subgroups. *Journal of the American Academy of Child and Adolescent Psychiatry, 40,* 147-158.

Kane, R., Mikalac, C., Benjamin, S., and Barkley, R. (1990). Assessment and treatment of adults with ADHD. In (Ed) Barkley, R. *Attention Deficit Hyperactivity Disorder. A Handbook for Diagnosis and Treatment.* New York: Guildford Press.

Karp, S. A., and Konstadt, N. L. (1963). *Children's Embedded Figures Test.* New York: Cognitive Tests.

Kendall, P., and Norton-Ford, J. (1982). Therapy outcome research methods. In Kendall, P., and Butcher, J. (Ed) *Handbook of Research Methods in Clinical Psychology.* New York: A Wiley-Interscience Publication.

Keogh, B. K., and Margolis, J. (1976). A component analysis of attentional problems of educationally handicapped boys. *Journal of Abnormal Child Psychology, 4,* 349-359.

Levin, H. S. (1990). Cognitive rehabilitation. Unproved but promising. *Archives of Neurology, 47,* 223-224.

Lezak, M. (1982). Problems of assessing executive functions. *International Journal of Psychology, 17,* 281-297.

Lezak, M. (1995). *Neuropsychological Assessment.* Third Edition. New York: Oxford University Press.

Lira, F. T., Carne, W., and Masri, A. M. (1983). Treatment of anger and impulsivity in a brain damaged patient: A case study applying stress inoculation. *Clinical Neuropsychology, 5,* 159-160.

Lovibond, S. H., and Lovibond, P. F. (1995). *Manual for the Depression Anxiety Stress Scales.* Sydney: Psychology Foundation Mongraph.

Mannuzza, S., Gittelman-Klein, R., and Addalli, K. A. (1991). Young adult mental status of hyperactive boys and their brothers: A Prospective follow up study. *Journal of the American Academy of Child and Adolescent Psychiatry, 30,* 743-751.

Mannuzza, S., Klein, R., Bessler, A., Malloy, P., and LaPadula, M. (1998). Adult psychiatric status of hyperactive boys grown up. *American Journal of Psychiatry, 155,* 493-498.

Mannuzza, S., Klein, R., Bonagura, N., Malloy, P., Giampino, T., and Addalli, K. (1991). Hyperactive boys almost grown up V. Replication of psychiatric status. *Archives of General Psychiatry, 48*, 77-83.

Marrs, R. (1995). A meta-analysis of bibliotherapy studies. *American Journal of Community Psychology, 23,* 843-864.

Meichenbaum, D., and Goodman, J. (1971). Training impulsive children to talk to themselves: A means of developing self control. *Journal of Abnormal Psychology, 77,* 115-126.

Moore, S. F., and Cole, S. O. (1978). Cognitive self-mediation training with hyperkinetic children. *Bulletin of the Psychonomic Society, 12 (1),* 18-20.

MTA Co-operative group. (1999). A 14-month randomised trial of treatment strategies for attention deficit hyperactivity disorder. *Archives of General Psychiatry, 56,* 1073-1086.

Nadeau, K. (1995). Life management skills for the adult with ADD. In Nadeau, K. (Ed). *A Comprehensive Guide to Attention Deficit Disorder in Adults. Research. Diagnosis. Treatment.* New York: Brunner/Mazel Publishers.

National Health and Medical Research Council (1996). *Attention Deficit Hyperactivity Disorder.* Australia: Commonwealth Department of Health and Family Services.

Neimann. H., Ruff, R. R., Baser, C. A. (1990). Computer assisted attention retraining in head injured individuals: A controlled efficacy study of an out-patient program. *Journal of Consulting and Clinical Psychology, 58,* 811-7.

Pekarik, E., Prinz, R., Liebert, D., Weintraub, S., and Neil, J. (1976). The pupil evaluation inventory: A sociometric technique for assessing children's social behaviour. *Journal of Abnormal Child Psychology, 4,* 83-97.

Pfiffner, L. J., and McBurnett, K. (1997). Social skills training with parent generalisation: Treatment effects for children with attention deficit disorder. *Journal of Consulting and Clinical Psychology, 65,* 749-757.

Ponsford, J. L., and Kinsella, G. (1988). Evaluation of a remedial programme for attentional deficits following closed head injury. *Journal of Clinical and Experimental Neuropsychology, 10,* 693-708.

Richters, J. E., Arnold, L. E., Jensen, P. S., Abikoff, H., Conners, C. K., Greenhill, L .L., Hechtman, L., Hinshaw, S. P., Pelham, W. E., and Swanson, J. M. (1995). NIMH collaborative multisite multimodal treatment study of children with ADHD: I. Background and rationale. *Journal of the Academy of Child and Adolescent Psychiatry, 34),* 987-999.

Rossini, E. D., and O'Conner, M. A. (1995). Retrospective self-reported symptoms of attention-deficit hyperactivity disorder: Reliability of the wender utah rating scale. *Psychological Reports, 77,* 751-754.

Satterfield, J. H., Satterfield, B. T., and Cantwell, D. P. (1980). Multimodality treatment. A two-year evaluation of 61 hyperactive boys. *Archives of General Psychiatry, 37,* 915-919.

Satterfield, J. H., Satterfield, B. T., and Cantwell, D. P. (1981). Three year treatment study of 100 hyperactive boys. *Journal of Pediatrics, 98,* 650-655.

Scherzer, B .P. (1986). Rehabilitation following severe head trauma: Results of a three year program. *Archives of Physical Medicine and Rehabilitation, 67,* 366-374.

Shekim, W. O., Asarnow, R. F., Hess, E., Zaucha, K., and Wheeler, N. (1990). A clinical and demographic profile of a sample of adults with attention deficit hyperactivity disorder, residual state. *Comprehensive Psychiatry, 31,* 416-425.

Smith, A. (1982). *Symbol-Digit Modalities Test-Revised.* Los Angeles: Western Psychological Services.

Sohlberg, M. M., and Mateer, C. A. (1987). Effectiveness of an attention-training program. *Journal of Clinical and Experimental Neuropsychology, 9,* 117-130.

Sohlberg, M. M., and Mateer, C. A. (1989). *Introduction to Cognitive Rehabilitation. Theory and Practice.* New York: Guildford press.

Speilberger, C. D. (1991). *State-Trait Anger Expression Inventory. Revised Research Edition.* USA: Psychological Assessment Resources Inc.

Spencer, T., Biederman, J., Wilens, T., Harding, M., O'Donnell, D., and Griffin, S. (1996). Pharmacotherapy of attention-deficit hyperactivity disorder across the life cycle. *Journal of the American Academy of Child and Adolescent Psychiatry, 35,* 409-432.

Spencer, T., Wilens, T., Biederman, J., Faraone, S., Ablon, S., and Lapey, K. (1995). A double-blind, crossover comparison of methylphenidate and placebo in adults with childhood-onset Attention-deficit hyperactivity disorder. *Archives of General Psychiatry, 52,* 434-443.

Stein, M. A., Sandoval, R., Szumoski, E., Roizen, N., Reinecke, M. A., Blondis, T. A., and Klein, Z. (1995). Psychometric characteristics of the wender utah rating scale (WURS): Reliability and factor structure for men and women. *Psychopharmacology Bulletin, 31,* 425-433.

Stevenson, C., Whitmont, S., Bornholt, L., Livesey, D. and Stevenson, R. (2002). A cognitive remediation programme for adults with attention deficit hyperactivity disorder. *Australian and New Zealand Journal of Psychiatry, 36,* 610-616.

Stevenson, C., Stevenson, R. and Whitmont, S. (2003). A self-directed psychosocial intervention with minimal therapist contact for adults with ADHD. *Clinical Psychology and Psychotherapy, 10,* 93-101.

Still, G, (1902). The coulstonian lectures on some abnormal psychical conditions in children. *Lancet,* 1008-1012, 1077-1082, 1163-1168.

Ward, M., Wender, P., and Reimherr, F. (1993). The Wender Utah rating scale: An aid to retrospective diagnosis of childhood attention deficit hyperactivity disorder. *American Journal of Psychiatry, 150,* 885-890.

Webster, J. S., and Scott, R. R. (1983) The effects of self-instructional training on attentional deficits following head injury. *Clinical Neuropsychology, 5,* 69-74.

Weinstein, C. S. (1994). Cognitive remediation strategies. An adjunct to the psychotherapy of adults with attention-deficit hyperactivity disorder. *Journal of Psychotherapy Practice and Research, 3,* 44-57.

Weiss, G., and Hechtman, L. (1986). *Hyperactive Children Grown Up. Empirical Findings and Theoretical Considerations.* London: Guildford Press.

Weiss, G., and Hechtman, L. (1993). *Hyperactive Children Grown Up. Second Edition.* New York: Guildford Press.

Weiss, G., Hechtman, L., Milroy, T., and Perlman, T. (1985). Psychiatric status of hyperactives as adults: A controlled prospective 15-year follow-up of 63 hyperactive children. *Journal of the American Academy of Child Psychiatry, 24,* 211-220.

Weiss, G., Hechtman, L., and Perlman, T. (1978). Hyperactive as young adults: School, employer and self rating scales obtained during ten year follow-up evaluations. *American Journal of Orthopsychiatry, 48,* 438-445.

Weiss, G., Hechtman, L., Perlman, T., Hopkins, J., and Wener, A. (1979) Hyperactives as young adults. A controlled prospective ten year follow up of 75 children. *Archives of General Psychiatry, 36,* 675-681.

Weiss, G., Minde, K., Werry, J., Douglas, V., and Nemeth, E. (1971). Studies on the hyperactive. Five year follow up. *Archives of General Psychiatry, 24,* 409-414.

Weiss, M.D., and Weiss. J.R. (2004). A guide to the treatment of adults with ADHD. *Journal of Clinical Psychiatry, 65,* 27-37.

Weschler, D. (1981). *Manual for the Weschler Adult Intelligence Scale-Revised.* San Antonio: The Psychological Corporation of Harcourt, Brace, Jovanovich.

Weschler, D. (1987). *Manual for the Weschler Memory Scale-Revised.* New York: Psychological Corporation.

Wiggins, D. (1999). Effects of a brief intervention for adults with attention deficit hyperactivity disorder. *Journal of Mental Health Counselling, 21,* 82-90.

Wilens, T., Spencer, T., and Biederman, J. (1994). Psychopharmacology of adult ADHD. In Nadeau, K. (Ed) *A Comprehensive Guide to Attention Deficit Hyperactivity Disorder in Adults. Research. Diagnosis. Treatment.* New York: Brunner/Mazel Publishers

Zentall, S. S., Harper, G. W., and Stormont-Spurgen, M. (1993). Children with hyperactivity and their organisational abilities. *Journal of Educational Research, 87,* 112-117.

In: Attention Deficit Hyperactivity Disorder
Editor: Marvin C. Shriner, pp. 47-66

ISBN: 1-60021 321-9

Chapter II

Stimulant Dosing in Adults with Attention Deficit Hyperactivity Disorder

Julian N. Trollor [1,2] ***and Perminder S. Sachdev*** [2]

[1] School of Psychiatry, University of New South Wales, and Senior Staff Specialist, Neuropsychiatric Institute, Prince of Wales Hospital, Sydney

[2] School of Psychiatry, University of New South Wales, and Director, Neuropsychiatric Institute, Prince of Wales Hospital, Sydney

Introduction

Even though it is often considered to be disorder of childhood, attention deficit hyperactivity disorder (ADHD) is recognized to persist well into adulthood. An age-dependent decline in retention of diagnosis [1 2] has been noted, with approximately one-third of ADHD children experiencing ADHD symptoms persistent into adulthood. As the current cohort of children and teenagers treated with psychostimulants is maturing, increasing numbers are seeking continuation of treatment in adulthood. Popularization of ADHD has also resulted in a large number of individuals coming forward for assessment for the first time in adulthood. However, despite its increasing recognition, concerns remain regarding the validity of the adult diagnosis and the appropriateness of long-term management with psychostimulants.

Treatment with stimulants in adulthood raises a number of issues peculiar to this age group. In patients who are continuing treatment from childhood and in those commencing treatment for the first time as adults, an endpoint for stimulant treatment can be difficult to identify. The potentially open-ended nature of the treatment therefore provokes concerns

[2] Correspondence: Dr J. Trollor, Neuropsychiatric Institute, Euroa Centre, Prince of Wales Hospital, Randwick, NSW 2031.Tel 61-2-93823763; Fax: 61-2-93823774; Email: *J.Trollor@unsw.edu.au*

about long-term exposure to stimulant medication, in terms of its efficacy, toxicity and the potential for psychological 'dependence' on the drug. Whether age renders individuals more susceptible to adverse effects is an unanswered question. As with the use of stimulants in adolescence, there is concern about the potential for abuse in adults. As society demands a 'quick fix' to most problems, there is pressure on both clinicians and patients to use the most rapidly effective treatment, often at the expense of development of non-pharmacological methods of symptom control (for example skills training or cognitive behavioural strategies). Despite these obvious issues, there are as yet no widely adopted guidelines for stimulant prescription and dosing in adults with ADHD.

In this chapter, we review the literature on the efficacy of stimulants in adults, particularly in relation to dose. The pharmacokinetics and behavioural pharmacology of stimulants are examined in order to better identify factors that may assist in determine an appropriate stimulant dose for adults. The potential risks of using high doses of stimulant are explored. We present some clinical guidelines for the use of stimulants in adults, focusing on dosing strategies. We define stimulant dose in units of milligram per kilogram per day (mg/kg/day), with low dose stimulant treatment as equal to or less than 0.5mg/kg/day of dexamphetamine or 1.0mg/kg/day of methylphenidate; high dose as between 0.5.0 mg/kg/day of dexamphetamine or 1.0-2.0 mg/kg/day of methylphenidate; and very high as equal to or greater than 1.0 mg/kg/day of dexamphetamine or 2.0mg/kg/day of methylphenidate. This arbitrary definition is derived from what are generally considered low, high and very high dose in the human and animal literature.

CONTEXT OF STIMULANT USE IN ADULTS

The treatment of adult ADHD with psychostimulants is a growing phenomenon in clinical practice [3]. Most psychiatrists approach the prescription of stimulants with some trepidation. Stimulants are more commonly thought of as drugs of abuse rather than therapy, their long-term effects are not known and beneficial effects are hard to quantify objectively. When a patient makes a request for an increasing dose of the drug for the treatment of ADHD, it immediately arouses the suspicion of abuse or fear of adverse consequences. The problem is particularly acute in adults because the validity of the diagnosis of ADHD in adults is often questioned [4], the empirical basis for treatment is less well-established than for children [3 4], the co-occurrence of drug abuse is common [5] and many patients have the additional diagnosis of personality disorder [5]. If one does accept the legitimacy of stimulant drug treatment in adult ADHD, is there a maximum daily dosage that should not be exceeded? The answer to this question needs to be sought from the efficacy data available, the neuroscientific information that underpins the treatment, the pharmacokinetics and bioavailability data on stimulants in adults in comparison with children and the differential likelihood of long-term side effects with higher doses.

In contradistinction to this clinical imperative is the limited data on the long-term use of psychostimulants in ADHD adults. The majority of studies are short or medium term and the issue of long-term tolerability and safety in adults has not been systematically addressed. As yet, there are no well-defined clinical guidelines regarding the doses of stimulants appropriate to the adult population. In Australia as in other parts of the world, the degree of regulation of stimulant prescription varies. In a phenomenon mirrored in other parts of the world, some Australian regulatory authorities notionally specify maximum permissible dose for use in adults but the regulations concerning stimulant prescription vary markedly from State to State. In the absence of clear guidelines, the titration and dosing process with stimulants is likely to vary considerably from clinician to clinician. This chapter aims to puts forward some of the theoretical and practical issues pertaining to stimulant dosing in adults with ADHD.

Studies of Efficacy

The treatment of ADHD with stimulants has been extensively investigated in children. A recent meta-analysis of the effect of methylphenidate in children included 62 randomised trials with a total of 2897 participants [6]. This review highlighted the short duration of most studies which had an average duration of just over three weeks. Less than 15% of studies lasted longer than four weeks. Overall, the quality of these trials was assessed as low. Significant effects of methylphenidate were demonstrated as rated by teachers and parents of affected children. Positive effect sizes were seen for core features of ADHD, and were highest for hyperactivity and a combined inattention and overactivity rating. Other features such as aggression and conduct problems also showed a favorable response. For both teacher and parent estimates, there was no significant effect of methylphenidate demonstrable on separate attention ratings. The most prominent adverse effects were decreased appetite, insomnia and stomach ache. Across these trials, various dosing schedules were used and no conclusions could be drawn regarding relationship between dose and efficacy or side effects.

The effectiveness of stimulant treatment in adults with ADHD has been studied in a very limited manner. The efficacy of stimulants, in particular methylphenidate, in adult ADHD has been examined in at least seven studies (N=193 subjects), five of which were controlled, with an overall report of significant reduction of symptoms of ADHD [7]. Within these studies, there was considerable variability in response rates ranging from 25% to 73%. Some of this variability could be explained by differences in methodology between studies, such as poorly standardized diagnostic procedures, variability in stimulant dose, variable rates of comorbidity and differing methods in determining efficacy of medication. Convincing evidence for dose effect is not apparent in these initial studies. For example, the highest response rate in the fixed dose studies was seen in the study in which the lowest milligram per kilogram dose of methylphenidate was used [8]. The majority of these studies used a relatively low dose of methylphenidate. In four of the five controlled studies [8 9 10 11], the average daily dose of methylphenidate used was 0.6 mg/kg and the average response rate was about 50%. A double-blind placebo-controlled randomized crossover trial by Spencer et al [12] utilized a variety of doses of methylphenidate in the same patient in a crossover design. An average daily dose of methylphenidate in the initial week of 0.51 mg/kg was used, followed by a second week dose of 0.75 mg/kg and a final week dose of 0.92 mg/kg. A significant effect of methylphenidate on ADHD symptoms was apparent as well as a significant interaction between time and drug response. An overall response rate of 78%

(versus 4% for placebo) was observed as determined by a reduction of at least 30% in individual rating scale scores. Average one hour serum methylphenidate levels were 4.6 +/- 0.8 ng/mL, a level approximately half that of levels reported in pediatric samples. No clear association between serum level and clinical response was observed, although the authors argue for the prescription of higher doses on the basis of their overall high response rates. However, there is an obvious limitation of such data i.e. differential improvement rates in studies utilizing different doses in the same patients cannot be accepted as evidence that higher doses are more efficacious. For this to be shown, a direct head-to head comparison of different doses is required. Furthermore, the maximum dose examined in the Spencer et al study [12] was 1 mg/kg, thereby providing no information on even higher doses, the question that is raised by many clinicians and patients.

Higher doses were used in one open study treating predominantly children [13], with the daily dosage range for dexamphetamine being 1.6 to 3.6 mg/kg and for methylphenidate 1.4 to 7.7 mg/kg. The highest dose of dexamphetamine used in this report was 230 mg/day. The open nature of this report is a serious limitation and makes it an unlikely basis to guide therapy [14]. More recently, Bouffard et al [15] undertook a direct comparison of the efficacy of two different doses of methylphenidate in 30 adult ADHD subjects. This study was a double blind placebo crossover trial administered 10 mg of methylphenidate t.i.d. for two weeks, followed by 15 mg t.i.d. for two weeks. Following a one week washout, the process was repeated with either placebo or methylphenidate. Although significant improvements in ADHD symptoms were noted and there were significant improvements on computerised tests, there was no difference between the two doses.

There has been only one controlled trial of dexamphetamine in adult ADHD [16]. This randomized double-blind placebo-controlled trial (N=45; mean age 35.5 years, range 19-57 years) used a number of efficacy measures including self and relative's reports, clinician ratings and a general measure of psychological well-being. Compliance was monitored by urinalysis. Dexamphetamine was gradually increased over a three week period to 15 mg/day and then titrated by the patient up to a maximum of 30 mg/day in weeks four to six. Patients were reviewed at the end of week six. The mean titrated daily dose of the dexamphetamine was 23.85 mg (0.34 mg/kg). Although both groups improved significantly, the dexamphetamine group had lower self ratings of symptoms, and performed better on the Global Improvement Scale and measures of patient satisfaction. No patients ceased dexamphetamine as a result of side effects. This study and some anecdotal reports [17] support the proposition that dexamphetamine shares similar efficacy to methylphenidate in ADHD adults. Furthermore, the effective dose of dexamphetamine, if usage in children is a guide, is about one-half the methylphenidate dose [18,19].

Horrigan et al [20] examined the effectiveness of mixed amphetamine salt (i.e. a mix of *d*-amphetamine and *l*-amphetamine) in an open label study of 24 ADHD adults. Treatment was commenced at 5 mg twice daily and titrated according to clinical response over a 16 week period. Fifty four percent of patients were classified as responders based on the clinical global impression improvement scale. Mean dose for responders was very small at 10.77 mg/day (0.14 mg/kg/day). Significant reductions in other measures of ADHD symptoms including the Copeland symptom checklist and Brown Attention Deficit Disorder scales were noted. This study provides preliminary evidence of the effectiveness of mixed amphetamine salt in adult ADHD.

The above studies suggest that chronic low-dose stimulant treatment is as effective in adult ADHD as in the childhood disorder, and that methyphenidate and dexamphetamine have similar efficacy. There is no empirical evidence to suggest that the use of high dose stimulant treatment in adults is superior to the average dose. There are however deficiencies in the literature including no head-to-head comparison of different stimulant doses, a lack of correlation of efficacy with serum stimulant levels, and in many studies a lack of comprehensive assessment of stimulant response on neuropsychological measures.

Behavioural Pharmacology

An examination of the behavioural pharmacology of dopaminomimetic drugs is instructive in determining the theoretical rationale for stimulant dosing. It has been hypothesised that stimulants such as methylphenidate and dexamphetamine have a biphasic response in animals. At lower doses these drugs are thought to reduce locomomotor activity, whereas at high doses they stimulate locomotor activity [21 22, 23]. The dose of amphetamine that reduces activity in mice is in the range of 0.5 to 1.0 mg/kg, with activity levels increasing progressively with doses from 1.0 to 5.0 mg/kg [23]. The same biphasic response is seen in humans. However, the precise doses required to produce an increase in locomotor activity is uncertain and is subject to individual variation. The commonly used clinical dose of dexamphetamine (0.2 to 0.6 mg/kg) is in the same range as that of the hypo-locomotor animal model, and in the vast majority of patients does not produce significant increase in motor activity or agitation. Furthermore, as it is common practice to titrate the dose of stimulant medication at the time of initiation, (e.g. by introducing a dose of approximately 0.15 mg/kg/day of dexamphetamine or 0.30 mg/kg/day of methylphenidate), an increase in locomotor activity is unlikely to be seen.

The activation of postsynaptic dopamine receptors is thought to mediate most of the locomotor activating effects of stimulant medications. However, there is some debate regarding how the reduction in locomotor activity in hyperactive animal models and ADHD humans may be mediated. Both methylphenidate and dexamphetamine are indirectly acting stimulants. They augment catecholaminergic transmission through the blockade of catecholamine uptake at high affinity uptake sites. Dexamphetamine also promotes the release of newly synthesized dopamine from catecholaminergic terminals, the resulting dopamine being free to act on both presynaptic and postsynaptic receptors. Low-dose directly acting dopamine agonists such as apomorphine preferentially activate autoreceptors leading to a reduction in dopamine release. At high doses, this is overridden by stimulation of postsynaptic receptors [24 25]. This differential responsiveness for directly acting dopamine agonists may explain why a biphasic behavioral response is seen with these agents. While the above observation has been used to argue for the biphasic response to stimulant medication [26], there are several problems in applying this theory to indirectly acting stimulants such as methylphenidate and dexamphetamine.

The first difficulty with this theory is that not all investigators have demonstrated a reduction in locomotor activity in response to stimulant medication in animal models. Although supported by some studies of spontaneously active rodents [27], other investigators have demonstrated a failure of low doses of dexamphetamine to reduce locomotion scores in normal animals [28 29]. However, in studies of rats made hyperactive with a neonatal dopaminergic lesion [30], support for a biphasic response is evident. An additional problem is that some electrophysiological studies of the effect of dexamphetamine suggest that there is no differential between its presynaptic and postsynaptic effects [25 31] in the healthy state.

Another theory, put forward by Seeman and Madras [32], suggests that the differential effects of dexamphetamine are due to relative rather than absolute increases in synaptic dopamine levels. There is a differential effect of the drug on the resting level of extracellular dopamine compared to the increase it produces in pulsatile dopamine release associated with the nerve impulse [32]. In a drug-free condition, a nerve impulse produces a transient 60-fold rise in synaptic dopamine level above the baseline level of about 4 nM [33]. Methylphenidate and dexamphetamine, like cocaine, block the dopamine transporter, and dexamphetamine additionally has a direct dopamine releasing action [34]. These drugs therefore raise the baseline level of extracellular dopamine as well as the nerve impulse-associated rise. At low doses of stimulants in the rat, the rise in baseline values is about six-fold and that in the impulse-related values two-fold [35 36]. The relative rise of dopamine, when expressed as a percentage of the baseline value, is therefore lowered by stimulants at low doses. At higher doses of dexamphetamine (> 1 mg/kg), the rise in baseline is 7 to 35-fold and that in the pulsatile output about 7-fold [37]. This differential effect of low and high doses may account for the biphasic response of stimulants. However, this explanation has been criticized by Ruskin et al [31] on the basis that the effect would require a differential sensitivity of presynaptic and postsynaptic dopamine receptors, which in their opinion does not exist.

It is possible that there is a differential effect of stimulants on dopamine neurotransmission in the healthy versus diseased states. Abnormalities of the structure and function of the basal ganglia in ADHD subjects [38] raises the possibility that in humans, as in hyperactive animal models, there may be alterations in pre or postsynaptic dopamine receptor sensitivity. Direct measurement of dopaminergic function in humans with and without ADHD would be required to consolidate this theory. However, the biphasic response model in ADHD continues to be a useful one. It could be argued that higher dexamphetamine doses (for example greater than 1 mg/kg) will have a stimulating effect and could possibly worsen the features of ADHD.

Functional Imaging Studies

The above argument can be further informed by recent work using positron emission tomography (PET) and single photon emission computerised tomography (SPECT). The effects of methylphenidate have been extensively studied in the brains of healthy adults. At oral doses of approximately 0.8 mg/kg, methylphenidate significantly increases the extracellular dopamine concentrations in the striatum [39]. Commonly used doses of methylphenidate result in blockade of at least 50% of dopamine transporters and the peak concentration of methylphenidate in the brain is reached after 60 min [40]. Plasma levels of methylphenidate correspond to the dopamine transporter occupancy [40]. Methylphenidate produces a 50% blockade at an oral dose of 0.25 mg/kg. Clinical doses of methylphenidate, therefore, can be expected to produce a greater than 50% occupancy which should be pharmacologically meaningful. At a dose of 1 mg/kg, 80% or greater occupancy should be expected [40], arguing against the value of further increases in clinical doses. In fact, adverse effects are likely to outweigh an advantage at very high doses. For example, it has been shown that for cocaine to produce a "high", at least 60% of the dopamine transporters must be blocked and this effect should occur and dissipate rapidly [41]. A similar effect would be anticipated for methylphenidate, giving a narrow therapeutic range in which to capitalize on clinical effects without inducing euphoria.

At optimal clinical doses in ADHD adults, methylphenidate has been shown to reverse relative increases in rCBF in the precentral gyrus and left caudate nucleus when compared with the baseline drug-free state [42]. These effects have been correlated with improvements on ADHD symptom ratings, suggesting that at usual clinical doses, methylphenidate produces a meaningful change in brain blood flow and associated motor behavior.

The *in vivo* effects of dexamphetamine administration on the brain are less well studied. Using FDG-PET to study the effects of an intravenous dose of 0.15 mg/kg of dexamphetamine in healthy humans, an increase in glucose utilization in subcortical limbic, frontal and cerebellar regions was observed [43]. Using a similar protocol, these authors noted inconsistent changes in glucose utilization in a small number of ADHD subjects during intravenous administration of dexamphetamine [44]. In healthy humans subjects studied with ^{11}C raclopride PET, a differential effect of amphetamine on striatal D_2 receptor availability has been demonstrated [45]. Amphetamine induced a significantly larger reduction in D_2 receptor availability in limbic and sensorimotor striatum than in other regions. Using SPECT and a specific dopamine transporter ligand, a reduction in availability of the dopamine transporter has been observed following four weeks of low dose (15mg/day) dexamphetamine treatment in ADHD adults [46]. These data suggest that low dose dexamphetamine in healthy subjects and in ADHD adults produces substantial and regionally specific alteration in dopaminergic neurotransmission and glucose utilization.

In summary, the functional neuroimaging data for methylphenidate and dexamphetamine suggests that acute and long-term dosing induces a significant alteration in dopaminergic neurotransmission. In addition, clear effects of low dose stimulants are apparent on cerebral blood flow and glucose metabolism. There is inadequate information to address differential effects of different doses of stimulant on these parameters. However, the evidence suggests a relatively narrow therapeutic window in which a stimulant medication produces beneficial cognitive effects without inducing euphoria. This observation would suggest that modest stimulant dosing should be the goal for the majority of patients.

The Question of Tolerance

Whether tolerance develops to chronic low dose stimulant administration is an important question. If such a phenomenon existed, there may be an argument for dose escalation when these drugs are used long term in clinical practice, or alternatively an argument for extended 'drug holidays'. Tolerance to some actions of stimulant drugs has been demonstrated in animal studies [47 48]. Long-term administration of dexamphetamine induces long-lasting down regulation of D_2 dopamine receptors in monkeys [49]. However, tolerance does not develop to all actions of these drugs [47]. There is experimental evidence that long-term use of dopamine agonists leads to a reduced density of D_2 receptors [50]. It is also possible that chronic stimulant treatment could alter the functional state of both D_1 and D_2 receptors, but the significance of this is not known [32]. Whether long-term changes in dopamine receptors occur when stimulants are used clinically in humans is unknown. Furthermore, the practical implications of any long-term changes in dopaminergic function remain unclear. In clinical practice, in parallel with other forms of psychotropic medication, both dexamphetamine and methylphenidate appear to maintain their effectiveness long-term. This is evidenced by continued effectiveness of medication across the developmental lifespan of children and, where appropriate, through to adulthood [18]. In a recent randomized, double-blind, placebo-controlled study of dexamphetamine treatment in children with ADHD, no evidence of tolerance to therapeutic effect was noted over a period of 15 months [51]. Clearly, such a study is of sufficient length to demonstrate tolerance if it was going to develop. In summary, the empirical basis is weak but clinical experience argues against the need for an escalation of dose with continuing treatment once the therapeutic effect has been established. Furthermore, based on the available data, chronic low dosing rather than an intermittent dose schedule appears to be a reasonable proposition.

PHARMACOKINETICS

The pharmacokinetic profile of orally administered stimulant medication is important in determining a rationale for dosing regimes. With oral administration, both methylphenidate and dexamphetamine are almost completely absorbed [52] with food having little impact on this process [53 54]. When administered to adults, methylphenidate has a pharmacokinetic profile similar to that of children [52 53], reaching a peak concentration in 1.5-2.5 hours and having an elimination half-life of 2-3.5 hours after oral administration of a single dose [52 53 55]. Non-linear kinetics have been observed with higher doses of methylphenidate [56 57] and have also been proposed with repeated doses [58]. A proposed mechanism of the non-linear kinetics is saturation of presystemic metabolism [56] which may itself be stereoselective [59]. In theory, therefore, dose escalation carries the potential for sudden increase in adverse effects. Dexamphetamine typically takes 2-3 hours to reach peak concentration after a single oral dose [52], but with a half-life of approximately 7 hours is considerably longer acting than the equivalent measure for methylphenidate. In adults, as with children, serum concentrations of both stimulants may vary greatly between individuals. For example, one hour serum levels of methylphenidate may show inter-individual variation of up to thirty fold [53]. Peak serum levels of methylphenidate show less but still substantial inter-individual variation of between four to five fold [53 54 56]. Such variability may arise from a number of pharmacokinetic factors. Substantial differences in presystemic metabolism have been noted between individuals [56]. Considerable inter-individual variability in plasma clearance is seen with both drugs [52]. Contrary to earlier suggestions [60], the latter does not appear to be less likely with methylphenidate. There are no reliable ways to assess individual differences in pharmacokinetics, leaving the clinician in a somewhat difficult situation. However, inter-individual differences in pharmacokinetics may be less dramatic when dose is adjusted for body weight [54]. Therefore, it would seem appropriate to use mg/kg as a general guide for determining maximum dose in individual patients.

Inter-individual variability might provide an argument for high dosing of individuals failing to respond to conventional dosing strategies. However, as with other psychotropics, there may be a number of reasons why an individual fails a particular trial of medication. Many of these reasons do not relate to pharmacokinetic considerations but may relate more to issues of accuracy of diagnosis, expectation of the degree of effect of medication on symptoms, poor compliance, and the experience of distressing side effects such as anxiety which may mask clinical benefit. Furthermore, it remains unclear whether clinical response to stimulant medication is related to peak brain concentration or the rate of increase of the drug in the brain [61]. Therefore, dose escalation purely on the basis of 'inadequate' response cannot be recommended. Whilst there may be an argument for examining the individual pharmacokinetics of stimulants in those patients failing to respond to conventional dosing strategies, this requires ready access to a laboratory with an established assay, and is not feasible in routine clinical practice. Furthermore, earlier data from children suggest that mean serum levels do not differ between drug responders and nonresponders [53]. Clearly, further study of the relationship between serum levels and clinical response to stimulants in adults is necessary in order to progress this issue.

Side Effects

The clinical dose of stimulants is significantly associated with side effects [62 63], which range from those of mostly nuisance value such as dry mouth to more substantial ones such as psychosis. Examination of the side effect profile of stimulants and particularly the relationship of side effects to dose is an important step in determining whether high dose stimulant treatment caries a substantially higher risk. In this section, major side effects are reviewed and evidence for association with dose examined.

Anorexia and Insomnia

The ability of stimulants to produce anorexia and insomnia is well established. In clinical trials, as the dose of methylphenidate exceeds 0.5 mg/kg, the risk of appetite suppression and insomnia increases [63]. The mechanism of induction of anorexia is by no means clear. However, tolerance to this effect may develop [64] and may be mediated by both dopaminergic and noradrenergic effects [65]. Insomnia is often encountered in clinical practice and is minimised by reducing the dose and ensuring lack of proximity to sleep initiation. At low doses, severe anorexia and insomnia are rarely seen.

Tics

The ability of stimulant medications to induce tics and obsessive compulsive symptoms is widely known. Early concerns [66 67] that stimulants were highly likely to induce tics have been generally unfounded [68]. Emergent tics are seen in less than 10% of children treated with stimulant medication, with the vast majority being transient in nature [69]. Short term trials of stimulant medication in children with comorbid tic disorder indicate that the risk of exacerbation of tics is low [70 71] and that abrupt discontinuation of stimulant medications is unlikely to exacerbate tics [72]. Long term follow up of children with comorbid ADHD and tic disorder also suggest that chronic low dose stimulant treatment does not exacerbate tic disorder [72 73]. A vexing question is whether the ability of stimulants to induce such phenomena is dose dependent. Within a small dose range, this appears to not be the case [74 70]. However, there have been no studies of the emergence or exacerbation of tics in children given very high doses of stimulant medication. It could be argued that the risk of inducing tics in adults is low, given that the onset of tic disorder in early childhood. However, in treating ADHD adults as with ADHD children, comorbidity with tic disorders should be borne in mind. Low dose stimulant treatment remains the most prudent measure for adults, particularly when treating ADHD adults with comorbid tic disorder.

Cardiovascular Effects

The cardiovascular effects of stimulants, e.g. increases in pulse and blood pressure, have not been well-examined but they cannot be ignored at higher doses. Such effects will be of most importance in adults with pre-existing cardiovascular disease. There are no clear guidelines for managing this risk. However, good clinical practice dictates that cardiovascular parameters are regularly reviewed during stimulant prescription. Furthermore, as the risk is likely to increase with age, an argument can be made for minimising stimulant dose, particularly in at risk individuals (e.g., those with family history of essential hypertension or with personal risk factors for cardiovascular disease).

Effects on Seizure Threshold

Although stimulant medications are commonly believed to lower the seizure threshold, there is no data on the propensity of stimulant medication to induce seizures in adults. In children, the seizure risk in nonepileptic children treated with stimulants appears negligible. However, epileptiform activity on electroencephalography has been observed in approximately 15% of children with ADHD prior to treatment [75]. For children with both epilepsy and ADHD, low dose stimulant medication does not appear to significantly alter seizure control [76 77]. However, the risk of convulsions may escalate with higher doses [62]. Given the risks associated with seizures, it would be prudent to adopt a low dose strategy to minimise any risk of the seizure induction, particularly in at risk individuals.

ABUSE POTENTIAL

In adults and adolescents, the therapeutic use of stimulant medication is open to potential abuse. Adults with ADHD are known to have high rates of comorbid disorders, including substance use [5]. It is possible that stimulant medications, as a result of their potential to increased extracellular dopamine concentrations, could be powerfully reinforcing. Furthermore, there are parallels between the effect of stimulant medication and cocaine on the dopamine transporter. Indeed, repeated administration of methylphenidate in adult rats results in decreased latency for the acquisition of cocaine self administration and this effect is dose dependent [78]. Could such an effect encourage abuse of prescribed stimulant medication in humans? Direct evidence regarding the potential for abuse of prescribed stimulants in adults is lacking. Only a handful of case reports in which adults appear to have abused stimulants have been published. The intranasal and intravenous abuse of prescription stimulants (ones own or from a friend) has been reported [79 80 81] and oral abuse has also been recognised [82]. A number of factors are likely to determine the reinforcing effects of stimulants. These include the rapidity of rise of dopamine levels together with the extent of dopamine increases, the context in which the drug is taken and individual factors determining sensitivity to the drug [83]. In theory, prescription of large doses of stimulant medication for ADHD, could increase potential for abuse due to the extent of rise of dopamine levels seen with higher doses. Overall, the likelihood of abuse of prescribed stimulant medications is probably reduced by virtue of the pharmacokinetics of orally administered stimulant, regular clinical review of patients, controlled prescription and use of relatively modest doses. It remains unknown whether slow-release stimulant preparations are less likely to be abused in routine clinical practice.

An additional question, also relevant to adults being treated with stimulants is whether previously treated children are more prone to stimulant abuse as a virtue of their exposure to stimulant medication. A number of studies now support the position that stimulant prescription does not increase substance abuse later in life [84]. Furthermore, some longitudinal studies demonstrate reduced rates of substance use disorders in those ADHD subjects previously medicated with stimulants [85 86 87]. It is likely that treatment for childhood ADHD minimizes the risk of later development of psychiatric conditions including substance abuse. Whilst the relevance of this observation to adults being treated is unclear, future studies will assist in determining whether adequate treatment of ADHD in adults is associated with a reduction in psychiatric comorbidity, including risk of substance abuse.

PSYCHOSIS

Stimulants are recognized to sometimes cause a psychosis characterized by persecutory delusions and auditory and visual hallucinations [88]. The development of psychosis is usually associated with intravenous usage of high doses and has been modeled in an escalating dose 'binge' model of amphetamine psychosis in the rodent [49]. Although psychosis is rarely seen in the context of low-dose prescription stimulants for ADHD, the use of large or very large doses raises this is a distinct possibility. Additionally, there has been recent interest in the overlap between ADHD and bipolar disorder in children [89]. Given the propensity of stimulants to induce psychosis or possible euphoria at higher doses, the purported comorbidity raises concerns about the safety of prescription stimulants in this subgroup, particularly in view of the propensity of some manic episodes to be associated with psychosis.

Central Nervous System (CNS) Toxicity

CNS toxicity of stimulant medications is seen in animals given high dose amphetamine. Behaviours such as extreme vigilance, tracking of non-apparent stimuli, constant checking, hyperresponsiveness and grasping in midair have been reported in non-human primates treated chronically with high dose amphetamine [90]. Other behaviours noted in monkeys include posturing and other catatonic features [91]. Intermittent but escalating doses of amphetamine given to monkeys have been associated with behavioral sensitization, an effect observed even at low doses [92]. While fixed, but low dose chronic treatment may produce similar behaviors at a lesser severity [92], high doses are more likely to cause such behaviors. Although both amphetamine and methylphenidate sensitize stereotypic behaviors in rats, only amphetamine induces locomotor sensitization [93]. The differential effect has been postulated to reflect the different methods by which these two drugs increase synaptic dopamine [93], although the precise mechanism mediating the difference remains obscure. There is increasing interest in elucidating precise alterations in dopamine-stimulated signal transducing mechanisms that may be responsible for different components of behavioural sensitization [94]. Chronic and high dose amphetamine exposure in monkeys and rodents has also been reported to produce nigrostriatal toxicity [90 95]. This can be prevented if an intermittent low dose schedule is used for amphetamine administration [96]. Of interest is the observation by Yuan et al [97] that methylphenidate appears to lack the dopaminergic neurotoxic effect shown by dexamphetamine in rats when examined 2 weeks after a high dose. The apparent contrast in neurotoxic potential of these two drugs at high doses suggests that dopaminergic efflux may not be the direct mediator of such damage [97]. The human implications of these laboratory findings remain unclear. However, in light of information regarding potential neurotoxic effects of high dose stimulants, careful review and strict justification of chronic stimulant treatment is necessary. In addition, stimulant doses should be restricted to the lowest effective doses.

Summary

In summary, there is clear evidence from studies of both children and adults that chronic low dose stimulant treatment is an appropriate, safe and effective treatment for ADHD. There are significant methodological limitations of the data for adults including the small number of studies in adulthood, lack of direct comparison of the effectiveness of different doses and the lack of high and very high dose studies. Examination of the behavioral pharmacology of stimulants suggests that chronic low stimulant treatment produces reduction in hyperkinesis without inducing euphoria. High doses cannot be justified on the basis of the pharmacokinetics of either methylphenidate or dexamphetamine and the potential to induce euphoria or other adverse effects. Given the chronic nature of stimulant treatment for ADHD, any such treatment must be well tolerated, with the perceived benefits outweighing the long-term risks. As high doses are associated with increased risk of both minor and major adverse events in humans, and behavioral sensitization and CNS toxicity at higher doses, a low dosing strategy should be adopted for ADHD adults. Whilst there is no clear upper limit that should be used in clinical practice, we recommend staying within the upper limits of 1 mg/kg for methylphenidate and 0.5 mg/kg for dexamphetamine. Clearly, this recommendation is not absolute and flexibility of dosing is required in some individuals who appear to only respond to higher doses. We recommend that these doses should be exceeded only after careful consideration and objective documentation of beneficial and adverse consequences. Furthermore, blood levels may be of some value if poor compliance or failure of the dose to produce adequate serum levels are being considered, as there is a direct relationship between blood and brain levels as well as dopamine transporter occupancy.

References

[1] Gittelman R, Mannuzza S, Shenker R, Bonagura N. Hyperactive boys almost grown up. I. Psychiatric status. *Archives of General Psychiatry* 1985; 42(10):937-947.

[2] Mannuzza S, Klein RG, Bonagura N, Malloy P, Giampino TL, Addalli KA. Hyperactive boys almost grown up. V. Replication of psychiatric status. *Archives of General Psychiatry* 1991; 48(1):77-83.

[3] Sachdev P. Attention deficit hyperactivity disorder in adults. [Review] [89 refs]. *Psychological Medicine* 1999; 29(3):507-514.

[4] Spencer T, Biederman J, Wilens T, Faraone SV. Is attention-deficit hyperactivity disorder in adults a valid disorder?. [Review] [88 refs]. *Harvard Review of Psychiatry* 1994; 1(6):326-335.

[5] Biederman J, Faraone SV, Spencer T, Wilens T, Norman D, Lapey KA et al. Patterns of psychiatric comorbidity, cognition, and psychosocial functioning in adults with attention deficit hyperactivity disorder. *American Journal of Psychiatry* 1993; 150(12):1792-1798.

[6] Schachter HM, Pham B, King J, Langford S, Moher D. How efficacious and safe is short-acting methylphenidate for the treatment of attention-deficit disorder in children and adolescents? A meta-analysis.[see comment]. *CMAJ Canadian Medical Association Journal* 2001; 165(11):1475-1488.

[7] Wilens TE, Biederman J, Spencer TJ, Prince J. Pharmacotherapy of adult attention deficit/hyperactivity disorder: a review. [Review] [81 refs]. *Journal of Clinical Psychopharmacology* 1995; 15(4):270-279.

[8] Wood DR, Reimherr FW, Wender PH, Johnson GE. Diagnosis and treatment of minimal brain dysfunction in adults: a preliminary report. *Archives of General Psychiatry* 1976; 33(12):1453-1460.

[9] Wender PH, Reimherr FW, Wood DR. Attention deficit disorder ('minimal brain dysfunction') in adults. A replication study of diagnosis and drug treatment. *Archives of General Psychiatry* 1981; 38(4):449-456.

[10] Mattes JA, Boswell L, Oliver H. Methylphenidate effects on symptoms of attention deficit disorder in adults. *Archives of General Psychiatry* 1984; 41(11):1059-1063.

[11] Gualtieri CT, Ondrusek MG, Finley C. Attention deficit disorders in adults. *Clinical Neuropharmacology* 1985; 8(4):343-356.

[12] Spencer T, Wilens T, Biederman J, Faraone SV, Ablon JS, Lapey K. A double-blind, crossover comparison of methylphenidate and placebo in adults with childhood-onset attention-deficit hyperactivity disorder. *Archives of General Psychiatry* 1995; 52(6):434-443.

[13] Kessler S. Drug therapy in attention-deficit hyperactivity disorder. *Southern Medical Journal* 1996; 89(1):33-38.

[14] Block RW. Medication for attention-deficit hyperactivity disorder: balancing art and science. *Southern Medical Journal* 1996; 89(1):95-96.

[15] Bouffard R, Hechtman L, Minde K, Iaboni-Kassab F. The efficacy of 2 different dosages of methylphenidate in treating adults with attention-deficit hyperactivity disorder. *Canadian Journal of Psychiatry - Revue Canadienne de Psychiatrie* 2003; 48(8):546-554.

[16] Paterson R, Douglas C, Hallmayer J, Hagan M, Krupenia Z. A randomised, double-blind, placebo-controlled trial of dexamphetamine in adults with attention deficit hyperactivity disorder.[see comment]. Australian and New Zealand *Journal of Psychiatry* 1999; 33(4):494-502.

[17] Wender PH. *Attention-deficit hyperactivity disorder in adults.* New York: Oxford University Press, 1995.

[18] Dulcan M. Practice parameters for the assessment and treatment of children, adolescents, and adults with attention-deficit/hyperactivity disorder. American Academy of Child and Adolescent Psychiatry. *Journal of the American Academy of Child and Adolescent Psychiatry* 1997; 36(10:Suppl):Suppl-121S.

[19] O'Toole K, Abramowitz A, Morris R, Dulcan M. Effects of methylphenidate on attention and nonverbal learning in children with attention-deficit hyperactivity disorder. *Journal of the American Academy of Child and Adolescent Psychiatry* 1997; 36(4):531-538.

[20] Horrigan JP, Barnhill LJ. Low-dose amphetamine salts and adult attention-deficit/hyperactivity disorder. *Journal of Clinical Psychiatry* 2000; 61(6):414-417.

[21] Hornykiewicz O. Dopamine (3-hydroxytyramine) and brain function. [Review] [250 refs]. *Pharmacological Reviews* 1966; 18(2):925-964.

[22] Boissier JR, Simon P. [On the potentiation of DOPA effects by monoamine oxidase inhibitors]. [French]. *Psychopharmacologia* 1966; 8(6):428-436.

[23] Helmeste DM, Seeman P. Amphetamine-induced hypolocomotion in mice with more brain D2 dopamine receptors. *Psychiatry Research* 1982; 7(3):351-359.

[24] Carlson JH, Bergstrom DA, Walters JR. Stimulation of both D1 and D2 dopamine receptors appears necessary for full expression of postsynaptic effects of dopamine agonists: a neurophysiological study. *Brain Research* 1987; 400(2):205-218.

[25] Piercey MF, Hyslop DK, Hoffmann WE. Excitation of type II caudate neurons by systemic administration of dopamine agonists. *Brain Research* 1996; 706(2):249-258.
[26] Solanto MV. Neuropsychopharmacological mechanisms of stimulant drug action in attention-deficit hyperactivity disorder: a review and integration. [Review] [290 refs]. Behavioural *Brain Research* 1998; 94(1):127-152.
[27] Steiner NO, Delay ER, Isaac W. Effects of drugs, age and illumination on response speed of squirrel monkeys. *Pharmacology, Biochemistry and Behavior* 1986; 24(3):503-506.
[28] Strombom U. Effects of low doses of catecholamine receptor agonists on exploration in mice. Journal of Neural Transmission 1975; 37(3):229-235.
[29] Taylor KM, Snyder SH. Differential effects of D- and L-amphetamine on behavior and on catecholamine disposition in dopamine and norepinephrine containing neurons of rat brain. *Brain Research* 1971; 28(2):295-309.
[30] Luthman J, Fredriksson A, Lewander T, Jonsson G, Archer T. Effects of d-amphetamine and methylphenidate on hyperactivity produced by neonatal 6-hydroxydopamine treatment. *Psychopharmacology* 1989; 99(4):550-557.
[31] Ruskin DN, Bergstrom DA, Shenker A, Freeman LE, Baek D, Walters JR. Drugs used in the treatment of attention-deficit/hyperactivity disorder affect postsynaptic firing rate and oscillation without preferential dopamine autoreceptor action. *Biological Psychiatry* 2001; 49(4):340-350.
[32] Seeman P, Madras BK. Anti-hyperactivity medication: methylphenidate and amphetamine.[see comment]. [Review] [105 refs]. *Molecular Psychiatry* 1998; 3(5):386-396.
[33] Parsons LH, Justice JB, Jr. Extracellular concentration and in vivo recovery of dopamine in the nucleus accumbens using microdialysis. *Journal of Neurochemistry* 1992; 58(1):212-218.
[34] Wall SC, Gu H, Rudnick G. Biogenic amine flux mediated by cloned transporters stably expressed in cultured cell lines: amphetamine specificity for inhibition and efflux. *Molecular Pharmacology* 1995; 47(3):544-550.
[35] Sharp T, Zetterstrom T, Ljungberg T, Ungerstedt U. A direct comparison of amphetamine-induced behaviours and regional brain dopamine release in the rat using intracerebral dialysis. *Brain Research* 1987; 401(2):322-330.
[36] Kuczenski R, Segal D. Concomitant characterization of behavioral and striatal neurotransmitter response to amphetamine using in vivo microdialysis. *Journal of Neuroscience* 1989; 9(6):2051-2065.
[37] Gonon FG. Nonlinear relationship between impulse flow and dopamine released by rat midbrain dopaminergic neurons as studied by in vivo electrochemistry. *Neuroscience* 1988; 24(1):19-28.
[38] Castellanos FX, Elia J, Kruesi MJ, Marsh WL, Gulotta CS, Potter WZ et al. Cerebrospinal fluid homovanillic acid predicts behavioral response to stimulants in 45 boys with attention deficit/hyperactivity disorder. *Neuropsychopharmacology* 1996; 14(2):125-137.

[39] Volkow ND, Wang G, Fowler JS, Logan J, Gerasimov M, Maynard L et al. Therapeutic doses of oral methylphenidate significantly increase extracellular dopamine in the human brain. *Journal of Neuroscience* 2001; 21(2):RC121.

[40] Volkow ND, Wang GJ, Fowler JS, Gatley SJ, Logan J, Ding YS et al. Dopamine transporter occupancies in the human brain induced by therapeutic doses of oral methylphenidate. *American Journal of Psychiatry* 1998; 155(10):1325-1331.

[41] Volkow ND, Ding YS, Fowler JS, Wang GJ, Logan J, Gatley JS et al. Is methylphenidate like cocaine? Studies on their pharmacokinetics and distribution in the human brain. *Archives of General Psychiatry* 1995; 52(6):456-463.

[42] Schweitzer JB, Lee DO, Hanford RB, Tagamets MA, Hoffman JM, Grafton ST et al. A positron emission tomography study of methylphenidate in adults with ADHD: alterations in resting blood flow and predicting treatment response. *Neuropsychopharmacology* 2003; 28(5):967-973.

[43] Ernst M, Zametkin AJ, Matochik J, Schmidt M, Jons PH, Liebenauer LL et al. Intravenous dextroamphetamine and brain glucose metabolism. *Neuropsychopharmacology* 1997; 17(6):391-401.

[44] Ernst M, Zametkin AJ, Matochik JA, Liebenauer L, Fitzgerald GA, Cohen RM. Effects of intravenous dextroamphetamine on brain metabolism in adults with attention-deficit hyperactivity disorder (ADHD). *Preliminary findings. Psychopharmacology Bulletin* 1994; 30(2):219-225.

[45] Martinez D. Imaging human mesolimbic dopamine transmission with positron emission tomography. Part II: amphetamine-induced dopamine release in the functional subdivisions of the striatum. *Journal of Cerebral Blood Flow and Metabolism* 23(3):285-300, 2003 Mar 2003;(3):285-300.

[46] Krause KH, Dresel SH, Krause J, Kung HF, Tatsch K. Increased striatal dopamine transporter in adult patients with attention deficit hyperactivity disorder: effects of methylphenidate as measured by single photon emission computed tomography. *Neuroscience Letters* 2000; 285(2):107-110.

[47] Ginovart N, Farde L, Halldin C, Swahn CG. Changes in striatal D2-receptor density following chronic treatment with amphetamine as assessed with PET in nonhuman primates. *Synapse* 1999; 31(2):154-162.

[48] Persico AM, Schindler CW, O'Hara BF, Brannock MT, Uhl GR. Brain transcription factor expression: effects of acute and chronic amphetamine and injection stress. *Brain Research Molecular Brain Research* 1993; 20(1-2):91-100.

[49] Segal DS, Kuczenski R. An escalating dose "binge" model of amphetamine psychosis: behavioral and neurochemical characteristics. *Journal of Neuroscience* 1997; 17(7):2551-2566.

[50] Seeman P. Brain dopamine receptors. [Review] [999 refs]. *Pharmacological Reviews* 1980; 32(3):229-313.

[51] Gillberg C, Melander H, von Knorring AL, Janols LO, Thernlund G, Hagglof B et al. Long-term stimulant treatment of children with attention-deficit hyperactivity disorder symptoms. A randomized, double-blind, placebo-controlled trial.[see comment]. *Archives of General Psychiatry* 1997; 54(9):857-864.

[52] Patrick KS, Markowitz JS. Pharmacology of methylphenidate, amphetamine enantiomers and pemoline in attention-deficit hyperactivity disorder. *Human Psychopharmacology* Vol 12(6)()(pp 527-546), 1997 1997;(6):527-546.
[53] Gualtieri CT, Wargin W, Kanoy R, Patrick K, Shen CD, Youngblood W et al. Clinical studies of methylphenidate serum levels in children and adults. *Journal of the American Academy of Child Psychiatry* 1982; 21(1):19-26.
[54] Angrist B, Corwin J, Bartlik B, Cooper T. Early pharmacokinetics and clinical effects of oral D-amphetamine in normal subjects. *Biological Psychiatry* 1987; 22(11):1357-1368.
[55] Wargin W, Patrick K, Kilts C, Gualtieri CT, Ellington K, Mueller RA et al. Pharmacokinetics of methylphenidate in man, rat and monkey. *Journal of Pharmacology and Experimental Therapeutics* 1983; 226(2):382-386.
[56] Aoyama T, Sasaki T, Kotaki H, Sawada Y, Sudoh Y, Honda Y et al. Pharmacokinetics and pharmacodynamics of (+)-threo-methylphenidate enantiomer in patients with hypersomnia. *Clinical Pharmacology and Therapeutics* 1994; 55(3):270-276.
[57] Aoyama T, Kotaki H, Sasaki T, Sawada Y, Honda Y, Iga T. Nonlinear kinetics of threo-methylphenidate enantiomers in a patient with narcolepsy and in healthy volunteers. *European Journal of Clinical Pharmacology* 1993; 44(1):79-84.
[58] Shader RI, Harmatz JS, Oesterheld JR, Parmelee DX, Sallee FR, Greenblatt DJ. Population pharmacokinetics of methylphenidate in children with attention-deficit hyperactivity disorder. *Journal of Clinical Pharmacology* 1999; 39(8):775-785.
[59] Srinivas NR, Hubbard JW, Quinn D, Korchinski ED, Midha KK. Extensive and enantioselective presystemic metabolism of dl-threo-methylphenidate in humans. *Progress in Neuro-Psychopharmacology and Biological Psychiatry* 1991; 15(2):213-220.
[60] Hungund BL, Perel JM, Hurwic MJ, Sverd J, Winsberg BG. Pharmacokinetics of methylphenidate in hyperkinetic children. *British Journal of Clinical Pharmacology* 1979; 8(6):571-576.
[61] Birmaher B, Greenhill LL, Cooper TB, Fried J, Maminski B. Sustained release methylphenidate: pharmacokinetic studies in ADDH males. *Journal of the American Academy of Child and Adolescent Psychiatry* 1989; 28(5):768-772.
[62] Wilens TE, Biederman J. The stimulants. [Review] [121 refs]. *Psychiatric Clinics of North America* 1992; 15(1):191-222.
[63] Levy F. Side effects of stimulant use. [Review] [39 refs]. *Journal of Paediatrics and Child Health* 1993; 29(4):250-254.
[64] Heffner TG, Seiden LS. The effect of depletion of brain dopamine by 6-hydroxydopamine on tolerance to the anorexic effect of d-amphetamine and fenfluramine in rats. *Journal of Pharmacology and Experimental Therapeutics* 1979; 208(1):134-143.
[65] Sanghvi IS, Singer G, Friedman E, Gershon S. Anorexigenic effects of d-amphetamine and l-DOPA in the rat. *Pharmacology, Biochemistry and Behavior* 1975; 3(1):81-86.
[66] Lowe TL, Cohen DJ, Detlor J, Kremenitzer MW, Shaywitz BA. Stimulant medications precipitate Tourette's syndrome. *JAMA* 1982; 247(8):1168-1169.

[67] Golden GS. The relationship between stimulant medication and tics. *Pediatric Annals* 1988; 17(6):405-406.

[68] Kurlan R. Tourette's syndrome: are stimulants safe?. [Review] [35 refs]. *Current Neurology and Neuroscience Reports* 2003; 3(4):285-288.

[69] Lipkin PH, Goldstein IJ, Adesman AR. Tics and dyskinesias associated with stimulant treatment in attention-deficit hyperactivity disorder. *Archives of Pediatrics and Adolescent Medicine* 1994; 148(8):859-861.

[70] Gadow KD, Sverd J, Sprafkin J, Nolan EE, Ezor SN. Efficacy of methylphenidate for attention-deficit hyperactivity disorder in children with tic disorder.[erratum appears in Arch Gen Psychiatry 1995 Oct;52(10):836]. *Archives of General Psychiatry* 1995; 52(6):444-455.

[71] Castellanos FX, Giedd JN, Elia J, Marsh WL, Ritchie GF, Hamburger SD et al. Controlled stimulant treatment of ADHD and comorbid Tourette's syndrome: effects of stimulant and dose. *Journal of the American Academy of Child and Adolescent Psychiatry* 1997; 36(5):589-596.

[72] Gadow KD, Sverd J, Sprafkin J, Nolan EE, Grossman S. Long-term methylphenidate therapy in children with comorbid attention-deficit hyperactivity disorder and chronic multiple tic disorder.[see comment]. *Archives of General Psychiatry* 1999; 56(4):330-336.

[73] Law SF, Schachar RJ. Do typical clinical doses of methylphenidate cause tics in children treated for attention-deficit hyperactivity disorder? *Journal of the American Academy of Child and Adolescent Psychiatry* 1999; 38(8):944-951.

[74] Varley CK, Vincent J, Varley P, Calderon R. Emergence of tics in children with attention deficit hyperactivity disorder treated with stimulant medications. *Comprehensive Psychiatry* 2001; 42(3):228-233.

[75] Hemmer SA, Pasternak JF, Zecker SG, Trommer BL. Stimulant therapy and seizure risk in children with ADHD. *Pediatric Neurology* 2001; 24(2):99-102.

[76] Gross-Tsur V, Manor O, van der MJ, Joseph A, Shalev RS. Epilepsy and attention deficit hyperactivity disorder: is methylphenidate safe and effective?[comment][republished from J Pediatr. 1997 Jan;130(1):40-4; PMID: 9003849]. *Journal of Pediatrics* 1997; 130(4):670-674.

[77] Gucuyener K, Erdemoglu AK, Senol S, Serdaroglu A, Soysal S, Kockar AI. Use of methylphenidate for attention-deficit hyperactivity disorder in patients with epilepsy or electroencephalographic abnormalities. *Journal of Child Neurology* 2003; 18(2):109-112.

[78] Schenk S, Izenwasser S. Pretreatment with methylphenidate sensitizes rats to the reinforcing effects of cocaine. *Pharmacology, Biochemistry and Behavior* 2002; 72(3):651-657.

[79] Garland EJ. Pharmacotherapy of adolescent attention deficit hyperactivity disorder: challenges, choices and caveats. [Review] [79 refs]. *Journal of Psychopharmacology* 1998; 12(4):385-395.

[80] Jaffe SL. Intranasal abuse of prescribed methylphenidate by an alcohol and drug abusing adolescent with ADHD. *Journal of the American Academy of Child and Adolescent Psychiatry* 1991; 30(5):773-775.

[81] Parran TV, Jr., Jasinski DR. Intravenous methylphenidate abuse. Prototype for prescription drug abuse. *Archives of Internal Medicine* 1991; 151(4):781-783.

[82] Goyer PF, Davis GC, Rapoport JL. Abuse of prescribed stimulant medication by a 13-year-old hyperactive boy. *Journal of the American Academy of Child Psychiatry* 1979; 18(1):170-175.

[83] Volkow ND, Swanson JM. Variables that affect the clinical use and abuse of methylphenidate in the treatment of ADHD. [Review] [60 refs]. *American Journal of Psychiatry* 2003; 160(11):1909-1918.

[84] Barkley RA, Fischer M, Smallish L, Fletcher K. Does the treatment of attention-deficit/hyperactivity disorder with stimulants contribute to drug use/abuse? A 13-year prospective study.[see comment]. *Pediatrics* 2003; 111(1):97-109.

[85] Biederman J. Pharmacotherapy for attention-deficit/hyperactivity disorder (ADHD) decreases the risk for substance abuse: findings from a longitudinal follow-up of youths with and without ADHD. *Journal of Clinical Psychiatry 64 Suppl* 11:3-8, 2003 2003;3-8.

[86] Mannuzza S, Klein RG, Moulton JL, III. Does stimulant treatment place children at risk for adult substance abuse? A controlled, prospective follow-up study. *Journal of Child and Adolescent Psychopharmacology* 2003; 13(3):273-282.

[87] Wilens T, Pelham W, Stein M, Conners CK, Abikoff H, Atkins M et al. ADHD treatment with once-daily OROS methylphenidate: interim 12-month results from a long-term open-label study. *Journal of the American Academy of Child and Adolescent Psychiatry* 2003; 42(4):424-433.

[88] McConnell H. Catecholamine metabolism in the attention deficit disorder: implications for the use of amino acid precursor therapy. *Medical Hypotheses* 1985; 17(4):305-311.

[89] Kent L, Craddock N. Is there a relationship between attention deficit hyperactivity disorder and bipolar disorder? *Journal of Affective Disorders* 2003; 73(3):211-221.

[90] Ridley RM, Baker HF, Owen F, Cross AJ, Crow TJ. Behavioural and biochemical effects of chronic treatment with amphetamine in the vervet monkey. *Neuropharmacology* 1983; 22(4):551-554.

[91] Ellison G, Morris W. Opposed stages of continuous amphetamine administration: parallel alterations in motor stereotypies and in vivo spiroperidol accumulation. *European Journal of Pharmacology* 1981; 74(2-3):207-214.

[92] Castner SA, Goldman-Rakic PS. Long-lasting psychotomimetic consequences of repeated low-dose amphetamine exposure in rhesus monkeys. *Neuropsychopharmacology* 1999; 20(1):10-28.

[93] McNamara CG, Davidson ES, Schenk S. A comparison of the motor-activating effects of acute and chronic exposure to amphetamine and methylphenidate. *Pharmacology, Biochemistry and Behavior* 1993; 45(3):729-732.

[94] Crawford CA, McDougall SA, Meier TL, Collins RL, Watson JB. Repeated methylphenidate treatment induces behavioral sensitization and decreases protein kinase A and dopamine-stimulated adenylyl cyclase activity in the dorsal striatum. *Psychopharmacology* 1998; 136(1):34-43.

[95] Ellison G, Ratan R. The late stage following continuous amphetamine administration to rats is correlated with altered dopamine but not serotonin metabolism. *Life Sciences* 1982; 31(8):771-777.

[96] Robinson TE, Becker JB. Enduring changes in brain and behavior produced by chronic amphetamine administration: a review and evaluation of animal models of amphetamine psychosis. [Review] [321 refs]. *Brain Research* 1986; 396(2):157-198.

[97] Yuan J, McCann U, Ricaurte G. Methylphenidate and brain dopamine neurotoxicity. *Brain Research* 1997; 767(1):172-175.

In: Attention Deficit Hyperactivity Disorder
Editor: Marvin C. Shriner, pp. 67-98

ISBN: 1-60021 321-9

Chapter III

An Interdiscplinary Approach to ADHD

Jonna Kuntsi[3] and Philip Asherson
MRC Social, Genetic and Developmental Psychiatry Centre
Institute of Psychiatry King's College London, UK

Abstract

Since the initial demonstration of high heritability for attention deficit hyperactivity disorder (ADHD), a large number of genetic studies have been published. Quantitative genetic studies, such as twin studies, have moved beyond the simple estimation of heritability and address more complex multivariate questions, such as the etiology of co-occurrence between ADHD and other disorders and traits. Molecular genetic studies have obtained preliminary evidence for several genes that are likely to be implicated in the disorder.

The success of the genetic research opens many questions regarding the functionality of the genes that contribute to ADHD. A key level of functionality is that of psychological processes. Much progress has been made in cognitive-experimental research on ADHD, but a consensus is yet to emerge on the key underlying processes. Part of the difficulty in specifying the key processes relates to the inconsistency that often characterises the performance of children with ADHD on cognitive tasks. Within-task manipulations with variables such as incentives often influence whether or not a cognitive 'deficit' is observed. Such observations need to be incorporated within the theoretical frameworks.

An interdisciplinary approach, which combines cognitive, quantitative genetic and molecular genetic approaches, holds promise for progress in identifying causal pathways in ADHD. Quantitative genetic analyses can indicate which candidate endophenotypes are heritable and therefore candidates for molecular genetic analyses. Multivariate quantitative genetic analyses address whether the same or different sets of genes influence different candidate endophenotypes, helping further to define psychological theory, as well as informing molecular genetic analyses. Yet further methodological

[3] Correspondence to j.kuntsi@iop.kcl.ac.uk

approaches, such as environmental measures that may help capture gene-environment interactions or electrophysiological measures, could be incorporated to provide more detailed information on the underlying processes.

Here we provide a selective review of recent studies that are particularly informative on these issues, as well as summarising our own recent research on these topics.

GENETIC STUDIES ON ADHD

The long-established findings that attention deficit hyperactivity disorder (ADHD) aggregates within families (1-3) and has a high heritability (60-90%; reviewed in Biederman and Farone (4) and Thapar et al. (5)) have generated much research interest regarding the nature of the genetic influences. An increasing number of molecular genetic studies are being published. At the same time, quantitative genetic (twin and family) studies are moving beyond the simple estimation of heritability, to address more complex multivariate questions.

RECENT FINDINGS FROM QUANTITATIVE GENETIC RESEARCH

A topical question regarding heritability is whether the extent of genetic influences is similar across the whole distribution of ADHD symptom scores in the population and whether the genetic factors that increase risk for ADHD also correlate with levels of ADHD symptoms in the general population. Although ADHD is diagnosed using operational diagnostic criteria, measures of ADHD symptoms are continuously distributed in the general population and have an excellent correspondence with the categorical diagnosis (6-12). Mathematical modelling applied to twin data is also consistent with the hypothesis that ADHD is the extreme of a behaviour that varies genetically throughout the entire population (13-15). Price et al. (16) investigated early ADHD symptom scores in 6000 UK twin pairs at ages 2, 3 and 4 and found these to be highly heritable (~90%), regardless of twin age or the measurement cut-off used. Heritability was equally high at both the low and high ends of the distribution, again suggesting that the trait is continuously distributed (Price et al., unpublished data). Despite these findings, this remains an area that has not been adequately investigated in relation to ADHD, since as yet there are no published reports that estimate group heritability where the extreme group is defined using recognised operational criteria and reliable data capture tools, such as standardised interview. Unpublished data, however, of 97 probands with a research diagnosis of DSM-IV combined subtype and their unselected siblings estimated familial correlations of 0.29 for teacher-rated ADHD symptom scores and 0.27 for parent-rated symptom scores (The IMAGE Consortium, unpublished data), suggesting a familial relationship between ADHD in probands and continuous measures of ADHD symptoms among their siblings.

The existing quantitative genetic data are therefore consistent with the quantitative trait locus (QTL) hypothesis that the same genetic variants, which increase risk for ADHD, may also influence levels of ADHD symptoms in the general population. Yet these analyses represent but a first step in an investigation of the possibility that differences between individuals with and without ADHD may be quantitative rather than qualitative. In the sections that follow, we review also initial findings from molecular genetic and cognitive-experimental research on this topic. Nevertheless, the consistency in the quantitative genetic findings across different measurement approaches and cut-offs has influenced the decision of many a quantitative genetic investigator to adopt a dimensional approach to the study of ADHD symptomatology (including the majority of the studies reviewed here).

Multivariate twin analyses enable the investigation of possible shared genetic effects on ADHD and other phenotypes that frequently co-occur with ADHD; we review a selection of recent studies here. A particularly high level of comorbidity exists between ADHD and conduct disorder. Several studies indicate a considerable extent of shared genetic influences on the symptomatology of these two forms of externalising behaviours, across a wide age range (17-21). A recent example is the study by Nadder and colleagues (19), where ratings were obtained from mothers from a comprehensive interview, the Child and Adolescent Psychiatric Assessment (CAPA), and from teachers from a written questionnaire composed of items from the Rutter B and Conners' scales. The sample consisted of 494 male and 603 female same-sex twin pairs between the ages of 8 and 16. A key finding was that genetic effects predominated in the liability to the co-occurrence of ADHD and oppositional-defiant disorder/conduct disorder (ODD/CD). This is consistent both with the possibility of ADHD behaviours predisposing to ODD/CD symptomatology or with both phenotypes representing different manifestations of the same genetic liability. The latter, the authors note, could reflect a genetically influenced temperamental trait, such as sensation seeking. Environmental risk factors could also contribute to the finding, insofar as these would either arise as a result of ADHD (gene-environment correlation) or if the susceptibility to the environmental risk factors was genetically moderated (gene-environment interaction); within the twin model-fitting it was not possible to exclude these possibilities.

ADHD frequently co-occurs not only with conduct problems, but also with a range of other problem behaviours, such as substance use. Young et al. (22) studied the etiology of co-occurrence between ADHD symptoms, conduct disorder symptoms, substance experimentation and novelty seeking. A sample of 334 adolescent twin pairs were assessed using standardised psychiatric interviews (including DSM-IV symptom counts for ADHD and conduct disorder) and personality assessments. The analyses suggested that the co-occurrence between these behaviours was largely due to additive genetic factors. The latent underlying characteristic, which captured the shared variance amongst the behavioural measures, was highly heritable (84%). A residual correlation between ADHD symptoms and novelty seeking, which was not accounted for by the latent characteristic, was attributed to genetic dominance. A residual correlation between conduct disorder symptoms and substance experimentation was attributed to environmental effects common to both twins in a pair.

In our recent investigation we examined the etiology of the association between ADHD and lower IQ scores in a large population-based sample of 5-year-old twins (23). The twins were individually assessed on an IQ test and data on ADHD symptoms were obtained from mother interviews and teacher ratings. Confirming previous reports, the phenotypic correlation between ADHD symptom scores and IQ was -.3 and, in a categorical analysis, children with a DSM-IV ADHD research diagnosis obtained IQ scores 9 points lower, on average, than comparison children. Analysis of these data suggested that the co-occurrence of ADHD and lower IQ has genetic origins: 86% of the association between ADHD symptom scores and IQ, and 100% of the association between ADHD diagnosis and IQ, was accounted for by genetic influences that are shared by ADHD and IQ.

MOLECULAR GENETIC RESEARCH

The high heritability of ADHD is likely to be due to multiple genes of small effect size (QTLs or susceptibility genes) (24). Based on the known response of ADHD symptoms to stimulant medication and other evidence implicating monoamine neurotransmitter pathways, molecular research has largely focused on the analysis of candidate genes that regulate monoamine neurotransmitter pathways.

The association between ADHD and the 7-repeat allele of a 48-base pair repeat within the D4 receptor gene (DRD4) is the most widely reported, although negative reports have also been published (25-39). A number of studies reported a pattern of findings suggestive of population genetic stratification (29;36;37). Each of these studies found a significant excess of the 7-repeat allele in cases compared to independent controls, although none were able to replicate this finding using within-family tests of association. These observations are reflected, to some extent, in the relative strength of association in the meta-analysis of case-control (OR=1.9, 95% CI=1.4-2-2, p=.00000008) versus within-family tests (OR=1.4, 95% CI=1.1-1.6, p=.02) (35). Systematic differences between the samples used for the two types of analysis may account for the observed differences: the requirement in within-family tests for genotype data from both parents and the ADHD probands may bring bias to the selection procedures (40). Ding et al. (41) have raised the possibility that the 7-repeat allele may carry some evolutionary advantage. The analyses on ADHD also leave open the possibility that the association would not be due to the 7-repeat allele itself, but to another nearby polymorphism or to sequence changes within the repeat sequence.

The association to the 7-repeat allele had previously been reported to novelty seeking in adults, although the majority of studies are negative and meta-analyses are not supportive of a general effect across all samples, so this finding remains far from conclusive (42;43-61). Associations have also been reported between DRD4 and substance abuse, heroin addiction, smoking and gambling in some studies (62-65), but not in others (66-70). The possibility therefore exists that functional variation of dopamine pathway genes, such as DRD4, may influence a range of related behavioural disorders and temperamental traits, although the inconsistency in the findings across studies remains to be addressed and firm conclusions cannot be drawn.

Association between ADHD and the 10-repeat allele of a 40-base pair variable number tandem repeat polymorphism (VNTR) in the 3'-untranslated region of DAT1 has also been reported in numerous studies and meta-analyses, although the net effect across studies appears to be small, with an average odds ratio of around 1.2 (29;36;71-81). Since the high-risk allele occurs on around 70% of Caucasian chromosomes and even higher in some other populations (79), it might be better to conceive of the less common 9-repeat allele of the DAT1 polymorphism as conferring a protective effect against ADHD. There is significant evidence for heterogeneity across the various datasets (81). Unpublished work reported by Irwin Waldman on the meta-analyses of available datasets suggests that a subtype-specific association to the combined subtype (with both hyperactivity-impulsivity and inattentiveness symptoms) may explain the apparent heterogeneity. This is consistent with his earlier report, where he concluded that the DAT1 association was especially strong with the combined, but not the inattentive subtype (73), and a recent report from Loo et al. (82) that the risk genotype may differentiate combined type ADHD from inattentive ADHD.

There is now increasing evidence to suggest that genetic variants within SNAP-25 (synaptosomal associated protein) also influence the risk for ADHD, although discrepancies in the particular alleles associated with ADHD have been reported. Whereas an early study found no linkage between ADHD and markers in the chromosome 20p11-12 region containing SNAP-25 (83), there are to date no negative association-based studies of SNAP-25 markers and ADHD. Barr et al. (84) were the first to investigate two single nucleotide polymorphisms (SNPs) that they had identified within the 3'UTR of the human gene, obtaining evidence that a specific haplotype (T-C haplotype) was associated with ADHD in a Canadian sample. This finding was partially supported by Kustanovich et al. (85) using a US Caucasian sample, who found evidence for the same haplotype, but only when paternal transmissions were considered. Brophy et al. (86), using an Irish sample, investigated the same SNPs: although they found no evidence to support biased transmission of the haplotype nominated by Barr et al. (84), they did find that one of the SNPs (C-allele of second SNP) was individually associated with ADHD, as well as evidence for increased transmission of the risk allele from paternal chromosomes. Finally, Mill et al. (87) found no association to the individual SNPs, but found significant association to a different allelic combination of the two markers (T-T haplotype), as well as further evidence for paternal transmission. A more in-depth analysis of SNAP-25 was also carried out by Mill et al. (87) who screened the coding, UTR and promotor regions for common polymorphisms and identified 12 genetic variants. Association analysis in a UK Caucasian sample found associations with three of these markers, including a multi-allelic tetra-nucleotide repeat polymorphism in the first intron with both risk and protective alleles (88).

Further research has focused on DRD5, an intronless gene that shows high structural and functional homology to the dopamine D1 receptor gene. Association studies of this gene have focused on a dinucleotide repeat polymorphism (89) that lies around 19,000 base pairs from the start of transcription. Following an initial report of an association between the common allele of this polymorphism and ADHD (74), other groups have reported the same significant association or a non-significant trend of association to the same allele. These data have been collated and a formal meta-analysis of 14 independent studies performed that shows a combined association of the DRD5 locus with no evidence of heterogeneity ($p=0.00005$; OR=1.24, 95% CI 1.12-1.38) (90). Analysis of ADHD subtypes found similar strength of the association to the DSM-IV combined (CT) and inattentive (I) subtypes, but not to the hyperactive-impulsive (HI) subtypes; a finding that is in keeping with twin studies that find cross-concordance between the CT and I subtypes, but not between these and the HI subtype (91).

In addition to the focus on dopamine system genes, there have been a few studies focusing on genes that regulate the serotonin neurotransmitter system. Interaction between the two neurotransmitter systems is well recognised and was neatly demonstrated in the paradoxical calming effects of stimulants on the DAT1 knockout mouse, through the effects of stimulants on serotonergic transmission (92). Several investigators have examined polymorphisms in the serotonin transporter gene (SERT) for associations with ADHD. Of particular interest is an insertion/deletion polymorphism in the promoter region and a VNTR within intron 2, both of which appear to have functional effects on SERT expression (93;94). Kent et al. (95) investigated both of these polymorphisms and, in keeping with two earlier studies (96;97), found increased transmission of the long allele of the promotor polymorphism from parents to their ADHD offspring that was significant in a combined analysis of the three datasets (p=.008). A Turkish study using a case-control design reported a similar association, with a lower frequency of the short homozygous genotype among their ADHD cases compared to controls (p=.02) (98). However, in another study of 150 ADHD probands Langley et al. (99) found no evidence for the association with either of the SERT polymorphisms alone or combined as a haplotype. The evidence for association with the intron 2 VNTR is particularly inconsistent, suggesting that this polymorphism is unlikely to have a direct influence on risk for ADHD.

The serotonin 1B receptor gene (5HT1B) has also shown evidence of association with ADHD in several datasets. Two studies published at around the same time reported association to the same SNP allele. The first study from Hawi et al. (100) combined datasets from four independent groups in the UK and Ireland and found preferential transmission of a SNP polymorphism (allele 861G; p = 0.01). The only other study to look at this particular SNP using a sample of ADHD probands from Canada reported a similar result (p=.09) (101). Combining the two studies enhanced the finding (p=0.001), suggesting the possible involvement of this locus in ADHD susceptibility. Despite the obvious interest in both the SERT and 5HT1B findings, these findings remain uncertain until they have been investigated more widely.

In addition to candidate gene association studies of ADHD, genome-wide linkage scans have recently been completed (102-104). These studies report several target regions that warrant further investigation, although only one region of chromosome 5 showed overlap between the studies.

To date only a few quantitative trait loci (QTL) studies that focus on continuous measures of ADHD symptom scores in general population samples have been published. Mill et al. (105) looked for QTL association with several ADHD risk alleles (DAT1, DRD4, DRD5, SNAP-25, 5HT1B) using a population sample of 329 male dizygotic twin pairs unselected for phenotype. Parent-rated ADHD symptom scores had been gathered at ages 2, 3, 4 and 7 years and teacher ratings at age 7 years, and these were combined in various ways to generate a series of composite scores. They found some evidence for the QTL association with the DAT1 10-repeat allele (p<0.01) and a protective effect of the SNAP-25 microsattelite-allele-2 (p<0.05). Two additional studies using population samples compared allele frequency differences between individuals with high and low scores on continuous measures of ADHD symptoms. One of the studies found a trend in favour of the DAT1 association in a small sample of 50 high-scoring and 42 low-scoring individuals (106), but the second larger study failed to find evidence for the association (Curran et al., personal communication). Finally, Todd et al. (75) used 100 randomly selected families and 413 families in which at least one twin passed an initial screening interview for ADHD; of these, 219 had a full DSM-IV diagnosis. Using conventional within-family tests of association to analyse both latent class criteria and DSM-IV ADHD subtypes, they failed to find any significant association or trend for association with the DAT1 10-repeat allele. The QTL approach to ADHD is in its early stages and careful phenotypic definition is required for future studies. The differences between teacher and parent ratings (discussed on p. 16), illustrate the type of methodological issues that require careful consideration.

Neurobiological Environmental Risk Factors and Potential Interactions with Genes

The most striking demonstration of how genetic factors cannot completely account for the behavioural manifestation of ADHD is MZ (monozygotic or identical) twins who are discordant for the disorder: about 20% of MZ twins with ADHD have a co-twin without the disorder (reviewed in Thapar et al. (5); Kuntsi and Stevenson (107)). Because MZ twins do not differ genetically, behavioural differences between them must have an environmental origin. (The term 'environment' refers here to all non-genetic influences, including intrauterine environment and epigenetic factors.)

The heritability estimates obtained from model-fitting analyses on twin data similarly leave some of the variance in ADHD unaccounted for. Most twin studies attribute the variance in ADHD symptoms that is not due to genetic influences to child-specific environmental influences (plus measurement error), rather than environmental influences common to both twins. A small caveat here is, though, that the studies with smaller samples, and those using scales particularly susceptible to rater bias, may have lacked power to detect shared environmental influences. In our recent analyses on ADHD symptoms (measured by Parent Conners' Rating Scale) in a general population sample of approx. 4000 7-9-year-old twin pairs we obtained evidence for modest, but significant, shared environmental effects that were of the same magnitude as the child-specific environmental influences (both 14%; Kuntsi, Rijsdijk, Asherson and Plomin, unpublished data). There was no evidence of contrast effects (possible rater bias) in these data.

Neurobiological environmental risk factors that have been implicated in ADHD include prematurity/low birth weight, pregnancy and birth complications, and mother's use of alcohol or cigarettes during pregnancy. In a study of extremely low birth weight (ELBW, <1000g) children, ADHD was more than twice as common at age 5 than in controls (108). Among adolescent ELBW survivors the prevalence rate for ADHD symptoms was 9%, compared to 2% among controls (109). Based on prospective data from four countries, Hille et al. (110) reported increased attention problems, as measured by the Child Behavior Checklist, in the ELBW group.

The same pattern holds for the larger group of very low birth weight (VLBW, <1500g) children. The Scottish Low Birth Weight Study (111) reported poor attention span among 47% of the sample at age 4.5 years. In a study in the UK, 23% of the VLBW children met clinical criteria for ADHD at age 12, compared to 6% of the normal birth weight controls (112). Nadeau and colleagues (113) reported higher ratings of inattentiveness and hyperactivity for VLBW children born extremely preterm (<29 weeks gestation) than for the control children. Other studies similarly report increased ADHD symptoms among VLBW or very preterm children (114-117). In contrast, Goodman and Stevenson (118) found no differences in ADHD symptoms between children with birth weights below and above 2000g.

In a regional cohort of low birth weight (LBW, <2500g) children, 15.6% had ADHD at age 6 (119). Breslau et al. (120) similarly reported a higher prevalence of ADHD among LBW children at age 6. Reassessments at age 11, now using rating scales rather than diagnostic interviews, indicated continuing attention problems (121). However, these problems were limited to LBW children from an urban, as opposed to suburban, setting. Using gestational age as the criterion, a ten-year follow-up of children born extremely preterm found a prevalence rate for ADHD of 20%, compared to 8% in the full-term group (122). An increased rate of ADD was also found in a study of mildly preterm children (123).

A recent retrospective ADHD case-control comparison found that ADHD was associated with a three-fold increase in having been born LBW (124). Prenatal exposure to alcohol and cigarettes, parental ADHD, social class and comorbid disruptive behavior disorders in parents and offspring did not account for the finding. The authors estimated that, if the association was causal, 13.8% of all ADHD cases could be attributed to LBW.

The association between prematurity/low birth weight and ADHD may be due, at least in part, to central nervous system insult (125;126). ADHD is linked to brain abnormalities, particularly in the dopamine-rich frontal-striatal region (127), which may be particularly vulnerable to perinatal adverse events (128). Animal research suggests that perinatal complications involving anoxia may lead to dopamine function alteration in the nucleus accumbens and prefrontal cortex (129;130). Brake and colleagues (131) suggest, based on their animal data, that subtle alterations in birth procedure may be sufficient to increase the sensitivity of the dopamine neurons to the effects of repeated subsequent stress. Decker et al. (132) reported increased striatal expression of vesicular monoamine transporter and D1 receptor proteins in post-hypoxic rats, suggesting depressed dopaminergic signalling. In humans, specific pregnancy and delivery complications that have been associated with later ADHD symptoms include maternal bleeding (133), antepartum haemorrhage (134) and length of labour (135).

Younger age of mother has also emerged as a risk factor for ADHD in some studies, but does not seem to act as a confounding variable that would explain the association between ADHD and pregnancy, labour and birth outcomes (124;136); On the other hand, in another investigation (137) attention problems were limited to LBW children from urban areas, leading to the suggestion of an interaction between biological risk associated with prematurity and environmental risk associated with social disadvantage.

Maternal smoking during pregnancy has emerged as another risk factor for ADHD. A case-control study found an increased risk for ADHD associated with maternal smoking (138) and this applied to their siblings too (139). Socioeconomic status, parental IQ, parental ADHD status or low birth weight did not account for the effect. Mick and colleagues (140) reported that mothers of children with ADHD were twice as likely to have smoked during pregnancy and 2.5 times more likely to have abused alcohol. Familial psychopathology, social adversity and comorbid conduct disorder did not account for these findings. In a large, population-based prospective follow-up study in Finland maternal smoking during pregnancy was associated with ADHD symptoms in children at age 8, even after adjustment for sex, family structure, socio-economic status, maternal age and maternal alcohol use (141). The reason for the association between ADHD and cigarette smoking is not known, but one hypothesis relates this to the role for nicotinic receptors in modulating dopaminergic activity (reviewed in Faraone and Biederman (142)). Possible genetic mediation of the association has also not been completely ruled out. A recent twin study (143), however, reported an association between maternal smoking and offspring ADHD symptoms that was additional to the effects of genetic influences on offspring ADHD symptoms.

Few studies have examined whether neurobiological or other environmental risk factors interact with genetic risk factors in ADHD. The high heritability estimates for ADHD in twin model-fitting analyses could potentially 'hide' gene-environment interactions. The potential importance of gene-environment interactions in contributing to complex behavioural disorders has recently been demonstrated by findings from the Dunedin Multidisciplinary Health and Development Study on antisocial behaviour and depression. Caspi et al. (144;145) reported that functional polymorphisms in candidate genes had an effect only in groups subjected to specific environmental stressors. The first study described the neurotransmitter-metabolizing enzyme monoamine oxidase A (MAOA) as a moderating influence on the effects of maltreatment on antisocial behaviour (144) and the second described the serotonin transporter gene (SERT) as a moderator of stressful life events on depression (146). Neither of the two genes investigated showed main effects with the behavioural phenotypes, so that the genetic associations would have been missed entirely, had the environmental risk factors not been taken into account.

A potential gene-environment interaction has emerged also for ADHD, if exposure to maternal prenatal smoking indicates an environmentally rather than genetically mediated risk. Kahn et al. (147) followed up 161 children from the age of 6 months up to 5 years of age. Child hyperactivity-impulsivity and oppositional behaviour was associated with DAT1 10-repeat allele, but only when the child was also exposed to maternal prenatal smoking.

Recent Cognitive-Experimental Research

The success of genetic research opens many questions regarding the functionality of the genes that contribute to ADHD. A key level of functionality is that of psychological processes. Much progress has been made in cognitive-experimental research on ADHD, but a consensus is yet to emerge on the key underlying processes. Part of the difficulty in specifying the key processes relates to the inconsistency that often characterises the performance of children with ADHD on cognitive tasks. Within-task manipulations with variables such as incentives often also influence whether or not a cognitive 'deficit' is observed. Such observations need to be incorporated within the theoretical frameworks. Here we provide a selected review of cognitive-experimental studies that help to address some of these questions. (We will not provide a detailed summary of different executive function theories, and recommend previous reviews for further details; for example Castellanos and Tannock (148); Kuntsi and Stevenson (149); Sergeant et al. (150); Sergeant et al. (151).)

Much of cognitive research on ADHD has focused on possible impairments in attention and executive functions, especially in response inhibition. A meta-analysis of studies using the stop task, a response inhibition measure, concluded that children with ADHD have a slower inhibitory process, though are not less likely to trigger the inhibitory process (152). Other studies have, however, failed to replicate this association between ADHD and a slower inhibitory process (153-155). Further evidence from studies that have combined an inhibition measure (the go/no-go task) with physiological measures suggests that children with ADHD can inhibit their responding as well as control children under certain conditions (156;157). The presentation rate of the stimuli (158), as well as incentives (see below), strongly affect their performance.

Two stop task studies illustrate how incentives can critically influence inhibition performance in children with ADHD. The first study (159) compared 33 children with ADHD to 33 psychiatric control children and 33 healthy control children (ages 6-14). In a low incentive condition the children with ADHD were less able to inhibit their reactions and had a slower inhibitory process, but in a high incentive condition they performed as well as the control groups. The incentives were points earned for successful inhibition and points lost for failures to inhibit a response to the stop signal. In the second study (160) the participants were 31 children with ADHD and 26 healthy control children, between the ages of 8 and 12 years (a third group of children with traumatic brain injury will not be considered here). Baseline performance was obtained from a condition with no feedback and this was compared to an incentive condition that consisted of positive feedback only (one point for each successful inhibition). The points earned were later exchanged for small prizes. Despite the differences in the exact incentive contingencies between the two studies, the second study similarly found that the performance of children with ADHD was brought up to the level of the control group in the incentive condition. A third study (161) did not find effects of reward and response cost on inhibition in ADHD, but the lack of comparison to a non-contingency condition limits the conclusions that can be made.

In contrast to an impulsive style of *fast* and inaccurate responding, on many tasks children with ADHD are slow and vary variable in their speed of responding, as well as inaccurate (153;155;156). As Castellanos and Tannock point out, "*response variability is the one ubiquitous finding in ADHD research across a variety of speeded-reaction-time tasks, laboratories and cultures*" (p. 624) (148). They tentatively suggest that the response variability could indicate a temporal processing deficit; a more common interpretation of this finding within the arousal and activation regulation model is discussed below. A detailed statistical analysis of response times demonstrated explicitly how a greater proportion of abnormally slow responses, mixed with fast responses on some trials, leads to the inconsistent pattern of responding in ADHD (162). Leth-Steensen et al. (162) attribute the periodic attentional 'lapses' to "*a deficient allocation of energetic resources (i.e., the effortful maintenance of optimal arousal and activation levels)*" which are needed for maintaining "*a consistent state of preparation for the processing of the stimulus information and for the generation of the accompanying response*" (p. 186). A faster presentation rate of stimuli improves the speed and the variability of responding of children with ADHD more than that of control children (155;156).

These findings of highly variable cognitive performance and of the interaction between cognitive performance and factors affecting the energetic state (incentives, presentation rate and predictability of stimuli) have led to the proposal, which provides an alternative to the pure cognitive accounts, that the key underlying characteristic in ADHD is a regulation problem. For example, the optimal stimulation theory placed the emphasis on the regulation of arousal (163) and, more recently, the state regulation theory proposes a critical role for the regulation of activation and effort (reviewed in van der Meere (164); see also Sergeant et al. (165)). We similarly interpreted the findings from our initial twin study as supporting this theoretical view; it was the variability in the speed of responding, out of several variables which included response inhibition and working memory variables, that was most strongly linked to ADHD in both genetic and non-genetic analyses (17;153). The model of poor regulation of arousal or activation suggests that ADHD is associated with a heightened need for stimulation and reinforcement, and may therefore be related to novelty and sensation seeking tendencies.

A recent study by Banaschewski et al. (166), using both cognitive and event-related potential data from the continuous performance test, similarly supports the hypothesis of an underlying deficit in state regulation in ADHD (without comorbidity); they suggest that poor attentional orienting, allocation of attentional capacity and response preparation in ADHD may indicate secondary deficits that stem from the state regulation deficit. (See p. 18-19 for a discussion of EEG data on activation and arousal in ADHD.) Mason et al. (167) also studied attentional processes in ADHD in detail. Children with ADHD and a control group performed a visual search task in three conditions. The children with ADHD showed the typical pattern of slow and variable reaction times, suggesting momentary lapses in performance. However, the analyses on the mechanisms of visual search provided no support for the hypothesis of a selective attention deficit in children with ADHD: the processes involved in visual selection, both in serial search and in guiding search over time, seemed intact. The differences that emerged between the groups suggested an adoption of an earlier response deadline in children with ADHD. The authors conclude that the findings indicate difficulties with state regulation of performance and 'delay aversion'.

Sonuga-Barke (168;169) coined the term 'delay aversion' to describe the sensitivity to delays in ADHD; the timing of reinforcement seems important. Children with ADHD tend to choose small, immediate rewards, as opposed to control children who tend to maximise their reward earnings by choosing larger rewards obtained after a delay (153;169). Whether such a tendency is a secondary consequence of some other underlying process or reflects a separate psychological process remains to be explored empirically.

Most of the research on psychological processes in ADHD has focused on group comparisons between children with ADHD and control children. To investigate psychological processes from within the QTL perspective of a continuous dimension of ADHD symptoms, we recently tested a general population sample of 49 children on experimental tasks and obtained ratings of ADHD symptoms from parents and teachers (170). The children performed the go/no-go task under three conditions: slow presentation time of stimuli, fast presentation time of stimuli and incentives with slow presentation time of stimuli. In the incentive condition the children earned points for successful performance and lost points for unsuccessful performance. The second key task, the 'fast task', consisted of two conditions: a standard four-choice reaction time task (baseline) and a novel comparison condition with fast presentation time of stimuli and incentives. In the comparison condition consistently faster reaction times were specifically rewarded (with smiley faces representing points earned). The aim here was to investigate the extent to which the association between slow and variable reaction times and ADHD can be maximally reduced with these manipulations. In both tasks the points earned were later exchanged for small prizes.

The associations with teacher ratings of ADHD symptoms were overall in line with the predictions from the model of arousal and activation regulation regarding effects of presentation time of stimuli and incentives on performance (170). The strongest associations were obtained for reaction time variability. In both tasks the decrease in reaction time variability from baseline condition to a condition with a faster event rate or incentives (or both) was significantly associated with teacher ratings of ADHD symptoms (correlations of .4-.6). Teacher ratings of ADHD symptoms were associated with slow and variable reaction times, and higher number of commission errors (measure of inhibition) in the go/no-go task, only in the baseline conditions and not in conditions with faster presentation time or incentives. The only exception was a correlation between teacher ratings of AHD symptoms and commission errors, which remained significant (when controlling for age) in the incentive condition. This may have been due to a speed-accuracy trade-off in children with more ADHD symptoms (ie the data from the incentive condition indicated relatively *fast* rather than slow responding, as well as a relatively higher rate of commission errors). The data on the go/no-go task and teacher (or parent) ratings of ADHD symptoms were not consistent with an inhibition deficit hypothesis that predicts an association between ADHD symptoms and commission errors across all conditions. We similarly obtained no evidence for an association between ADHD symptom scores and working memory, as measured by the digit span backward score. In contrast to the encouraging findings with teacher ratings, no clear pattern of findings emerged for parent ratings of ADHD symptoms. We discuss the issue of parent vs teacher ratings of ADHD below.

Recent cognitive-experimental research on ADHD, some of which we have reviewed here, indicates several promising lines of enquiry. Despite this, a consensus is yet to emerge on the key underlying processes. The possibility remains that multiple psychological processes, both cognitive and state regulation or reward-related processes, are affected (148). For future progress carefully designed tasks are required, which allow a detailed manipulation of variables proposed to be critical in ADHD. Group differences frequently emerge between children with and without ADHD on standard neuropsychological tasks, but without disentangling the effects of the multiple factors that influence performance on such tasks, the meaning of the group differences remains uncertain. Study designs are required that enable the hypotheses under investigation not only to be proved, but also potentially disproved.

PARENT VS TEACHER RATINGS OF ADHD

In line with our recent data (170), Oosterlaan et al. (171) similarly reported that only teacher ratings of ADHD symptoms predicted performance on cognitive tasks that were sensitive to ADHD, with parent ratings not contributing to the association. The sample in their study included children with research diagnoses of pervasive ADHD and control children.

In general, teacher and parent ratings of ADHD symptoms tend to correlate only to a modest degree (around .3). Twin analyses on ratings on the Conners' scales by Martin et al. (172) indicated that only 31% of the variance in teacher and parent ratings of ADHD symptoms were due to genetic effects common to both ratings, whereas 41% of the variance in parent ratings and 50% of the variance in teacher ratings were due to additional genetic effects that were unique to each. Therefore the ratings by parents and teachers reflect only partially overlapping phenotypes and genotypes.

Potential strengths of teacher ratings of ADHD symptoms include a better awareness of population norms, observing children in situations that are challenging for children with ADHD symptomatology and greater objectivity. Gomez and colleagues (173) reported that teacher ratings of ADHD symptoms were more likely to be confirmed by parent ratings, than vice versa. Teacher ratings also indicated higher internal consistency and stability, leading Gomez et al. (173) to support the greater reliability of teacher ratings over parent ratings. Twin analyses further indicate that teacher ratings are free of the rater bias typically found in parent ratings (174-176) and show greater genetic stability (19).

Nadder et al. (19), although generally supportive of the potential greater validity of teacher ratings, also point out the need for caution here. Their data indicated notably higher correlations between teacher ratings of ADHD and oppositional defiant disorder/conduct disorder symptoms than between parent ratings of these two types of externalising behaviours. It is not clear whether this reflects teachers being less able to distinguish between the two forms of disruptive behaviours, or them being better at identifying comorbidity.

Many questions remain to be answered regarding differences between parent and teacher ratings of ADHD. Pervasiveness of the ADHD symptoms across situations is an important criterion in DSM-IV and both teachers and parents will undoubtedly continue to be important informants. The methodological challenge remains of how best to obtain and combine information from the different sources that maximises the strengths of each informant, whilst minimising the potential biases.

An Interdisciplinary Approach to Studying Causal Pathways in ADHD

Research Combining Genetic and Cognitive-Experimental Approaches

To enable an investigation of the links between the genetic risk factors and psychological processes – to study candidate endophenotypes – an interdisciplinary approach is required. An initial set of studies on ADHD have emerged that have combined genetic and cognitive-experimental approaches.

In our initial twin study we investigated, using the group heritability method (177;178), whether the same genes that influence ADHD symptoms also affect performance on the tasks that discriminated between ADHD and control groups (17). The only variable for which we obtained evidence of shared genetic effects was the variability in the speed of responding on a reaction time task (primary task of the stop task), suggesting that a state regulation problem could be the psychological process that mediates the genetic effects on ADHD symptomatology. However, statistical power for these bivariate genetic analyses was limited, emphasising the need for replication and extension of this work.

In addition to the twin design, sibling or family designs can be used to explore quantitative genetic questions. Such designs can give an indication of 'familiality' of a specific trait, which refers to the combined influences from genetic and shared environmental factors. Seidman et al. (179) reported poor performance on executive function tasks among siblings of ADHD probands who also received an ADHD diagnosis themselves, but not among unaffected siblings. In contrast, Slaats-Willemse et al. (180) found poor performance on inhibition tasks among unaffected siblings of ADHD probands. In a larger-scale study, Nigg et al. (181) studied the performance of 307 parents and 79 siblings of children with ADHD and control children on a variety of tasks. They found familial effects on five of the tasks and further analyses led to the suggestion that the strongest candidates for endophenotypes were set shifing (Trails B), the variability in the speed of responding and the speed of the inhibition process (stop signal reaction time). However, some of the effects were only seen in females. An interesting further avenue for future research using the sibling design is to apply model-fitting techniques to analyse ADHD symptom scores as a continuous dimension in the siblings of ADHD probands. This will provide a complementary approach to the categorical focus on affected vs unaffected siblings.

Possible associations between specific genes and task performance in ADHD have been studied in an initial set of molecular genetic analyses. Swanson et al. (182) reported an association, contrary to their prediction, between *lack* of the DRD4 7-repeat allele and slow and variable responses on tasks designed to probe attentional processes in an ADHD sample. Manor et al. (183) found preferential transmission of *short* (2-5 repeats) DRD4 alleles to ADHD probands, and an association in the probands between the short alleles and worse performance on commission errors and response time variability on a continuous performance task. In contrast, a recent study (184) reported a mixed pattern of more errors on a Matching Familiar Figures test, but faster responses on this task and the stop task in children with the DRD4 7-repeat allele. (Interpretation of the data is complicated here by the observation of an opposite pattern of associations for speed of responding between the two groups of children with ADHD and comparison children across two different inhibition tasks.) The initial data on the links between specific alleles of the DRD4 gene and putative psychological processes are therefore inconsistent. Fewer studies have focused on the DAT polymorphism that is associated with ADHD: an initial study with an ADHD sample (Oh et al., 2003) reported an association between the 10-repeat allele and fewer omission errors in the *first quarter* of the TOVA (test of variables of attention) only; the remaining 15 comparisons on performance on this task were negative.

The inconsistency across studies may be due, in part, to small sample sizes and methodological limitations. Caution is therefore required when interpreting data from these initial studies. Future studies would benefit from a more focused theoretical approach to the psychological processes under investigation. Establishing differences between age- and sex-matched ADHD and control groups on the tasks to be used in genetic investigations, and the theoretical interpretation of such differences, are essential initial steps. The cognitive-experimental data, reviewed above, indicate how task performance in children with ADHD is often sensitive to minor changes in task parameters, leading to different theoretical interpretations. Such nuances and the theoretical context have equally important implications for the interpretation of molecular genetic data on task performance.

A recent molecular genetic study (185), focusing on the DAT polymorphism, made interesting links to EEG data. Previous studies have indicated excessive frontal and central slow-wave EEG (θ) activity in ADHD, indicating under-arousal, as well as several (though not all) studies reporting decreased fast-wave (β) activity in these regions, indicating under-activation (see Loo et al. (185)). Such EEG measures are good candidates for endophenotypes, as they have high heritabilities (around 70-90%) (186). Loo et al. (185) investigated EEG patterns and cognitive performance in 24 children with ADHD within a double-blind, placebo-controlled methylphenidate study. The cognitive data indicated greater response variability and a higher number of commission errors on a continuous performance task among children with two copies of the 10-repeat alleles (10R), compared to those with one or two copies of the 9-repeat allele (9R). Medication led to increased central and parietal β activity, decreased right frontal θ activity and lower θ/β ratios in children with 10R, whereas children with 9R showed the opposite pattern. This indicates that DAT1 alleles may mediate medication-related EEG changes in ADHD, with 10R being associated with increased and 9R with decreased cortical activation and arousal. The authors highlight the convergence of the EEG and cognitive data, as the response variability observed in the 10R group during the cognitive assessments is thought to reflect levels of arousal. Though awaiting replication, these initial data suggest a potentially fruitful direction for future studies on the functional effects of genes associated with ADHD.

Research on Reward and the Dopamine System

Given that the positive molecular genetic findings that have emerged to date in ADHD research implicate dopamine pathway genes, we may look for further insight into possible psychological processes that may be linked with such genetic variation in research on the dopamine system.

The dopamine system has long been implicated in reward, with animal research suggesting a role in anticipatory and approach phases of motivated behaviour, in incentive motivational phenomena and novelty (reviewed in Berridge and Robinson (187); Wise (188)). These findings have led to several hypotheses, including a critical role for the dopamine system in mediating incentive salience (‘wanting’ incentives) (187;189), in reward learning (190;191) and in mediating reward specifically when in a state of physiological deprivation (192;193). Parallel findings are also beginning to emerge from human neuroimaging studies on dopamine release (194;195) and brain activity in response to rewards (196;197). The brain area most consistently implicated in these studies is the striatum, but its interactions with other brain areas, including the prefrontal cortex, are also emphasised. Brain imaging studies on ADHD also consistently implicate the frontal-striatal network (reviewed in Castellanos and Swanson (198); Hale et al.(127); Swanson et al. (199)): anatomical MRI (magnetic resonance imaging) studies on ADHD indicate reduced size in the frontal lobes and basal ganglia, as well as in posterior inferior cerebellar vermis, and in functional MRI studies differences between ADHD and control groups have emerged in prefrontal cortex and striatum. Using SPECT (single photon emission computed tomography) elevated dopamine transporter density has been found in striatum in individuals with ADHD (200-203), but see also (204) for a non-significant finding); this decreased following treatment with low-dose methylphenidate (201).

Given these findings and other findings on ADHD reviewed throughout this chapter, we may speculate that genes affecting dopamine pathways, and in particular the regulation of dopamine in the frontal-striatal circuits, would be linked to the regulation of activation and arousal, and to the processing of rewards and other salient stimuli. Other interpretations are also of course possible and the picture may yet turn out to be complex. However, such potential emergence of the research literatures seems worth exploring further. There is undoubtedly a need for further refinement of the proposed models. The activation/arousal regulation model, amongst others, is currently poorly defined, with various brain areas speculated upon and the links between different levels of explanation remaining vague. Interdisciplinary approaches that incorporate further methods, such as electrophysiological measures or brain imaging, are required for more precise model building.

A Combined Quantitative and Molecular Genetic Design: Added Benefits

In most ADHD studies published to date, which have combined genetic and cognitive-experimental approaches, the genetic design has been *either* quantitative genetic (sibling pairs or twins) *or* molecular genetic (DNA collection). Using a combination of the two genetic designs brings added benefits. First, quantitative genetic analyses can indicate which candidate endophenotypes are heritable (or familial) and therefore candidates for molecular genetic analyses. Second, multivariate quantitative genetic analyses can indicate whether there are shared genetic effects on performance across different tasks, and whether there are shared genetic effects on performance on the tasks and ADHD symptoms. Such analyses will be informative theoretically, regarding possible causal pathways, as well as providing further information for molecular genetic analyses. With regard to helping molecular genetic analyses, this process may be thought of as genetically-informative data reduction. A cognitive-experimental test battery is likely to consist of several tasks, each of which will produce multiple variables. Data reduction is required to restrict the number of associations tested with candidate genes, and it may be beneficial for such process to be guided by both theory and genetically informative prior analyses.

We have currently two such projects underway: a twin study and a sibling-pair study. Both projects involve individual assessments on a theory-driven cognitive-experimental test battery, as well as the collection of behavioural data and DNA samples. Crucially, the projects differ in terms of their subject populations: the sibling-pair study focuses on probands with ADHD DSM-IV combined subtype diagnoses and their nearest-age siblings who are unselected for phenotype (plus an age- and sex-matched sibling-pair control group), whereas the participants in the twin study consist of a general population sample. This will enable us to conduct detailed analyses of the QTL hypothesis of a continuously distributed ADHD symptom dimension. Although the most encouraging molecular genetic findings to date have emerged in relation to diagnosed ADHD, the diagnostic approach has undoubtedly also its limitations. A focus on the functionality – at the level of psychological processes – of candidate genes in an unselected population will complement the top-down approach that takes ADHD diagnosis as the starting point. It will also enable an unbiased investigation of potential association of the genetic risk factors with other disorders and temperamental traits that commonly co-occur with ADHD symptoms. Whereas heterogeneity in etiological factors contributing to possible subgroups within the ADHD diagnosis is often speculated upon and remains plausible, there may yet also be heterogeneity at the behavioural level amongst associated disorders and traits that can be traced to shared genetic roots.

Acknowledgements

The authors are currently supported with grants from the Wellcome Trust, Medical Research Council, British Academy and the National Institute of Mental Health.

References

[1] Biederman J, Faraone SV, Keenan K, Benjamin J, Krifcher B, Moore C et al. Further evidence for family-genetic risk factors in attention deficit hyperactivity disorder. Patterns of comorbidity in probands and relatives psychiatrically and pediatrically referred samples. Arch Gen Psychiatry 1992; 49:728-738.

[2] Biederman J, Faraone SV, Keenan K, Knee D, Tsuang MT. Family-genetic and psychosocial risk factors in DSM-III attention deficit disorder. J Am Acad Child Adolesc Psychiatry 1990; 29:526-533.

[3] Cantwell DP. Psychiatric illness in the families of hyperactive children. Arch Gen Psychiatry 1972; 27:414-417.

[4] Biederman J, Faraone SV. Current concepts on the neurobiology of Attention-Deficit/Hyperactivity Disorder. J Atten Disord 2002; 6 Suppl 1:S7-16.

[5] Thapar A, Holmes J, Poulton K, Harrington R. Genetic basis of attention deficit and hyperactivity. Br J Psychiatry 1999; 174:105-11:105-111.

[6] Biederman J, Faraone SV, Doyle A, Lehman BK, Kraus I, Perrin J et al. Convergence of the Child Behavior Checklist with structured interview-based psychiatric diagnoses of ADHD children with and without comorbidity. J Child Psychol Psychiatry 1993; 34:1241-1251.

[7] Biederman J, Faraone S, Mick E, Moore P, Lelon E. Child Behavior Checklist findings further support comorbidity between ADHD and major depression in a referred sample. J Am Acad Child Adolesc Psychiatry 1996; 35:734-742.

[8] Bird HR, Canino G, Gould MS, Ribera J, Rubio-Stipec M, Woodbury M et al. Use of the Child Behavior Checklist as a screening instrument for epidemiological research in

child psychiatry: results of a pilot study. J Am Acad Child Adolesc Psychiatry 1987; 26(2):207-213.

[9] Boyle MH, Offord DR, Racine YA, Szatmari P, Sanford M, Fleming JE. Adequacy of interviews vs checklists for classifying childhood psychiatric disorder based on parent reports. Arch Gen Psychiatry 1997; 54(9):793-799.

[10] Chen WJ, Faraone SV, Biederman J, Tsuang MT. Diagnostic accuracy of the Child Behavior Checklist scales for attention-deficit hyperactivity disorder: a receiver-operating characteristic analysis. J Consult Clin Psychol 1994; 62:1017-1025.

[11] Edelbrock C. Behavioral ratings of children diagnosed for attention deficit disorder. Psychiatric Annals 1986; 16:36-40.

[12] Goodman R, Scott S. Comparing the Strengths and Difficulties Questionnaire and the Child Behavior Checklist: is small beautiful? J Abnorm Child Psychol 1999; 27(1):17-24.

[13] Gjone H, Stevenson J, Sundet JM. Genetic influence on parent-reported attention-related problems in a Norwegian general population twin sample. J Am Acad Child Adolesc Psychiatry 1996; 35(5):588-596.

[14] Levy F, Hay DA, McStephen M, Wood C, Waldman I. Attention-deficit hyperactivity disorder: a category or a continuum? Genetic analysis of a large-scale twin study. J Am Acad Child Adolesc Psychiatry 1997; 36(6):737-744.

[15] Willcutt EG, Pennington BF, DeFries JC. Etiology of inattention and hyperactivity/impulsivity in a community sample of twins with learning difficulties. J Abnorm Child Psychol 2000; 28(2):149-159.

[16] Price TS, Simonoff E, Waldman I, Asherson P, Plomin R. Hyperactivity in preschool children is highly heritable. J Am Acad Child Adolesc Psychiatry 2001; 40(12):1362-1364.

[17] Kuntsi J, Stevenson J. Psychological mechanisms in hyperactivity: II The role of genetic factors. J Child Psychol Psychiatry 2001; 42(2):211-219.

[18] (18) Nadder TS, Silberg JL, Eaves LJ, Maes HH, Meyer JM. Genetic effects on ADHD symptomatology in 7- to 13-year-old twins: results from a telephone survey. Behav Genet 1998; 28:83-99.

[19] Nadder TS, Rutter M, Silberg JL, Maes HH, Eaves LJ. Genetic effects on the variation and covariation of attention deficit-hyperactivity disorder (ADHD) and oppositional-defiant disorder/conduct disorder (ODD/CD) symptomatologies across informant and occasion of measurement. Psychological Medicine 2002; 32(1):39-53.

[20] Silberg J, Rutter M, Meyer J, Maes H, Hewitt J, Simonoff E et al. Genetic and environmental influences on the covariation between hyperactivity and conduct disturbance in juvenile twins. J Child Psychol Psychiatry 1996; 37(7):803-816.

[21] Thapar A, Harrington R, McGuffin P. Examining the comorbidity of ADHD-related behaviours and conduct problems using a twin study design. Br J Psychiatry 2001; 179:224-229.

[22] Young SE, Stallings MC, Corley RP, Krauter KS, Hewitt JK. Genetic and environmental influences on behavioral disinhibition. Am J Med Genet 2000; 96(5):684-695.

[23] Kuntsi J, Eley TC, Taylor A, Hughes C, Asherson P, Caspi A et al. Co-occurrence of ADHD and low IQ has genetic origins. Am J Med Genet 2004; 124B(1):41-47.

[24] Plomin R, Owen MJ, McGuffin P. The genetic basis of complex human behaviors. Science 1994; 264:1733-1739.

[25] Castellanos FX, Lau E, Tayebi N, Lee P, Long RE, Giedd JN et al. Lack of an association between a dopamine-4 receptor polymorphism and attention-deficit/hyperactivity disorder: genetic and brain morphometric analyses. Mol Psychiatry 1998; 3(5):431-434.

[26] Smalley SL, Bailey JN, Palmer CG, Cantwell DP, McGough JJ, Del'Homme MA et al. Evidence that the dopamine D4 receptor is a susceptibility gene in attention deficit hyperactivity disorder. Mol Psychiatry 1998; 3(5):427-430.

[27] Swanson JM, Sunohara GA, Kennedy JL, Regino R, Fineberg E, Wigal T et al. Association of the dopamine receptor D4 (DRD4) gene with a refined phenotype of attention deficit hyperactivity disorder (ADHD): a family-based approach. Mol Psychiatry 1998; 3(1):38-41.

[28] Faraone SV, Biederman J, Weiffenbach B, Keith T, Chu MP, Weaver A et al. Dopamine D4 gene 7-repeat allele and attention deficit hyperactivity disorder. Am J Psychiatry 1999; 156(5):768-770.

[29] Holmes J, Payton A, Barrett JH, Hever T, Fitzpatrick H, Trumper AL et al. A family-based and case-control association study of the dopamine D4 receptor gene and dopamine transporter gene in attention deficit hyperactivity disorder. Mol Psychiatry 2000; 5(5):523-530.

[30] Tahir E, Yazgan Y, Cirakoglu B, Ozbay F, Waldman I, Asherson PJ. Association and linkage of DRD4 and DRD5 with attention deficit hyperactivity disorder (ADHD) in a sample of Turkish children. Mol Psychiatry 2000; 5(4):396-404.

[31] Sunohara GA, Roberts W, Malone M, Schachar RJ, Tannock R, Basile VS et al. Linkage of the dopamine D4 receptor gene and attention-deficit/hyperactivity disorder. J Am Acad Child Adolesc Psychiatry 2000; 39(12):1537-1542.

[32] Kotler M, Manor I, Sever Y, Eisenberg J, Cohen H, Ebstein RP et al. Failure to replicate an excess of the long dopamine D4 exon III repeat polymorphism in ADHD in a family-based study. Am J Med Genet 2000; 96(3):278-281.

[33] Muglia P, Jain U, Macciardi F, Kennedy JL. Adult attention deficit hyperactivity disorder and the dopamine D4 receptor gene. Am J Med Genet 2000; 96(3):273-277.

[34] Hawi Z, McCarron M, Kirley A, Daly G, Fitzgerald M, Gill M. No association of the dopamine DRD4 receptor (DRD4) gene polymorphism with attention deficit hyperactivity disorder (ADHD) in the Irish population. Am J Med Genet 2000; 96(3):268-272.

[35] Faraone SV, Doyle AE, Mick E, Biederman J. Meta-analysis of the association between the 7-repeat allele of the dopamine D(4) receptor gene and attention deficit hyperactivity disorder. Am J Psychiatry 2001; 158(7):1052-1057.

[36] Roman T, Schmitz M, Polanczyk G, Eizirik M, Rohde LA, Hutz MH. Attention-deficit hyperactivity disorder: a study of association with both the dopamine transporter gene and the dopamine D4 receptor gene. Am J Med Genet 2001; 105(5):471-478.

[37] Mill J, Curran S, Kent L, Richards S, Gould A, Virdee V et al. Attention deficit hyperactivity disorder (ADHD) and the dopamine D4 receptor gene: evidence of association but no linkage in a UK sample. Mol Psychiatry 2001; 6(4):440-444.

[38] Payton A, Holmes J, Barrett JH, Hever T, Fitzpatrick H, Trumper AL et al. Examining for association between candidate gene polymorphisms in the dopamine pathway and attention-deficit hyperactivity disorder: a family-based study. Am J Med Genet 2001; 105(5):464-470.

[39] Qian Q, Wang Y, Li J, Yang L, Wang B, Zhou R. [Association studies of dopamine D4 receptor gene and dopamine transporter gene polymorphisms in Han Chinese patients with attention deficit hyperactivity disorder]. Beijing Da Xue Xue Bao 2003; 35(4):412-418.

[40] West A, Langley K, Hamshere ML, Kent L, Craddock N, Owen MJ et al. Evidence to suggest biased phenotypes in children with Attention Deficit Hyperactivity Disorder from completely ascertained trios. Mol Psychiatry 2002; 7(9):962-966.

[41] Ding YC, Chi HC, Grady DL, Morishima A, Kidd JR, Kidd KK et al. Evidence of positive selection acting at the human dopamine receptor D4 gene locus. Proc Natl Acad Sci U S A 2002; 99(1):309-314.

[42] Benjamin J, Li L, Patterson C, Greenberg BD, Murphy DL, Hamer DH. Population and familial association between the D4 dopamine receptor gene and measures of Novelty Seeking. Nat Genet 1996; 12(1):81-84.

[43] Ebstein RP, Belmaker RH. Saga of an adventure gene: novelty seeking, substance abuse and the dopamine D4 receptor (D4DR) exon III repeat polymorphism. Mol Psychiatry 1997; 2(5):381-384.

[44] Malhotra AK, Virkkunen M, Rooney W, Eggert M, Linnoila M, Goldman D. The association between the dopamine D4 receptor (D4DR) 16 amino acid repeat polymorphism and novelty seeking. Mol Psychiatry 1996; 1(5):388-391.

[45] Jonsson EG, Nothen MM, Gustavsson JP, Neidt H, Brene S, Tylec A et al. Lack of evidence for allelic association between personality traits and the dopamine D4 receptor gene polymorphisms. Am J Psychiatry 1997; 154(5):697-699.

[46] Sander T, Harms H, Dufeu P, Kuhn S, Rommelspacher H, Schmidt LG. Dopamine D4 receptor exon III alleles and variation of novelty seeking in alcoholics. Am J Med Genet 1997; 74(5):483-487.

[47] Ono Y, Manki H, Yoshimura K, Muramatsu T, Mizushima H, Higuchi S et al. Association between dopamine D4 receptor (D4DR) exon III polymorphism and novelty seeking in Japanese subjects. Am J Med Genet 1997; 74(5):501-503.

[48] Gelernter J, Kranzler H, Coccaro E, Siever L, New A, Mulgrew CL. D4 dopamine-receptor (DRD4) alleles and novelty seeking in substance-dependent, personality-disorder, and control subjects. Am J Hum Genet 1997; 61(5):1144-1152.

[49] Pogue-Geile M, Ferrell R, Deka R, Debski T, Manuck S. Human novelty-seeking personality traits and dopamine D4 receptor polymorphisms: a twin and genetic association study. Am J Med Genet 1998; 81(1):44-48.

[50] Noble EP, Ozkaragoz TZ, Ritchie TL, Zhang X, Belin TR, Sparkes RS. D2 and D4 dopamine receptor polymorphisms and personality. Am J Med Genet 1998; 81(3):257-267.

[51] Jonsson EG, Nothen MM, Gustavsson JP, Neidt H, Forslund K, Mattila-Evenden M et al. Lack of association between dopamine D4 receptor gene and personality traits. Psychol Med 1998; 28(4):985-989.

[52] Paterson AD, Sunohara GA, Kennedy JL. Dopamine D4 receptor gene: novelty or nonsense? Neuropsychopharmacology 1999; 21(1):3-16.

[53] Persson ML, Wasserman D, Geijer T, Frisch A, Rockah R, Michaelovsky E et al. Dopamine D4 receptor gene polymorphism and personality traits in healthy volunteers. Eur Arch Psychiatry Clin Neurosci 2000; 250(4):203-206.

[54] Gebhardt C, Leisch F, Schussler P, Fuchs K, Stompe T, Sieghart W et al. Non-association of dopamine D4 and D2 receptor genes with personality in healthy individuals. Psychiatr Genet 2000; 10(3):131-137.

[55] Lusher JM, Chandler C, Ball D. Dopamine D4 receptor gene (DRD4) is associated with Novelty Seeking (NS) and substance abuse: the saga continues.. Mol Psychiatry 2001; 6(5):497-499.

[56] Jonsson EG, Ivo R, Gustavsson JP, Geijer T, Forslund K, Mattila-Evenden M et al. No association between dopamine D4 receptor gene variants and novelty seeking. Mol Psychiatry 2002; 7(1):18-20.

[57] Strobel A, Lesch KP, Hohenberger K, Jatzke S, Gutzeit HO, Anacker K et al. No association between dopamine D4 receptor gene exon III and -521C/T polymorphism and novelty seeking. Mol Psychiatry 2002; 7(6):537-538.

[58] Strobel A, Spinath FM, Angleitner A, Riemann R, Lesch KP. Lack of association between polymorphisms of the dopamine D4 receptor gene and personality. Neuropsychobiology 2003; 47(1):52-56.

[59] Lee HJ, Lee HS, Kim YK, Kim SH, Kim L, Lee MS et al. Allelic variants interaction of dopamine receptor D4 polymorphism correlate with personality traits in young Korean female population. Am J Med Genet 2003; 118B(1):76-80.

[60] Lee HJ, Lee HS, Kim YK, Kim L, Lee MS, Jung IK et al. D2 and D4 dopamine receptor gene polymorphisms and personality traits in a young Korean population. Am J Med Genet 2003; 121B(1):44-49.

[61] Luciano M, Zhu G, Kirk KM, Whitfield JB, Butler R, Heath AC et al. Effects of dopamine receptor D4 variation on alcohol and tobacco use and on novelty seeking: multivariate linkage and association analysis. Am J Med Genet 2004; 124B(1):113-123.

[62] Franke P, Nothen MM, Wang T, Knapp M, Lichtermann D, Neidt H et al. DRD4 exon III VNTR polymorphism-susceptibility factor for heroin dependence? Results of a case-control and a family-based association approach. Mol Psychiatry 2000; 5(1):101-104.

[63] Li T, Zhu ZH, Liu X, Hu X, Zhao J, Sham PC et al. Association analysis of polymorphisms in the DRD4 gene and heroin abuse in Chinese subjects. Am J Med Genet 2000; 96(5):616-621.

[64] Perez de Castro I, Ibanez A, Torres P, Saiz-Ruiz J, Fernandez-Piqueras J. Genetic association study between pathological gambling and a functional DNA polymorphism at the D4 receptor gene. Pharmacogenetics 1997; 7(5):345-348.

[65] Vandenbergh DJ, Rodriguez LA, Hivert E, Schiller JH, Villareal G, Pugh EW et al. Long forms of the dopamine receptor (DRD4) gene VNTR are more prevalent in

substance abusers: no interaction with functional alleles of the catechol-o-methyltransferase (COMT) gene. Am J Med Genet 2000; 96(5):678-683.

[66] Adamson MD, Kennedy J, Petronis A, Dean M, Virkkunen M, Linnoila M et al. DRD4 dopamine receptor genotype and CSF monoamine metabolites in Finnish alcoholics and controls. Am J Med Genet 1995; 60:199-205.

[67] Chang FM, Ko HC, Lu RB, Pakstis AJ, Kidd KK. The dopamine D4 receptor gene (DRD4) is not associated with alcoholism in three Taiwanese populations: six polymorphisms tested separately and as haplotypes. Biol Psychiatry 1997; 41(4):394-405.

[68] Geijer T, Jonsson E, Neiman J, Persson ML, Brene S, Gyllander A et al. Tyrosine hydroxylase and dopamine D4 receptor allelic distribution in Scandinavian chronic alcoholics. Alcohol Clin Exp Res 1997; 21:35-39.

[69] Ishiguro H, Saito T, Shibuya H, Arinami T. Association study between genetic polymorphisms in the 14-3-3 eta chain and dopamine D4 receptor genes and alcoholism. Alcohol Clin Exp Res 2000; 24(3):343-347.

[70] Parsian A, Chakraverty S, Fisher L, Cloninger CR. No association between polymorphisms in the human dopamine D3 and D4 receptors genes and alcoholism. Am J Med Genet 1997; 74:281-285.

[71] Cook EH, Jr., Stein MA, Krasowski MD, Cox NJ, Olkon DM, Kieffer JE et al. Association of attention-deficit disorder and the dopamine transporter gene. Am J Hum Genet 1995; 56(4):993-998.

[72] Gill M, Daly G, Heron S, Hawi Z, Fitzgerald M. Confirmation of association between attention deficit hyperactivity disorder and a dopamine transporter polymorphism. Mol Psychiatry 1997; 2(4):311-313.

[73] Waldman ID, Rowe DC, Abramowitz A, Kozel ST, Mohr JH, Sherman SL et al. Association and linkage of the dopamine transporter gene and attention-deficit hyperactivity disorder in children: heterogeneity owing to diagnostic subtype and severity. Am J Hum Genet 1998; 63(6):1767-1776.

[74] Daly G, Hawi Z, Fitzgerald M, Gill M. Mapping susceptibility loci in attention deficit hyperactivity disorder: preferential transmission of parental alleles at DAT1, DBH and DRD5 to affected children. Mol Psychiatry 1999; 4(2):192-196.

[75] Todd RD, Jong YJ, Lobos EA, Reich W, Heath AC, Neuman RJ. No association of the dopamine transporter gene 3' VNTR polymorphism with ADHD subtypes in a population sample of twins. Am J Med Genet 2001; 105(8):745-748.

[76] Curran S, Mill J, Tahir E, Kent L, Richards S, Gould A et al. Association study of a dopamine transporter polymorphism and attention deficit hyperactivity disorder in UK and Turkish samples. Mol Psychiatry 2001; 6(4):425-428.

[77] Barr CL, Xu C, Kroft J, Feng Y, Wigg K, Zai G et al. Haplotype study of three polymorphisms at the dopamine transporter locus confirm linkage to attention-deficit/hyperactivity disorder. Biol Psychiatry 2001; 49(4):333-339.

[78] Muglia P, Jain U, Inkster B, Kennedy JL. A quantitative trait locus analysis of the dopamine transporter gene in adults with ADHD. Neuropsychopharmacology 2002; 27(4):655-662.

[79] Chen CK, Chen SL, Mill J, Huang YS, Lin SK, Curran S et al. The dopamine transporter gene is associated with attention deficit hyperactivity disorder in a Taiwanese sample. Mol Psychiatry 2003; 8(4):393-396.

[80] Kustanovich V, Ishii J, Crawford L, Yang M, McGough JJ, McCracken JT et al. Transmission disequilibrium testing of dopamine-related candidate gene polymorphisms in ADHD: confirmation of association of ADHD with DRD4 and DRD5. Mol Psychiatry 2003.

[81] Curran S, Mill J, Tahir E, Kent L, Richards S, Gould A et al. Association study of a dopamine transporter polymorphism and attention deficit hyperactivity disorder in UK and Turkish samples. Mol Psychiatry 2001; 6(4):425-428.

[82] Loo SK, Specter E, Smolen A, Hopfer C, Teale PD, Reite ML. Functional effects of the DAT1 polymorphism on EEG measures in ADHD. J Am Acad Child Adolesc Psychiatry 2003; 42(8):986-993.

[83] Hess EJ, Rogan PK, Domoto M, Tinker DE, Ladda RL, Ramer JC. Absence of linkage of apparently single gene mediated ADHD with the human syntenic region of the mouse mutant Coloboma. Am J Med Genet 1995; 60(6):573-579.

[84] Barr CL, Feng Y, Wigg K, Bloom S, Roberts W, Malone M et al. Identification of DNA variants in the SNAP-25 gene and linkage study of these polymorphisms and attention-deficit hyperactivity disorder. Mol Psychiatry 2000; 5(4):405-409.

[85] Kustanovich V, Merriman B, McGough J, McCracken JT, Smalley SL, Nelson SF. Biased paternal transmission of SNAP-25 risk alleles in attention-deficit hyperactivity disorder. Mol Psychiatry 2003; 8(3):309-315.

[86] Brophy K, Hawi Z, Kirley A, Fitzgerald M, Gill M. Synaptosomal-associated protein 25 (SNAP-25) and attention deficit hyperactivity disorder (ADHD): evidence of linkage and association in the Irish population. Mol Psychiatry 2002; 7(8):913-917.

[87] Mill J, Richards S, Knight J, Curran S, Taylor E, Asherson P. Haplotype analysis of SNAP-25 suggests a role in the aetiology of ADHD. Mol Psychiatry 2004.

[88] Mill J, Curran S, Kent L, Gould A, Huckett L, Richards S et al. Association study of a SNAP-25 microsatellite and attention deficit hyperactivity disorder. Am J Med Genet 2002; 114(3):269-271.

[89] Sherrington R, Mankoo B, Attwood J, Kalsi G, Curtis D, Buetow K et al. Cloning of the human dopamine D5 receptor gene and identification of a highly polymorphic microsatellite for the DRD5 locus that shows tight linkage to the chromosome 4p reference marker RAF1P1. Genomics 1993; 18(2):423-425.

[90] Lowe N, Kirley A, Hawi Z, Sham P, Wickham H, Kratochvil CJ et al. Joint Analysis of the DRD5 Marker Concludes Association with Attention-Deficit/Hyperactivity Disorder Confined to the Predominantly Inattentive and Combined Subtypes. Am J Hum Genet 2004; 74(2):348-356.

[91] Todd RD, Rasmussen ER, Neuman RJ, Reich W, Hudziak JJ, Bucholz KK et al. Familiality and heritability of subtypes of attention deficit hyperactivity disorder in a population sample of adolescent female twins. Am J Psychiatry 2001; 158(11):1891-1898.

[92] Gainetdinov RR, Wetsel WC, Jones SR, Levin ED, Jaber M, Caron MG. Role of serotonin in the paradoxical calming effect of psychostimulants on hyperactivity. Science 1999; 283(5400):397-401.

[93] Mortensen OV, Thomassen M, Larsen MB, Whittemore SR, Wiborg O. Functional analysis of a novel human serotonin transporter gene promoter in immortalized raphe cells. Brain Res Mol Brain Res 1999; 68(1-2):141-148.

[94] Lovejoy EA, Scott AC, Fiskerstrand CE, Bubb VJ, Quinn JP. The serotonin transporter intronic VNTR enhancer correlated with a predisposition to affective disorders has distinct regulatory elements within the domain based on the primary DNA sequence of the repeat unit. Eur J Neurosci 2003; 17(2):417-420.

[95] Kent L, Doerry U, Hardy E, Parmar R, Gingell K, Hawi Z et al. Evidence that variation at the serotonin transporter gene influences susceptibility to attention deficit hyperactivity disorder (ADHD): analysis and pooled analysis. Mol Psychiatry 2002; 7(8):908-912.

[96] Seeger G, Schloss P, Schmidt MH. Functional polymorphism within the promotor of the serotonin transporter gene is associated with severe hyperkinetic disorders. Mol Psychiatry 2001; 6(2):235-238.

[97] Manor I, Eisenberg J, Tyano S, Sever Y, Cohen H, Ebstein RP et al. Family-based association study of the serotonin transporter promoter region polymorphism (5-HTTLPR) in attention deficit hyperactivity disorder. Am J Med Genet 2001; 105(1):91-95.

[98] Zoroglu SS, Erdal ME, Alasehirli B, Erdal N, Sivasli E, Tutkun H et al. Significance of serotonin transporter gene 5-HTTLPR and variable number of tandem repeat polymorphism in attention deficit hyperactivity disorder. Neuropsychobiology 2002; 45(4):176-181.

[99] Langley K, Payton A, Hamshere ML, Pay HM, Lawson DC, Turic D et al. No evidence of association of two 5HT transporter gene polymorphisms and attention deficit hyperactivity disorder. Psychiatr Genet 2003; 13(2):107-110.

[100] Hawi Z, Dring M, Kirley A, Foley D, Kent L, Craddock N et al. Serotonergic system and attention deficit hyperactivity disorder (ADHD): a potential susceptibility locus at the 5-HT(1B) receptor gene in 273 nuclear families from a multi-centre sample. Mol Psychiatry 2002; 7(7):718-725.

[101] Quist JF, Barr CL, Schachar R, Roberts W, Malone M, Tannock R et al. The serotonin 5-HT1B receptor gene and attention deficit hyperactivity disorder. Mol Psychiatry 2003; 8(1):98-102.

[102] Bakker SC, van der Meulen EM, Buitelaar JK, Sandkuijl LA, Pauls DL, Monsuur AJ et al. A whole-genome scan in 164 Dutch sib pairs with attention-deficit/hyperactivity disorder: suggestive evidence for linkage on chromosomes 7p and 15q. Am J Hum Genet 2003; 72(5):1251-1260.

[103] Fisher SE, Francks C, McCracken JT, McGough JJ, Marlow AJ, MacPhie IL et al. A genomewide scan for loci involved in attention-deficit/hyperactivity disorder. Am J Hum Genet 2002; 70(5):1183-1196.

[104] Ogdie MN, MacPhie IL, Minassian SL, Yang M, Fisher SE, Francks C et al. A genomewide scan for attention-deficit/hyperactivity disorder in an extended sample: suggestive linkage on 17p11. Am J Hum Genet 2003; 72(5):1268-1279.

[105] Mill J, Xu X, Ronals A, Knight J, Plomin R, Asherson P. Association analysis of five candidate gene polymorphisms with chidhood hyperactivity in a population based sample of male dizygotic twins. Manuscript submitted for publication . 2004.

[106] Payton A, Holmes J, Barrett JH, Sham P, Harrington R, McGuffin P et al. Susceptibility genes for a trait measure of attention deficit hyperactivity disorder: a pilot study in a non-clinical sample of twins. Psychiatry Res 2001; 105(3):273-278.

[107] Kuntsi J, Stevenson J. Hyperactivity in children: a focus on genetic research and psychological theories. Clin Child Fam Psychol Rev 2000; 3(1):1-23.

[108] Szatmari P, Saigal S, Rosenbaum P, Campbell D, King S. Psychiatric disorders at five years among children with birthweights less than 1000g: a regional perspective. Dev Med Child Neurol 1990; 32(11):954-962.

[109] Saigal S, Stoskopf BL, Streiner DL, Burrows E. Physical growth and current health status of infants who were of extremely low birth weight and controls at adolescence. Pediatrics 2001; 108(2):407-415.

[110] Hille ET, den Ouden AL, Saigal S, Wolke D, Lambert M, Whitaker A et al. Behavioural problems in children who weigh 1000 g or less at birth in four countries. Lancet 2001; 357(9269):1641-1643.

[111] The Scottish low birthweight study: II. Language attainment, cognitive status, and behavioural problems. Arch Dis Child 1992; 67(6):682-686.

[112] Botting N, Powls A, Cooke RW, Marlow N. Attention deficit hyperactivity disorders and other psychiatric outcomes in very low birthweight children at 12 years. J Child Psychol Psychiatry 1997; 38(8):931-941.

[113] Nadeau L, Boivin M, Tessier R, Lefebvre F, Robaey P. Mediators of behavioral problems in 7-year-old children born after 24 to 28 weeks of gestation. J Dev Behav Pediatr 2001; 22(1):1-10.

[114] Breslau N, Klein N, Allen L. Very low birthweight: behavioral sequelae at nine years of age. J Am Acad Child Adolesc Psychiatry 1988; 27(5):605-612.

[115] Foulder-Hughes LA, Cooke RW. Motor, cognitive, and behavioural disorders in children born very preterm. Dev Med Child Neurol 2003; 45(2):97-103.

[116] Hack M, Breslau N, Aram D, Weissman B, Klein N, Borawski-Clark E. The effect of very low birth weight and social risk on neurocognitive abilities at school age. J Dev Behav Pediatr 1992; 13(6):412-420.

[117] McCormick MC, Gortmaker SL, Sobol AM. Very low birth weight children: behavior problems and school difficulty in a national sample. J Pediatr 1990; 117(5):687-693.

[118] Goodman R, Stevenson J. A twin study of hyperactivity.II. The aetiological role of genes, family relationships and perinatal adversity. J Child Psychol Psychiatry 1989; 30:691-709.

[119] Whitaker AH, Van Rossem R, Feldman JF, Schonfeld IS, Pinto-Martin JA, Tore C et al. Psychiatric outcomes in low-birth-weight children at age 6 years: relation to neonatal cranial ultrasound abnormalities. Arch Gen Psychiatry 1997; 54(9):847-856.

[120] Breslau N, Brown GG, DelDotto JE, Kumar S, Ezhuthachan S, Andreski P et al. Psychiatric sequelae of low birth weight at 6 years of age. J Abnorm Child Psychol 1996; 24(3):385-400.
[121] Breslau N, Chilcoat HD. Psychiatric sequelae of low birth weight at 11 years of age. Biol Psychiatry 2000; 47(11):1005-1011.
[122] Stjernqvist K, Svenningsen NW. Ten-year follow-up of children born before 29 gestational weeks: health, cognitive development, behaviour and school achievement. Acta Paediatr 1999; 88(5):557-562.
[123] Cherkes-Julkowski M. Learning disability, attention-deficit disorder, and language impairment as outcomes of prematurity: a longitudinal descriptive study. J Learn Disabil 1998; 31(3):294-306.
[124] Mick E, Biederman J, Prince J, Fischer MJ, Faraone SV. Impact of low birth weight on attention-deficit hyperactivity disorder. J Dev Behav Pediatr 2002; 23(1):16-22.
[125] Lou HC. Etiology and pathogenesis of attention-deficit hyperactivity disorder (ADHD): significance of prematurity and perinatal hypoxic-haemodynamic encephalopathy. Acta Paediatr 1996; 85(11):1266-1271.
[126] Wolke D. Psychological development of prematurely born children. Arch Dis Child 1998; 78(6):567-570.
[127] Hale TS, Hariri AR, McCracken JT. Attention-deficit/hyperactivity disorder: Perspectives from neuroimaging. Mental Retardation and Developmental Disabilities Research Reviews 2000; 6(3):214-219.
[128] Toft PB. Prenatal and perinatal striatal injury: A hypothetical cause of attention-deficit-hyperactivity disorder? Pediatr Neurol 1999; 21(3):602-610.
[129] Brake WG, Noel MB, Boksa P, Gratton A. Influence of perinatal factors on the nucleus accumbens dopamine response to repeated stress during adulthood: an electrochemical study in the rat. Neuroscience 1997; 77(4):1067-1076.
[130] Brake WG, Sullivan RM, Gratton A. Perinatal distress leads to lateralized medial prefrontal cortical dopamine hypofunction in adult rats. J Neurosci 2000; 20(14):5538-5543.
[131] Brake WG, Noel MB, Boksa P, Gratton A. Influence of perinatal factors on the nucleus accumbens dopamine response to repeated stress during adulthood: an electrochemical study in the rat. Neuroscience 1997; 77(4):1067-1076.
[132] Decker MJ, Hue GE, Caudle WM, Miller GW, Keating GL, Rye DB. Episodic neonatal hypoxia evokes executive dysfunction and regionally specific alterations in markers of dopamine signaling. Neurosci 2003; 117(2):417-425.
[133] Milberger S, Biederman J, Faraone SV, Guite J, Tsuang MT. Pregnancy, delivery and infancy complications and attention deficit hyperactivity disorder: issues of gene-environment interaction. Biol Psychiatry 1997; 41(1):65-75.
[134] Chandola CA, Robling MR, Peters TJ, Melville-Thomas G, McGuffin P. Pre- and perinatal factors and the risk of subsequent referral for hyperactivity. J Child Psychol Psychiatry 1992; 33(6):1077-1090.
[135] Chandola CA, Robling MR, Peters TJ, Melville-Thomas G, McGuffin P. Pre- and perinatal factors and the risk of subsequent referral for hyperactivity. J Child Psychol Psychiatry 1992; 33(6):1077-1090.

[136] Chandola CA, Robling MR, Peters TJ, Melville-Thomas G, McGuffin P. Pre- and perinatal factors and the risk of subsequent referral for hyperactivity. J Child Psychol Psychiatry 1992; 33(6):1077-1090.

[137] Breslau N, Chilcoat HD. Psychiatric sequelae of low birth weight at 11 years of age. Biol Psychiatry 2000; 47(11):1005-1011.

[138] Milberger S, Biederman J, Faraone SV, Chen L, Jones J. Is maternal smoking during pregnancy a risk factor for attention deficit hyperactivity disorder in children? Am J Psychiatry 1996; 153:1138-1142.

[139] Milberger S, Biederman J, Faraone SV, Jones J. Further evidence of an association between maternal smoking during pregnancy and attention deficit hyperactivity disorder: findings from a high-risk sample of siblings. J Clin Child Psychol 1998; 27(3):352-358.

[140] Mick E, Biederman J, Faraone SV, Sayer J, Kleinman S. Case-control study of attention-deficit hyperactivity disorder and maternal smoking, alcohol use, and drug use during pregnancy. J Am Acad Child Adolesc Psychiatry 2002; 41(4):378-385.

[141] Kotimaa AJ, Moilanen I, Taanila A, Ebeling H, Smalley SL, McGough JJ et al. Maternal smoking and hyperactivity in 8-year-old children. J Am Acad Child Adolesc Psychiatry 2003; 42(7):826-833.

[142] Faraone SV, Biederman J. Neurobiology of attention-deficit hyperactivity disorder. Biol Psychiatry 1998; 44(10):951-958.

[143] Thapar A, Fowler T, Rice F, Scourfield J, van den BM, Thomas H et al. Maternal smoking during pregnancy and attention deficit hyperactivity disorder symptoms in offspring. Am J Psychiatry 2003; 160(11):1985-1989.

[144] Caspi A, McClay J, Moffitt TE, Mill J, Martin J, Craig IW et al. Role of genotype in the cycle of violence in maltreated children. Science 2002; 297(5582):851-854.

[145] Caspi A, Sugden K, Moffitt TE, Taylor A, Craig IW, Harrington H et al. Influence of life stress on depression: moderation by a polymorphism in the 5-HTT gene. Science 2003; 301(5631):386-389.

[146] Caspi A, Sugden K, Moffitt TE, Taylor A, Craig IW, Harrington H et al. Influence of life stress on depression: moderation by a polymorphism in the 5-HTT gene. Science 2003; 301(5631):386-389.

[147] Kahn RS, Khoury J, Nichols WC, Lanphear BP. Role of dopamine transporter genotype and maternal prenatal smoking in childhood hyperactive-impulsive, inattentive, and oppositional behaviors. J Pediatr 2003; 143(1):104-110.

[148] Castellanos FX, Tannock R. Neuroscience of attention-deficit hyperactivity disorder: the search for endophenotypes. Nat Rev Neurosci 2002; 3:617-628.

[149] Kuntsi J, Stevenson J. Hyperactivity in children: a focus on genetic research and psychological theories. Clin Child Fam Psychol Rev 2000; 3(1):1-23.

[150] Sergeant JA, Geurts H, Huijbregts S, Scheres A, Oosterlaan J. The top and the bottom of ADHD: a neuropsychological perspective. Neurosci Biobehav Rev 2003; 27(7):583-592.

[151] Sergeant JA, Geurts H, Oosterlaan J. How specific is a deficit of executive functioning for Attention-Deficit/Hyperactivity Disorder? Behavioural Brain Research 2002; 130(1-2):3-28.

[152] Oosterlaan J, Logan GD, Sergeant JA. Response inhibition in AD/HD, CD, comorbid AD/HD + CD, anxious, and control children: a meta-analysis of studies with the stop task. J Child Psychol Psychiatry 1998; 39:411-425.

[153] Kuntsi J, Oosterlaan J, Stevenson J. Psychological mechanisms in hyperactivity: I response inhibition deficit, working memory impairment, delay aversion, or something else? J Child Psychol Psychiatry 2001; 42(2):199-210.

[154] Pliszka SR, Liotti M, Woldorff MG. Inhibitory control in children with attention-deficit/hyperactivity disorder: event-related potentials identify the processing component and timing of an impaired right-frontal response-inhibition mechanism. Biol Psychiatry 2000; 48(3):238-246.

[155] Scheres A, Oosterlaan J, Sergeant JA. Response execution and inhibition in children with AD/HD and other disruptive disorders: the role of behavioural activation. J Child Psychol Psychiatry 2001; 42(3):347-357.

[156] Borger N, Van der Meere J. Motor control and state regulation in children with ADHD: a cardiac response study. Biological Psychology 2000; 51(2-3):247-267.

[157] Yong-Liang G, Robaey P, Karayanidis F, Bourassa M, Pelletier G, Geoffroy G. ERPs and behavioral inhibition in a Go/No-go task in children with attention-deficit hyperactivity disorder. Brain Cogn 2000; 43(1-3):215-220.

[158] Van der Meere J, Stemerdink N, Gunning B. Effects of presentation rate of stimuli on response inhibition in ADHD children with and without tics [comment]. Percept Mot Skills 1995; 81(1):259-262.

[159] Slusarek M, Velling S, Bunk D, Eggers C. Motivational effects on inhibitory control in children with ADHD. J Am Acad Child Adolesc Psychiatry 2001; 40(3):355-363.

[160] Konrad K, Gauggel S, Manz A, Scholl M. Lack of inhibition: a motivational deficit in children with attention deficit/hyperactivity disorder and children with traumatic brain injury. Neuropsychol Dev Cogn Sect C Child Neuropsychol 2000; 6(4):286-296.

[161] Oosterlaan J, Sergeant JA. Effects of reward and response cost on response inhibition in AD/HD, disruptive, anxious, and normal children. J Abnorm Child Psychol 1998; 26:161-174.

[162] Leth-Steensen C, Elbaz ZK, Douglas VI. Mean response times, variability, and skew in the responding of ADHD children: a response time distributional approach. Acta Psychol (Amst) 2000; 104(2):167-190.

[163] Zentall SS, Zentall TR. Optimal stimulation: a model of disordered activity and performance in normal and deviant children. Psychol Bull 1983; 94:446-471.

[164] Van der Meere JJ. The role of attention in hyperactivity disorders. In: Sandberg S, editor. Hyperactivity and attention disorders of childhood. Cambridge: Cambridge University Press, 2002.

[165] Sergeant J, Oosterlaan J, Van der Meere J. Information processing and energetic factors in attention-deficit/hyperactivity disorder. In: Quay HC, Hogan AE, editors. Handbook of disruptive behavior disorders. New York: Plenum Press, 1999: 75-104.

[166] Banaschewski T, Brandeis D, Heinrich H, Albrecht B, Brunner E, Rothenberger A. Association of ADHD and conduct disorder--brain electrical evidence for the existence of a distinct subtype. J Child Psychol Psychiatry 2003; 44(3):356-376.

[167] Mason DJ, Humphreys GW, Kent LS. Exploring selective attention in ADHD: visual search through space and time. J Child Psychol Psychiatry 2003; 44(8):1158-1176.

[168] Sonuga-Barke EJ. On dysfunction and function in psychological theories of childhood disorder. J Child Psychol Psychiatry 1994; 35:801-815.

[169] Sonuga-Barke EJS, Taylor E, Sembi S, Smith J. Hyperactivity and delay aversion - I. The effect of delay on choice. J Child Psychol Psychiatry 1992; 33:387-398.

[170] Kuntsi J, Andreou P, Ma J, Borger, Van der Meere J. Testing assumptions for endophenotype studies in ADHD: Reliability and validity of tasks in a general population sample. Manuscript submitted for publication . 2004.

[171] Oosterlaan J, Scheres A, Sargeant J. Which executive functioning deficits are associated with AD/HD, ODD/CD and combordid AD/HD + ODD/CD? Manuscript submitted for publication. 2004.

[172] Martin N, Scourfield J, McGuffin P. Observer effects and heritability of childhood attention-deficit hyperactivity disorder symptoms. Br J Psychiatry 2002; 180:260-265.

[173] Gomez R, Harvey J, Quick C, Scharer I, Harris G. DSM-IV AD/HD: confirmatory factor models, prevalence, and gender and age differences based on parent and teacher ratings of Australian primary school children. J Child Psychol Psychiatry 1999; 40(2):265-274.

[174] Eaves LJ, Silberg JL, Meyer JM, Maes HH, Simonoff E, Pickles A et al. Genetics and developmental psychopathology: 2. The main effects of genes and environment on behavioral problems in the Virginia Twin Study of Adolescent Behavioral Development. J Child Psychol Psychiatry 1997; 38(8):965-980.

[175] Nadder TS, Silberg JL, Rutter M, Maes HH, Eaves LJ. Comparison of multiple measures of ADHD symptomatology: A multivariate genetic analysis. J Child Psychol Psychiatry 2001; 42(4):475-486.

[176] Thapar A, Harrington R, Ross K, McGuffin P. Does the definition of ADHD affect heritability? J Am Acad Child Adolesc Psychiatry 2000; 39(12):1528-1536.

[177] DeFries JC, Fulker DW. Multiple regression analysis of twin data. Behav Genet 1985; 15(5):467-473.

[178] DeFries JC, Fulker DW. Multiple regression analysis of twin data: etiology of deviant scores versus individual differences. Acta Genet Med Gemellol (Roma) 1988; 37(3-4):205-216.

[179] Seidman LJ, Biederman J, Monuteaux MC, Weber W, Faraone SV. Neuropsychological functioning in nonreferred siblings of children with attention deficit/hyperactivity disorder. J Abnorm Psychol 2000; 109(2):252-265.

[180] Slaats-Willemse D, Swaab-Barneveld H, de Sonneville L, van der ME, Buitelaar J. Deficient response inhibition as a cognitive endophenotype of ADHD. J Am Acad Child Adolesc Psychiatry 2003; 42(10):1242-1248.

[181] Nigg J, Blaskey L, Stawicki J, Sachek J. Evaluating the endophenotype model of ADHD neuropsychological deficit: results for parents and siblings of children with DSM-IV ADHD combined and inattentive subtypes. Journal of Abnormal Psychology in press. 2004.

[182] Swanson J, Oosterlaan J, Murias M, Schuck S, Flodman P, Spence MA et al. Attention deficit/hyperactivity disorder children with a 7-repeat allele of the dopamine receptor

D4 gene have extreme behavior but normal performance on critical neuropsychological tests of attention . Proc Natl Acad Sci U S A 2000; 97(9):4754-4759.

[183] Manor I, Tyano S, Eisenberg J, Bachner-Melman R, Kotler M, Ebstein RP. The short DRD4 repeats confer risk to attention deficit hyperactivity disorder in a family-based design and impair performance on a continuous performance test (TOVA). Mol Psychiatry 2002; 7(7):790-794.

[184] Langley K, Marshall L, van den BM, Thomas H, Owen M, O'Donovan M et al. Association of the dopamine D4 receptor gene 7-repeat allele with neuropsychological test performance of children with ADHD. Am J Psychiatry 2004; 161(1):133-138.

[185] Loo SK, Specter E, Smolen A, Hopfer C, Teale PD, Reite ML. Functional effects of the DAT1 polymorphism on EEG measures in ADHD. J Am Acad Child Adolesc Psychiatry 2003; 42(8):986-993.

[186] van Beijsterveldt CE, Molenaar PC, de Geus EJ, Boomsma DI. Heritability of human brain functioning as assessed by electroencephalography. Am J Hum Genet 1996; 58(3):562-573.

[187] Berridge KC, Robinson TE. What is the role of dopamine in reward: hedonic impact, reward learning, or incentive salience? Brain Res Brain Res Rev 1998; 28:309-369.

[188] Wise RA. Interactions between medial prefrontal cortex and meso-limbic components of brain reward circuitry. Prog Brain Res 2000; 126:255-262.

[189] Wyvell CL, Berridge KC. Intra-accumbens amphetamine increases the conditioned incentive salience of sucrose reward: enhancement of reward "wanting" without enhanced "liking" or response reinforcement. J Neurosci 2000; 20(21):8122-8130.

[190] Schultz W. Multiple reward signals in the brain. Nat Rev Neurosci 2000; 1(3):199-207.

[191] Schultz W, Dayan P, Montague PR. A neural substrate of prediction and reward. Science 1997; 275(5306):1593-1599.

[192] Bechara A, Harrington F, Nader K, van der KD. Neurobiology of motivation: double dissociation of two motivational mechanisms mediating opiate reward in drug-naive versus drug-dependent animals. Behav Neurosci 1992; 106(5):798-807.

[193] Nader K, Bechara A, van der KD. Neurobiological constraints on behavioral models of motivation. Annu Rev Psychol 1997; 48:85-114.

[194] Fuente-Fernandez R, Ruth TJ, Sossi V, Schulzer M, Calne DB, Stoessl AJ. Expectation and dopamine release: mechanism of the placebo effect in Parkinson's disease. Science 2001; 293(5532):1164-1166.

[195] Koepp MJ, Gunn RN, Lawrence AD, Cunningham VJ, Dagher A, Jones T et al. Evidence for striatal dopamine release during a video game. Nature 1998; 393:266-268.

[196] Berns GS, McClure SM, Pagnoni G, Montague PR. Predictability modulates human brain response to reward. J Neurosci 2001; 21(8):2793-2798.

[197] Pagnoni G, Zink CF, Montague PR, Berns GS. Activity in human ventral striatum locked to errors of reward prediction. Nat Neurosci 2002; 5(2):97-98.

[198] Castellanos FX, Swanson J. Biological underpinnings of ADHD. In: Sandberg S, editor. Hyperactivity and attention disorders in childhood. Cambridge, UK: Cambridge University Press, 2002: 336-366.

[199] Swanson JM, Sergeant JA, Taylor E, Sonuga-Barke EJS, Jensen PS, Cantwell DP. Seminar: attention-deficit hyperactivity disorder and hyperkinetic disorder. Lancet 1998; 351:429-433.

[200] Dougherty DD, Bonab AA, Spencer TJ, Rauch SL, Madras BK, Fischman AJ. Dopamine transporter density is elevated in patients with attention deficit hyperactivity disorder. Lancet 1999; 354(9196):2132-2133.

[201] Krause KH, Dresel SH, Krause J, Kung HF, Tatsch K. Increased striatal dopamine transporter in adult patients with attention deficit hyperactivity disorder: effects of methylphenidate as measured by single photon emission computed tomography. Neurosci Lett 2000; 285(2):107-110.

[202] Dresel S, Krause J, Krause KH, LaFougere C, Brinkbaumer K, Kung HF et al. Attention deficit hyperactivity disorder: binding of [^{99m}Tc]TRODAT-1 to the dopamine transporter before and after methylphenidate treatment. Eur J Nucl Med 2000; 27(10):1518-1524.

[203] Cheon KA, Ryu YH, Kim YK, Namkoong K, Kim CH, Lee JD. Dopamine transporter density in the basal ganglia assessed with [123I]IPT SPET in children with attention deficit hyperactivity disorder. Eur J Nucl Med Mol Imaging 2003; 30(2):306-311.

[204] van Dyck CH, Quinlan DM, Cretella LM, Staley JK, Malison RT, Baldwin RM et al. Unaltered dopamine transporter availability in adult attention deficit hyperactivity disorder. Am J Psychiatry 2002; 159(2):309-312.

In: Attention Deficit Hyperactivity Disorder
Editor: Marvin C. Shriner, pp. 99-127
ISBN: 1-60021 321-9

Chapter IV

Relationships between Attention Deficit/Hyperactivity Disorder, Conduct Disorder, Psychopathy, and Aggression: The Fledgling Psychopath Hypothesis

Waisam Hoong, Stephen Houghton[1] and Elaine Chapman
Graduate School of Education
The University of Western Australia

Abstract

It has been proposed that children with conduct problems who also show symptoms of hyperactivity, impulsivity, and inattention constitute a unique subgroup who may be considered "fledgling psychopaths". This study was designed to test the predictions implied by the fledgling psychopath hypothesis. In the study, levels of psychopathy and aggression were compared in four groups of adolescent males (n = 129): three clinical samples and one non-diagnosed community sample. The first clinical sample comprised boys with conduct disorder who had also been diagnosed with attention deficit/hyperactivity disorder. The second and third clinical samples comprised boys diagnosed either with attention deficit/hyperactivity disorder or conduct disorder only. In general, results of group comparison and multiple regression analyses did not support the predictions implied by the fledgling psychopath hypothesis. Implications for the status of the hypothesis and for the measurement of psychopathy in adolescent populations are discussed.

[1] Corresponding Author:Professor Stephen Houghton,The Centre for Attention Related Disorders The Graduate School of Education,The University of Western Australia,Crawley 6009, Australia Tel: ++ 618 6488 2391,Fax: ++ 618 6488 1052,Email: *stephen.houghton@uwa.edu.au*

INTRODUCTION

Psychopathy, which was first described by Cleckley (1976), is a disorder characterised in part by an unemotional interpersonal style, the absence of empathy, and a callous disregard for the rights, feelings or welfare of others (Frick, Bodin, Barry, 2000). According to Loney, Frick, Clements, Ellis, and Kerlin (2003), psychopathy refers to a constellation of affective (e.g., poverty of emotions, lack of empathy, and guilt), interpersonal (e.g., callous use of others for one's own gain), self-referential (e.g., inflated sense of one's own importance) and behavioural (e.g., impulsive behavior and inadequately motivated violence) characteristics that have proven important in designating a severe, chronic, and difficult-to-treat group of antisocial adults. Although studies conducted with incarcerated adults have suggested that the onset of psychopathy may occur early in development (Forth Burke, 1998; Saltaris, 2002), and that longitudinal research has indicated that adult psychopathy can often be traced back to childhood (Lahey, Loeber, Quay, Frick, Grimm, 1992), the focus has almost exclusively been on adult samples and forensic populations.

Recently, however, it has been recognised that there exists a subgroup of children and adolescents who show severe antisocial behaviour and who also exhibit characteristics that are similar to psychopathic adults (Frick, et al., 2000). Like adults with psychopathy, children and adolescents who also display callous and unemotional traits show a much more severe and aggressive pattern of Conduct Problems (CP) than other children with Conduct Disorder (CD) (Caputo, Frick, Brodsky, 1999). Furthermore, the majority of children with CP show symptoms of Hyperactivity, Impulsivity and Inattention (HIA). It is this combination (HIA plus CP) which, according to Lynam (1996), constitutes a unique subgroup of "fledgling psychopaths", who possess a "virulent strain" of CP. Lynam (1996) suggested that during childhood, signs of HIA are exhibited, which develop into Oppositional Defiant Disorder behaviors (e.g., non compliance, arguing). On entry to school, the child has difficulty remaining seated, being quiet, and listening to the teacher. Interpersonally, the child shows signs of CP (e.g., bullying, fighting, and stealing). To date, this hypothesis has received limited research attention. Recently, however, Abromowitz, Kosson, and Seidenberg (2003) concluded from a retrospective study of 275 adult male inmates that childhood CP emerged as the most powerful predictor of adult psychopathy scores, and that while childhood ADHD also predicted psychopathy, its contribution was smaller than that of CP.

In summarising a review of the literature pertaining to the fledgling psychopath hypothesis, Gresham, Lane, and Lambros (2000) stated that the prognosis for children becomes markedly worse when comorbidity of HIA and CP is present. Specifically, children with HIA + CP possess the worst features of both domains, and evidence "a variety of delinquent acts in adolescence, more severe aggression in adolescence, and more violent offending in adulthood than those who are not comorbid for these diagnoses" (p. 85). Gresham et al. continued that, "children with HIA + CP are at heightened risk for the development of future psychopathology, as well as a host of additional adult adjustment problems including substance abuse, unemployment, divorce, accidents, and dependence on welfare"(p. 85). Gresham et al. concluded that what is particularly disturbing about this group is the impulsive response style coupled with the tendency to engage in severe aggression and violent offending.

The question remains however, as to what distinguishes this subgroup of ADHD comorbid CP children, who reportedly commit a disproportionate amount of crime, appear unperturbed when confronted with the destructive nature of their behaviour (Blair, Colledge, Murray, Mitchel, 2001), and are more likely to re-offend (Forth Burke, 1998) or resist efforts at rehabilitation (Salekin, Rogers, Ustad, Sewell, 1998), from others who have CP. Barry, Frick, DeShazo, McCoy, Ellis, and Loney (2000) suggested that it is the presence of Callous and Unemotional traits (C/U) which is necessary to designate a group of youth who show characteristics similar to adults with psychopathy. Frick and colleagues have also highlighted the presence or absence of C/U traits, coupled with deficits in emotional reactivity as the difference between individuals who are both psychopathic and antisocial, and those who are antisocial but not psychopathic (see Frick, 1998; Frick, Cornell, Loney, Bodin, Dane, Barry, 2003; Loney, Frick, Clements, Ellis, Kerlin, 2003; Silverthorn Frick, 1999).

Recently, Barry, Frick, DeShazo, McCoy, Ellis, and Loney (2000) provided support for Lynam's (1996) fledgling psychopath hypothesis. The findings from a study with clinic referred children (ADHD only, ADHD + ODD/CD with low C/U, ADHD + ODD/CD high C/U, and clinic referred controls) aged 6 to 13 years revealed that those with symptoms of ADHD with severe CP were most likely to show features associated with psychopathy. However, within this group, only the children who also showed high rates of C/U traits exhibited these features.

Frick, Cornell, Loney, Bodin, Dane and Barry (2003) further examined C/U traits and developmental pathways to severe conduct problems in non-referred children with and without C/U traits. The findings from this research extended the earlier work with forensic populations by showing that the presence of C/U traits in mainstream children may designate a distinct, behaviorally dysregulated group of children with conduct problems, who may have unique processes underlying their dysregulation that make them more similar to adults with psychopathy. The authors further commented on this, stating that a callous and unemotional interpersonal style combined with impulsive and antisocial behavior is similar to the traits exhibited by adults with psychopathy. It may be, therefore, that the presence or absence of C/U traits (absence of guilt, constricted display of emotion) and related interpersonal behaviours (failure to show empathy, use of other's for one's own gain) are the key markers for psychopathy in children and adolescents.

The research reported here was designed to test the predictions implied by the fledgling psychopath hypothesis. In the study, levels of psychopathy and aggression were compared in four groups of adolescent males: three clinical samples and one non-diagnosed community sample. The first clinical sample comprised boys with Conduct Disorder (CD) who had also been diagnosed with ADHD. The second and third clinical samples comprised boys diagnosed either with ADHD or CD only. Thus, this design meets the criteria posited by Gresham et al. (2000), who argued that in order to examine the presence of psychopathy within the ADHD and CD populations, it is ideal to have four groups (CD only, ADHD only, ADHD+CD, and a non-diagnosed community sample) to use in contrast.

For all participants in the study, a battery of measures was taken, including the *Psychopathy Screening Device* (PSD: Frick, O'Brien, Wootton, McBurnett, 1994), the *Aggression Questionnaire* (AQ: Buss Warren, 2000), and the *Swanson, Nolan and Pelham Teacher and Parent Rating Scale-IV* (SNAP-IV: Swanson, 1995). Two approaches were taken in the analysis of the data. One was based on comparing levels of psychopathy and aggression across diagnostic groups. The other examined correlations between scores on these measures with symptom severity ratings on the SNAP-IV. Based on the fledgling psychopath hypothesis, it was anticipated that the presence of comorbid ADHD and CD symptoms (manifested either in diagnostic classifications or symptom severity ratings) would be associated with higher scores on the psychopathy and aggression questionnaires.

METHOD

Participants

The sample comprised 129 male adolescents between the ages of 14 and 20 (*M* = 16.50, *SD* = 1.65). Of these, 42 were non-diagnosed adolescents drawn from the general community, 35 were diagnosed with ADHD only, 34 with CD only, and 18 with comorbid ADHD and CD (ADHD+CD). The age distribution of the sample is shown in Table 1. Participants were excluded from the research if they had other developmental or neurological disorders. All participants were native English speakers, had normal hearing and normal or corrected vision. None had major sensori-motor difficulties.

Table 1. Age distribution of sample by diagnostic category

Age	ADHD	CD	ADHD +CD	Community	Total
14	10	1	0	11	22
15	7	0	1	9	17
16	9	2	1	12	24
17	6	9	3	2	20
18	3	17	8	6	34
19	0	4	5	1	10
20	0	1	0	1	2
Total	35	34	18	42	129

ADHD Only

Adolescents with ADHD were aged between 14 and 20 years (*M* = 15.57, *SD* = 1.31), had been clinically diagnosed by a paediatrician as meeting DSM-IV criteria for ADHD, and had no diagnosed comorbid disorders (as assessed by clinical psychologists). Twenty-three participants were recruited through one consultant paediatrician, while 12 were recruited from the Centre for Attention Related Disorders, located at the University of Western Australia. All of the boys were free of stimulant medication for a minimum period of 20 hours prior to the testing.

CD With and Without ADHD

Adolescents with CD only and CD with comorbid ADHD were recruited from the main juvenile detention centre and main remand centre of the capital city of Perth,

Western Australia. To be included in this group, it was necessary for participants to have met appropriate DSM-IV criteria as determined by the institutional medical staff and clinical/forensic psychologists. Aboriginals were not included in this study because of cultural issues. The mean age of the CD only participants was 17.68 years (SD = 1.07), while for the CD with comorbid ADHD group it was 17.83 years (SD = 1.10). The types of offences committed by these individuals included theft and burglary, assault, and stealing of motor vehicles. The length of incarceration for these adolescents ranged from 2 days to 2.5 years (average 52 weeks).

Community Comparison Group

The community comparison sample comprised 42 boys from years 8 to 12 (M = 15.76, SD = 1.57) in one low to middle SES state high school situated in Perth, Western Australia. All students in this school are screened each year to identify those who are "at risk of educational failure". None of the participants in the community group had been identified as "at risk" in the screening procedure, and according to school records, had not been identified during their school experience as having any academic or behavioural problems.

SETTINGS

All adolescents with ADHD were tested in the Centre for Attention Related Disorders, within the University of Western Australia. Those with CD (with and without ADHD) were tested in their respective Detention and Remand Centres. Individuals in the community sample were tested in a room set aside by the school for the purposes of the study. In each of the settings, the testing area was quiet and free from extraneous distractions. Furniture layout and equipment was identical, with seating arranged in an informal manner so that participants and interviewers were facing each other. Each participant was tested individually.

INSTRUMENTATION

All participants completed three questionnaires: The *Psychopathy Screening Device* (PSD: Frick, et al., 1994), the *Aggression Questionnaire* (AQ: Buss Warren, 2000), and the *Swanson, Nolan and Pelham Teacher and Parent Rating Scale-IV* (SNAP-IV: Swanson, 1995).

The 20-item PSD was developed as an extension of the adult *Psychopathy Checklist–Revised* (PCL-R: Hare, 1991), and is administered to the primary caregiver of the child. The PSD is designed to assess three dimensions of psychopathy: (i) a lack of empathy and a callous and unemotional interpersonal style, (ii) impulsivity, and (iii) narcissism. The items on the PSD are arranged on a 3-point scale anchored with the words "Not at all True", "Sometimes True", and "Definitely True". Previous factor analyses have revealed two highly interrelated dimensions in the psychopathy construct with clinic-referred children and adolescents. Frick et al. (1994) labelled these as Impulsivity-Conduct Problems (defined by characteristics such as poor impulse control and delinquent behaviours) and Callous-Unemotional interpersonal style (defined by affective and interpersonal traits such as superficial charm, and a lack of guilt and empathy).

In a validation study of the PSD, Frick et al. (2000) used both exploratory and confirmatory factor analyses to examine the underlying structure of the PSD in two samples of children: a non-diagnosed community sample, and a clinic-referred sample of children from approximately the same age range. These analyses indicated very similar factor structures across the two samples. In both cases, either a two- or a three-factor solution could be justified, with the two-factor model being somewhat more justifiable in the clinic-referred sample. In the two-factor model, PSD items grouped into a callous/unemotional factor (C/U) and a narcissism/impulsivity factor (NARC/IMP), while in the three-factor, narcissism and impulsivity items separated into two highly correlated dimensions (NARC and IMP, respectively). There was, however, no significant improvement in model fit with the addition of a third factor, hence supporting the use of the more parsimonious two-factor solution. In both analyses, one item (lies easily and skilfully) failed to load, and this item was thus labelled "unclassified". In light of the ambiguous nature of this item, the scale used in the present study used only the remaining 19 PSD items.

The AQ (Buss Warren, 2000) assesses an individual's aggressive responses and ability to channel these responses in a safe and constructive manner. The full-scale AQ includes 34 self-report items, organised into five subscales that measure physical aggression (e.g., use of physical force when expressing anger or aggression), verbal aggression (e.g., quarrelsome and hostile speech), indirect aggression (e.g., expressing anger in actions that avoid direct confrontation), hostility (e.g., pervasive social maladjustment, and severe psychopathology and mental illness), and anger (e.g., difficulties controlling one's temper, getting angry for no good reason). Participants respond on a five-point scale anchored with the response options "Not at all like me" to "Completely like me".

Results of the initial AQ standardization with a large sample of college students suggested the presence of five possible subscales: Physical Aggression, Verbal Aggression, Hostility, Anger, and Indirect Aggression. This factor structure was not supported, however, in a second standardization with a younger community sample. In particular, the second analysis indicated high cross-loadings for items in the scale, suggesting that the scale components were not well differentiated in this sample. Despite this, the AQ subscales have acceptable internal consistency, as indexed by Cronbach's alpha, with estimates of .88, .76, .82, .78, and .71 for the Physical, Verbal, Hostility, Anger, and Indirect subscales, respectively.

In the present study, only three of the AQ subscales were used. These components were those that focused on different manifestations of aggression (i.e., Physical, Verbal, and Indirect) rather than its antecedent psychological or affective states (i.e., Anger and Hostility). These subscales were considered the most relevant for use in the study in light of the hypotheses tested. Further, as indicated in the validation study (Buss Warren, 2000), items in both of these subscales cross-load significantly on the three manifest aggression subscales within this age group.

The scale used to confirm the presence or absence of ADHD and/or CD symptoms was based on items from the *SNAP-IV Teacher and Parent Rating Scale* (Swanson, 1995). In total, 23 items were drawn from the scale, each of which corresponded with a relevant DSM-IV diagnostic criterion. For each item, raters were asked to indicate whether the child exhibited the symptom "not at all", "just a little", "pretty much", or "very much". While previous evaluations have shown the SNAP-IV to have high levels of concurrent validity with other rating scales (see Swanson, 1995), few studies have been conducted to examine the underlying factor structure of the scale or the internal consistency of its subscales.

General Procedure

Prior to the research being conducted, permission was obtained from the Human Research and Ethics Committee of the University of Western Australia. The procedure for recruitment varied slightly for each of the diagnostic groups. For the ADHD only participants, individuals were recruited through a paediatrician. For the community group, principals of three high schools were invited to participate, one of whom subsequently agreed. The CD and the ADHD+CD groups were recruited over a period of 12 months from one Detention Centre and one Remand Centre in Perth, Western Australia. The researchers administered all of the relevant tests to the ADHD and community groups. For the CD and ADHD+CD groups, it was decided that as teachers had established rapport with these individuals, they would be better placed to complete the testing procedures. As such, two teachers were trained by the researchers to administer the study instruments.

The caregivers of children with ADHD were asked not to give their child any stimulant medication on the afternoon or evening prior to testing (a minimum of 20 hours medication free). This was done to ensure that there were no masking effects in the testing sessions (Tannock, 1998). To confirm that all parents had complied with this request, a verbal check was made immediately prior to testing.

For the ADHD and community groups, children completed the AQ independently. In the two incarcerated groups, the questions were read aloud by the tester to compensate for any reading difficulties. Teachers and/or parents completed the PSD and SNAP-IV questionnaires for all participants.

Results

The data were analysed in three major stages. In Stage I, properties of the measuring instruments were explored. In Stage II, scores for the four diagnostic groups on the PSD and the AQ were compared to test predictions implied by the "fledgling psychopath" hypothesis. The Stage III analyses were designed to provide a further test of this hypothesis by examining correlations between subscale scores on the SNAP-IV, the PSD, and the AQ across the full study sample.

Properties of the Measuring Instruments

The Stage I analyses examined properties of the SNAP-IV, PSD, and AQ instruments within the context of the study sample. The goal of these analyses was to identify any major digressions from proposed scale structures. Both confirmatory and exploratory factor analysis methods were used to address this goal. These models were tested using

LISREL 8.71 (Jöreskog Sörbom, 2004), and SPSS 12.0.1 (SSI International, 2003), respectively.

The Swanson, Nolan, and Pelham Teacher and Parent Rating Scale - IV

As indicated, the ADHD/CD screening instrument was based on a sample of items from the full SNAP-IV scale (Swanson, 1995). As no previous studies could be located which used precisely the same item combination (including the five drawn from the CD subscale), an exploratory factor analysis was used for this scale. Preliminary screening runs indicated varying levels of positive skew in the raw item distributions for all three subscales. These deviations from normality were modest for the Inattention subscale, and moderate to severe for the Hyperactivity/Impulsivity and the Conduct Disorder subscales. Transformations using PRELIS 2.72 produced some improvement in the item distributions, although some degree of positive skew remained evident for several items. Item-level descriptive statistics and bivariate correlations are presented in Tables 2 and 3, respectively. In the table, item labels indicate the original subscale from which each item was drawn (Inattention: IA; Hyperactivity/Impulsivity: H/I; and Conduct Disorder: CD).

Table 2. Descriptive statistics for items in the SNAP-IV

Item no.	Label	Abbreviated item wording	N	M	SD
SNAP1	IA1	Fails to give close attention to details	129	1.40	0.84
SNAP2	IA2	Has difficulty sustaining attention	129	1.27	1.00
SNAP3	IA3	Does not seem to listen when spoken to	129	1.19	1.08
SNAP4	IA4	Does not follow through on instructions	129	1.42	1.08
SNAP5	IA5	Has difficulty organising tasks/activities	129	1.26	1.07
SNAP6	IA6	Avoids tasks requiring sustained mental effort	129	1.40	1.09
SNAP7	IA7	Loses things necessary for activities	129	0.88	1.01
SNAP8	IA8	Is distracted by extraneous stimuli	129	1.52	1.03
SNAP9	IA9	Is forgetful in daily activities	129	1.02	1.02
SNAP10	H/I1	Fidgets/squirms in seat	129	0.96	1.09
SNAP11	H/I2	Leaves seat when remaining seated is expected	129	0.74	0.99
SNAP12	H/I3	Runs about/climbs when inappropriate	129	0.42	0.70
SNAP13	H/I4	Has difficulty engaging in activities quietly	129	0.57	0.85
SNAP14	H/I5	Is "on the go" or acts as if "driven by a motor"	129	0.71	0.99
SNAP15	H/I6	Talks excessively	129	0.88	1.08
SNAP16	H/I7	Blurts out answers	129	0.77	1.04
SNAP17	H/I8	Has difficulty awaiting turn	129	0.79	1.03
SNAP18	H/I9	Interrupts or intrudes on others	129	0.96	1.09
SNAP19	CD1	Is aggressive to other children	129	0.54	0.88
SNAP20	CD2	Is disruptive with property of others	129	0.38	0.74
SNAP21	CD3	Is deceitful	129	0.61	0.90
SNAP22	CD4	Seriously violates rules	129	0.64	1.04
SNAP23	CD5	Has a pattern of violating the rights of others	129	0.59	0.93

Table 3. Bivariate correlations for items in the SNAP-IV

	IA1	IA2	IA3	IA4	IA5	IA6	IA7	IA8	IA9	H/I1	H/I2	H/I3	H/I4	H/I5	H/I6	H/I7	H/I8	H/I9	CD1	CD2	CD3	CD4	CD5
IA1	--	.73**	.64**	.66**	.70**	.63**	.59**	.54**	.56**	.43**	.35**	.32**	.43**	.39**	.41**	.36**	.43**	.45**	.32**	.22*	.16	.17	.12
IA2		--	.68**	.77**	.74**	.78**	.68**	.71**	.66**	.56**	.40**	.32**	.45**	.42**	.48**	.39**	.41**	.47**	.35**	.27**	.26**	.25**	.19*
IA3			--	.74**	.70**	.69**	.69**	.64**	.67**	.51**	.46**	.43**	.40**	.45**	.48**	.47**	.44**	.56**	.48**	.40**	.42**	.37**	.33**
IA4				--	.80**	.80**	.67**	.69**	.65**	.57**	.46**	.41**	.46**	.42**	.50**	.40**	.43**	.51**	.41**	.36**	.39**	.33**	.24**
IA5					--	.77**	.72**	.62**	.69**	.56**	.41**	.36**	.34**	.38**	.47**	.40**	.47**	.53**	.31**	.24**	.26**	.24**	.09
IA6						--	.66**	.66**	.62**	.44**	.40**	.37**	.38**	.36**	.45**	.33**	.45**	.49**	.41**	.35**	.38**	.32**	.28**
IA7							--	.62**	.78**	.55**	.45**	.34**	.46**	.46**	.48**	.45**	.43**	.54**	.26**	.27**	.27**	.23**	.04
IA8								--	.63**	.47**	.50**	.37**	.44**	.39**	.51**	.41**	.37**	.46**	.27**	.24**	.35**	.28**	.19*
IA9									--	.55**	.34**	.38**	.40**	.40**	.46**	.41**	.34**	.46**	.22*	.26**	.22*	.20*	.07
H/I1										--	.55**	.49**	.49**	.56**	.56**	.58**	.53**	.55**	.17	.17	.11	.13	.02
H/I2											--	.70**	.56**	.56**	.53**	.53**	.60**	.55**	.44**	.40**	.39**	.43**	.39**
H/I3												--	.62**	.61**	.54**	.49**	.55**	.50**	.44**	.42**	.34**	.42**	.41**
H/I4													--	.68**	.60**	.55**	.66**	.61**	.43**	.38**	.26**	.27**	.31**
H/I5														--	.66**	.62**	.66**	.63**	.33**	.28**	.12	.14	.16
H/I6															--	.75**	.66**	.72**	.32**	.17	.18*	.15	.14
H/I7																--	.68**	.69**	.25**	.06	.09	.14	.10
H/I8																	--	.77**	.46**	.35**	.22*	.26**	.31**
H/I9																		--	.46**	.34**	.32**	.24**	.23**
CD1																			--	.62**	.59**	.48**	.59**
CD2																				--	.58**	.66**	.65**
CD3																					--	.78**	.69**
CD4																						--	.74**
CD5																							--

**Significant at $\alpha = .01$ (two-tailed); *Significant at $\alpha = .05$ (two-tailed).

Maximum Likelihood estimation was used in the initial extraction of factors from responses to the 23 SNAP-IV items. Given that the SNAP-IV subscales are assumed to represent relatively independent dimensions of ADHD and CD symptomatology, the resulting solution was then rotated to approximate simple structure using an orthogonal (Varimax) procedure. Results of this analysis are presented in Table 4. Based on Kaiser's criterion and Cattell's scree test, the items separated into three factors, which together accounted for 70.84% of the total score variance. As indicated in Table 4, these represented the IA, H/I, and CD dimensions of the scale. All items loaded strongly on anticipated dimensions, showing minimal cross-loadings on other factors. Thus, response patterns to the SNAP-IV items used in the present study were well aligned with the original scale structure.

Table 4. Communalities and rotated factor loadings for items in the SNAP-IV

Item no.	Item label	*Communalities (h^2)*		*Rotated Factor Loadings*		
		Initial	Extraction	Factor I	Factor II	Factor III
SNAP5	IA5	.80	.78	***.84***	.25	.09
SNAP4	IA4	.80	.80	***.82***	.25	.24
SNAP2	IA2	.80	.76	***.82***	.24	.14
SNAP6	IA6	.77	.76	***.81***	.19	.27
SNAP7	IA7	.76	.67	***.75***	.33	.07
SNAP9	IA9	.72	.62	***.74***	.27	.06
SNAP3	IA3	.74	.70	***.71***	.31	.31
SNAP1	IA1	.65	.58	***.71***	.26	.07
SNAP8	IA8	.67	.59	***.69***	.28	.19
SNAP16	H/I7	.73	.68	.26	***.78***	-.01
SNAP17	H/I8	.77	.71	.24	***.78***	.21
SNAP14	H/I5	.66	.66	.25	***.77***	.08
SNAP15	H/I6	.71	.69	.35	***.76***	.05
SNAP18	H/I9	.75	.70	.36	***.73***	.19
SNAP13	H/I4	.68	.60	.24	***.69***	.25
SNAP12	H/I3	.67	.56	.19	***.62***	.38
SNAP11	H/I2	.67	.57	.26	***.60***	.38
SNAP10	H/I1	.64	.56	.49	***.56***	-.02
SNAP23	CD5	.74	.77	.00	.13	***.87***
SNAP22	CD4	.76	.74	.14	.08	***.84***
SNAP21	CD3	.75	.71	.21	.04	***.82***
SNAP20	CD2	.66	.58	.17	.17	***.73***
SNAP19	CD1	.63	.52	.21	.30	***.62***

The solution in Table 4 was also used to generate uncorrelated SNAP-IV factor scores for use in subsequent analyses. This procedure was used rather than taking simple subscale means because later analyses relied on distinguishing between symptoms on the three ADHD/CD indices. The factor scores correlated very highly with the raw subscale scores (all *r*s ≥ .92), suggesting that use of the factor scores would not produce marked discrepancies in the interpretation of results. Internal consistencies were also high for the three resulting subscales, with αs = .95, .93, and .89 for the IA, H/I, and CD subscales, respectively.

To examine whether the pattern of scores on the SNAP-IV across the four study samples was consistent with diagnostic classifications, three univariate analyses of variance (ANOVAs) were performed. Preliminary screening tests for conformity to ANOVA assumptions generally produced satisfactory results. An examination of standard scores within groups indicated no univariate outliers at the $\alpha = .001$ level. Some degree of positive skew and leptokurtosis was still evident for the H/I and the CD subscales, particularly in the community comparison group. As noted by Tabachnick and Fidell (2001), F is generally robust to violations of the normality assumption given a sample size of around 20 in the smallest design cell. As this criterion was met in the present case, these violations would have minimal impact on the analysis outcomes. Levene's tests also indicated significant heterogeneity in score variances on the H/I and CD subscales, $Fs(3,125) \geq 6.47$, $ps \leq .001$. Further inspection indicated relatively modest variance discrepancies on the H/I subscale ($F_{MAX} = 3.38$), but larger discrepancies on the CD subscale ($F_{MAX} = 6.07$), with larger variances apparent for smaller-n cells. While this would generally produce liberal F ratios, previous studies (see Tabachnick Fidell, 2001) have indicated that F is generally robust to violations due to heterogeneity of up to $F_{MAX} = 10$, as long as sample sizes are within a ratio of 4:1 from largest to smallest. Again, as this criterion was met in the present study, the violation observed would have a minimal impact on the analysis outcomes. Means and standard deviations for SNAP-IV factor scores across the four diagnostic groups are shown in Table 5.

Table 5. Descriptive statistics for SNAP-IV subscales by diagnostic group

Subscale	Diagnostic group	*N*	*M*	*SD*
Inattention (IA)	ADHD	35	2.16	0.61
	Community	42	0.87	0.75
	ADHD+CD	18	1.10	0.59
	CD	34	0.91	0.68
	Total	129	1.26	0.87
Hyperactivity/Impulsivity (H/I)	ADHD	35	1.09	1.00
	Community	42	0.58	0.65
	ADHD+CD	18	0.89	0.84
	CD	34	0.55	0.54
	Total	129	0.76	0.79
Conduct Disorder (CD)	ADHD	35	0.21	0.46
	Community	42	0.17	0.34
	ADHD+CD	18	1.03	0.88
	CD	34	1.12	0.84
	Total	129	0.55	0.76

Results of the three ANOVAs performed are shown in Table 6. Based on Bonferroni-adjusted α levels of .016, these indicated highly significant differences across the groups on the IA and the CD dimensions, but surprisingly, only a marginally significant effect on H/I. This result is likely to reflect the very high levels of variability on this subscale within groups (see Table 5).

Table 6. Univariate ANOVAs on SNAP-IV subscale scores by diagnostic group

Source	Subscale	*Df*	*MS*	*F*	Partial η^2
Diagnostic group	IA	3	13.15	28.75*	.41
	H/I	3	2.34	4.01*	.09
	CD	3	8.44	21.77*	.34
Error	IA	125	0.46		
	H/I	125	0.59		
	CD	125	0.39		

* Significant at $\alpha = .016$

Tukey post-hoc tests indicated that on the IA subscale, ADHDs had significantly higher scores than the other three groups (*p*s < .016). Surprisingly, however, there were no significant differences between the community comparison, CD, and ADHD+CD groups on this subscale. On the H/I subscale, although the omnibus *F* test was significant, only two of the cell mean comparisons approached significance at the .016 level: ADHD versus community ($p = .02$) and ADHD versus CD ($p = .02$), both of which indicated somewhat higher scores for ADHDs. On the CD subscale, there were no significant differences between the ADHD+CDs and the CD group, or between ADHDs and the community group. All other differences were significant (*p*s < .016), confirming that ADHD+CD and CD only participants reported higher scores than did those in the ADHD and community groups.

These results indicate that participants' symptom ratings on the SNAP-IV were generally consistent with their diagnostic classifications, with a few minor discrepancies. For example, participants in the ADHD+CD group did not differ significantly from the CD only group on any of the three indices. There was also considerable variability within the groups, particularly on the H/I index. These results suggested the need for two kinds of analyses in examining the relationship between ADHD/CD and psychopathy/aggression levels; one based on diagnostic classifications, the other based directly on SNAP-IV symptom ratings.

The Psychopathy Screening Device

As indicated, a previous validation of the PSD (Frick et al., 2000) indicated that the scale comprised either two or three underlying factors. In the two-factor model, PSD items grouped into a callous/unemotional interpersonal style dimension (C/U) and a narcissism/impulsivity dimension (N/I), while in the three-factor, narcissism and impulsivity items split into separate, though highly correlated, factors (NARC and IMP, respectively). To determine which of these models was most suitable for use in the present study, PSD item scores were subjected to a confirmatory factor analysis using LISREL 8.72 (Jöreskog Sörbom, 2004). As in the original validation, three models were compared in this study: the two- and three-factor models outlined above, and a one-factor PSD model. Descriptive statistics and bivariate correlations for PSD items are shown in Tables 7 and 8, respectively. Again, item labels indicate the original subscales from which the items were drawn.

Table 7. Descriptive statistics for items on the PSD

Item no.	Label	Abbreviated question wording	*N*	*M*	*SD*
PSD16	NARC1	Thinks that he/she is more important	129	0.44	0.70
PSD8	NARC2	Brags excessively	129	0.51	0.74
PSD10	NARC3	Uses or "cons" others	129	0.59	0.68
PSD14	NARC4	Can be charming	129	0.57	0.69
PSD11	NARC5	Teases others	129	0.64	0.69
PSD15	NARC6	Becomes angry when corrected	129	0.88	0.75
PSD5	NARC7	Emotions seem shallow	129	0.48	0.66
PSD4	IMP1	Acts without thinking	129	1.10	0.73
PSD17	IMP2	Does not plan ahead	129	1.13	0.76
PSD13	IMP3	Engages in risky activities	129	0.89	0.80
PSD1	IMP4	Blames others for mistakes	129	0.81	0.74
PSD9	IMP5	Gets bored easily	129	1.19	0.73
PSD18r	C/U1	Concerned about feelings of others*	129	0.74	0.64
PSD12r	C/U2	Feels bad or guilty*	129	0.81	0.61
PSD3r	C/U3	Concerned about school or work*	129	0.74	0.69
PSD7r	C/U4	Good at keeping promises*	129	0.84	0.73
PSD19	C/U5	Does not show feelings	129	0.54	0.64
PSD20r	C/U6	Keeps the same friends*	129	0.61	0.69

Item reverse-scored.

The covariance matrix for PSD scores was used as input data. Fit statistics for the three initial models are summarized in Table 9. Several indices were used to assess model fit. As chi-squared (χ^2) significance levels depend heavily on sample size, the table presents χ^2/df ratios rather than probability values. In general, χ^2/df ratios ranging from two to five are considered to represent adequate model fit (Byrne, 1989). As the alternative models formulated were nested designs, the chi-squared change ($\Delta\chi^2$) statistic was used to test for differences in fit between the alternative models. Two absolute fit indices (the Standardised Root Mean Residual, SRMR, and the Goodness of Fit Index, GFI) and two incremental fit indices (the Non-Normed Fit Index, NNFI, and the Comparative Fit Index, CFI) are also presented for each model. In general, indices of around .05 for the SRMR and greater than .85-.90 for the GFI, NNFI, and CFI are deemed to indicate adequate model fit (e.g., Byrne, 1989).

As indicated in Table 9, fit indices for the one-factor model were adequate, but only on some indices (the χ^2/df, the NNFI, and the CFI). The two-factor produced a significant reduction in χ^2 over the one-factor ($\Delta\chi^2 = 63.31$, $\Delta df = 1$, $p < .001$), but the reduction in χ^2 associated with the addition of a third factor was not significant at $\alpha = .001$ ($\Delta\chi^2 = 9.97$, $\Delta df = 2$). The three-factor model also indicated a very high correlation between the NARC and IMP factors, $r(127) = .89$, $p < .001$. These results are consistent with those reported by Frick et al. (2000). In light of these outcomes, the two-factor model was considered to be more tenable for use in the present study.

Table 8. Bivariate correlations for items in the PSD

	NARC1	NARC2	NARC3	NARC4	NARC5	NARC6	NARC7	IMP1	IMP2	IMP3	IMP4	IMP5	C/U1	C/U2	C/U3	C/U4	C/U5	C/U6
NARC1	--	.62**	.50**	.47**	.49**	.41**	.42**	.26**	.15	.36**	.43**	.31**	.39**	.34**	.31**	.31**	.15	.14
NARC2		--	.49**	.47**	.46**	.41**	.49**	.31**	.18*	.38**	.45**	.40**	.31**	.22*	.28**	.35**	.02	.20*
NARC3			--	.59**	.56**	.55**	.50**	.36**	.30**	.44**	.59**	.42**	.38**	.33**	.42**	.42**	.18*	.17
NARC4				--	.35**	.46**	.58**	.35**	.32**	.37**	.42**	.40**	.39**	.31**	.37**	.37**	.20*	.19*
NARC5					--	.44**	.34**	.37**	.25**	.30**	.52**	.43**	.36**	.24**	.31**	.35**	.02	.14
NARC6						--	.43**	.42**	.47**	.33**	.59**	.50**	.21*	.14	.25	.37	.13	.13
NARC7							--	.54**	.25**	.40**	.48**	.41**	.38**	.29	.44	.40	.30	.21
IMP1								--	.45**	.34**	.53**	.50**	.29**	.22*	.33**	.39**	.21*	.24**
IMP2									--	.05	.44**	.46**	.00	.05	.31**	.34**	.17	.09
IMP3										--	.28**	.33**	.31*	.19*	.22*	.18*	.19*	.09
IMP4											--	.45**	.27**	.21*	.33**	.52**	.07	.18*
IMP5												--	.19*	.10	.24**	.40**	.17	.10
C/U1													--	.55**	.49**	.47**	.25**	.35**
C/U2														--	.40**	.44**	.33**	.20*
C/U3															--	.47**	.24**	.25**
C/U4																--	.13	.31**
C/U5																	--	.13
C/U6																		--

**Significant at $\alpha = .01$ (two-tailed); *Significant at $\alpha = .05$ (two-tailed).

Table 9. Fit statistics and indices for four CFA models on the PSD

Model	χ^2	*df*	χ^2/df	SRMR	GFI	NNFI	CFI
One-factor (PSD)	302.69	135	2.24	.08	.77	.92	9 3
Two-factor (N/I, C/U)	239.38	134	1.79	.07	.82	.95	.96
Three-factor (NARC, IMP, C/U)	229.41	132	1.74	.07	.83	.95	.96
Modified two-factor (see Figure 1)	201.95	132	1.53	.07	.85	.97	.97

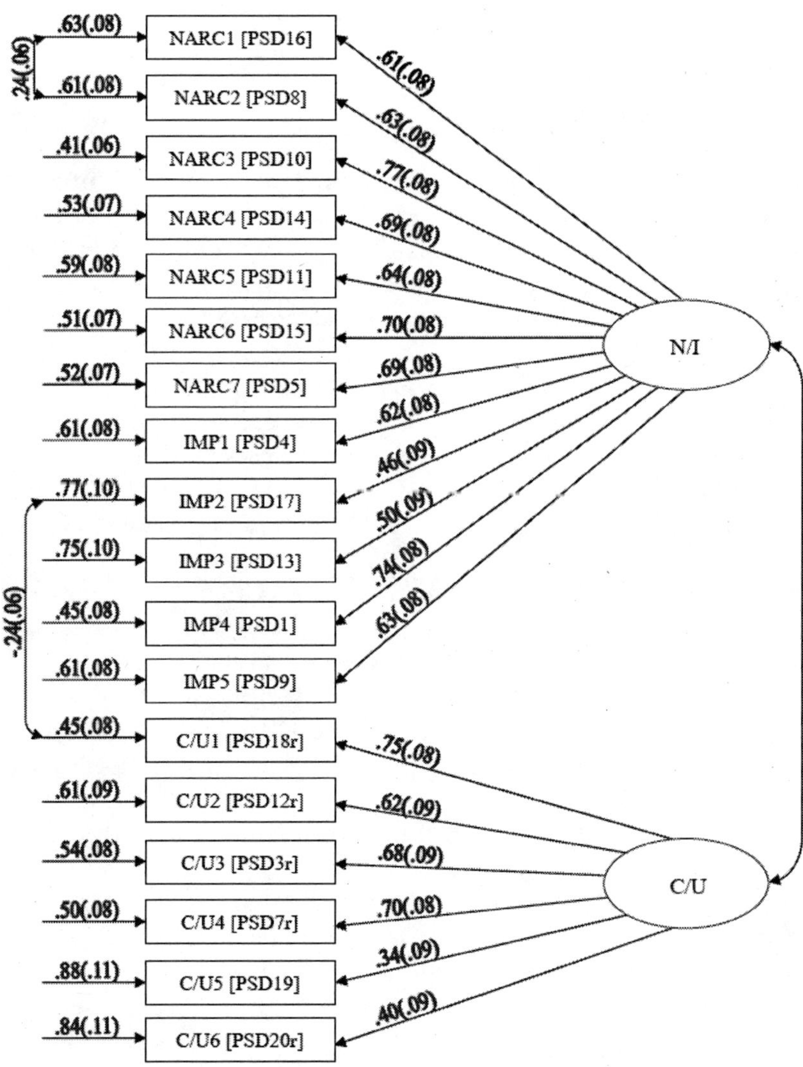

Figure 1. Standardized path coefficients for two-factor model of the PSD

As indicated in Table 9, the fit of the initial two-factor was moderately good, but fell just short of accepted cut-offs. Modification indices indicated no cross-loadings that would produce a significant reduction in χ^2. There were, however, large error covariances between two pairs of items (PSD17 and PSD18r; PSD16 and PSD8). As the purpose of this exercise was to assess broad conformity to the specified scale structure, these post-hoc modifications were then incorporated (Modified Two-Factor). Based on the outcomes shown in Table 9, this modified model approximated accepted fit criteria. It should be highlighted here, however, that the addition of the two error covariances was done on an entirely post-hoc basis. As a result, the modified model is unlikely to replicate precisely in subsequent studies. Standardized path coefficients for the final model are shown in Figure 1. All paths in the model were positive and significant, although a small number (e.g., the path between PSD19 and C/U) were somewhat low (.34). In broad terms, however, the results of these analyses did indicate good correspondence between response patterns within the current study sample and the specified PSD scale structure. This was further confirmed by the acceptable internal consistencies obtained for the combined Narcissism/Impulsivity and the C/U subscales (.89 and .75, respectively).

The Aggression Questionnaire

As indicated, only the three AQ subscales which focused on manifestations of aggression (PHY, VER, and IND) were included in the analyses. Given this, an exploratory approach was taken in examining the structure of the remaining items. In the original validation of the instrument, a principal components analysis (PCA) was used rather than common factor analysis. To facilitate comparisons between the two sets of results, a PCA was also used in this case. Again, as the three forms of aggression assessed by the AQ are presumed to be relatively independent, a Varimax rotation was then used to aid interpretation. Initial results indicated the presence of three components that were generally consistent with the original subscale compositions (Buss Warren, 2000), accounting for 53.73% of the total item variance. Descriptive statistics and bivariate correlations for items in the AQ PHY, VER, and IND subscales are shown in Tables 10 and 11, respectively.

Outcomes of the PCA on AQ scores are shown in Table 12. As indicated, loading patterns were consistent with the original subscale designations, although as found by Buss and Warren (2000), several items showed significant cross-loadings. Two items (AQ13 and AQ14) originally listed as part of the IND subscale also had somewhat higher loadings on PHY than on IND. As both items could be interpreted as acts of physical aggression, however (messing up another's work, slamming a door), both were retained in the scale as part of the PHY component. One of the IND subscale items ("I like to play practical jokes") also loaded on the VER subscale rather than on IND. It is possible that this occurred because "practical jokes" were interpreted by respondents more as verbal jokes than other kinds. This item was also retained, but as part of the VER subscale. One further item (AQ18) also had only a marginal loading on its reference factor. Again, however, this result is not surprising, because the content of the item (spreading gossip about others) differs somewhat from that of others in the subscale (e.g., giving others the 'silent treatment'). As this loading pattern was conceptually reasonable, however, AQ18 was retained as part of the IND component. Alpha coefficients were also acceptable for the final PHY and VER subscales (αs = .91 and .76, respectively), but low for the IND subscale (α = .48). This result may reflect the relatively low number of items in the latter scale. Thus, the outcomes of further analyses on this subscale may reflect some degree of power attenuation due to low internal consistency.

Table 10. Descriptive statistics for final items in the AQ

Item no.	Item Label	Abbreviated Item wording	*N*	*M*	*SD*
AQ8	PHY1	May hit someone if provoked	129	2.51	1.41
AQ10	PHY2	Have threatened people I know	129	2.22	1.27
AQ11	PHY3	Have hit someone when pushed	129	2.91	1.46
AQ17	PHY4	Have broken things when mad	129	2.57	1.46
AQ23	PHY5	Can't control the urge to hit someone	129	2.14	1.34
AQ24	PHY6	Get into fights more than most	129	1.88	1.27
AQ25	PHY7	Will hit back if someone hits me	129	3.35	1.44
AQ27	PHY8	Will resort to violence to protect rights	129	3.01	1.46
AQ1	VER1	Friends say I argue a lot	129	1.98	1.06
AQ4	VER2	Often disagree with people	129	2.64	1.15
AQ6	VER3	Can't help getting into arguments	129	2.71	1.26
AQ20	VER4	Tell people what I think when annoyed	129	3.15	1.43
AQ26	VER5	Tell friends openly when I disagree	129	3.24	1.31
AQ13	IND1	May mess up someone's work if angry	129	1.98	1.22
AQ14	IND2	Have been mad enough to slam a door	129	2.78	1.45
AQ15	IND3	Take my time when people are bossy	129	2.60	1.35
AQ18	IND4	Sometimes spread gossip about people	129	1.84	1.16
AQ30	IND5	Might give the silent treatment	129	2.38	1.26
AQ34	IND6	Like to play practical jokes	129	3.30	1.37

Table 11. Bivariate correlations for final items in the AQ

	PHY1	PHY2	PHY3	PHY4	PHY5	PHY6	PHY7	PHY8	VER1	VER2	VER3	VER4	VER5	IND1	IND2	IND3	IND4	IND5	IND6
PHY1	--	.54**	.73**	.52**	.59**	.51**	.52**	.39**	.16	.29**	.31**	.38**	.15	.43**	.47**	.25**	.21*	.02	.24**
PHY2		--	.55**	.63**	.57**	.48**	.36**	.48**	.27**	.34**	.42**	.36**	.18*	.49**	.52**	.44**	.17	.21*	.40**
PHY3			--	.60**	.63**	.50**	.52**	.60**	.19*	.28**	.36**	.36**	.25**	.38**	.48**	.34**	.19*	-.01	.29**
PHY4				--	.65**	.47**	.36**	.49**	.27**	.34**	.38**	.36**	.17	.54**	.56**	.53**	.32**	.22*	.25**
PHY5					--	.56**	.50**	.49**	.23**	.31**	.37**	.35**	.20*	.52**	.52**	.25**	.32**	.21*	.20*
PHY6						--	.42**	.32**	.24**	.28**	.26**	.24**	.07	.49**	.40**	.23**	.21*	-.02	.13
PHY7							--	.53**	.22*	.19*	.37**	.31**	.27**	.33**	.29**	.11	.23*	.13	.26**
PHY8								--	.14	.26**	.34**	.39**	.39**	.38**	.46**	.42**	.28**	.22*	.27**
VER1									--	.44**	.51**	.30**	.10	.20*	.30**	.16	.16	-.02	.25**
VER2										--	.46**	.48**	.21*	.28**	.30**	.21*	.26**	.07	.31**
VER3											--	.40**	.37**	.36**	.40**	.26**	.23**	.16	.37**
VER4												--	.57**	.25**	.45**	.31**	.27**	.16	.27**
VER5													--	.12	.27**	.20*	.14	.15	.24**
IND1														--	.44**	.33**	.48**	.17	.12
IND2															--	.42**	.29**	.20*	.28**
IND3																--	.17	.33**	.21*
IND4																	--	.20*	.17
IND5																		--	.10
IND6																			--

**Significant at α = .01 (two-tailed); *Significant at α = .05 (two-tailed).

Table 12. Communalities and rotated factor loadings for items in the AQ

Item No.	Subscale	*Communalities (h^2)*	*Rotated Component Loadings*		
		Extraction	I	II	III
AQ8	PHY1	.67	***.80***	.17	.00
AQ11	PHY3	.69	***.80***	.21	.08
AQ23	PHY5	.68	***.78***	.17	.21
AQ24	PHY6	.59	***.76***	.11	-.07
AQ17	PHY4	.67	***.70***	.18	.38
AQ10	PHY2	.59	***.65***	.27	.29
AQ13	IND1	.49	***.62***	.11	.30
AQ25	PHY7	.42	***.59***	.27	.04
AQ14	IND2	.52	***.53***	.33	.37
AQ27	PHY8	.53	***.52***	.24	.45
AQ6	VER3	.60	.27	***.71***	.14
AQ4	VER2	.53	.23	***.69***	.03
AQ1	VER1	.53	.17	***.69***	-.15
AQ20	VER4	.57	.22	***.65***	.32
AQ34	IND6	.34	.15	***.54***	.13
AQ26	VER5	.44	-.01	***.54***	.38
AQ30	IND5	.61	-.03	-.01	***.78***
AQ15	IND3	.53	.28	.14	***.66***
AQ18	IND4	.23	.27	.19	***.35***

Diagnostic Group Differences in Levels of Psychopathy and Aggression

The goal of the second analysis stage was to compare the scores of the four diagnostic groups (ADHD, CD, ADHD+CD, and community) on the psychopathy (PSD) and aggression (AQ) measures. Based on the "fledgling psychopath" hypothesis, adolescents in the ADHD+CD group (i.e., those with a comorbid diagnosis of ADHD and CD) were expected to have higher scores on both the PSD and the AQ than any of the other groups. The diagnostic group comparisons relied on a combination of multivariate and univariate analysis of variance (MANOVA and ANOVA) methods. Although each analysis initially incorporated age as a covariate, preliminary tests indicated that this did not produce a significant reduction in error variance on any of the dependent measures (all *ps* > .10). As a result, age was excluded from all of the final models.

Given the large age differences across groups, however, each full sample analysis was replicated on a subsample of age-matched participants from each diagnostic group. To create these subsamples, ADHD+CD participants (who represented the smallest *n* cell) were selected as the reference group. For each member of this group, one member of the same (or the closest available) age level was selected at random from each of the other three groups.

As no matches were available for the five 19 year-olds in the ADHD+CD group, these participants were excluded from the matched sample analysis, leaving $n = 13$ per group (total $n = 52$). A univariate ANOVA confirmed that there were no significant age differences across groups in the matched age sample ($F(3,48) < 1$). Given the reduced power levels that resulted from this process, the age-matched sample analyses provided stringent confirmatory tests of any group differences identified in the full sample analyses.

Psychopathy

As the two PSD subscales (N/I and C/U) were highly correlated, a MANOVA followed by univariate and stepdown analyses was used to compare the four groups on this measure. Preliminary screening tests generally indicated adequate conformity to all relevant underlying test assumptions. Mahalanobis distances, calculated separately for each of the four groups, indicated no multivariate or univariate outliers at $\alpha = .001$. Visual examinations of within-cell distributions and scatterplots of N/I and C/U scores suggested no notable deviations from normality or linearity, and determinants for within-cell correlation matrices suggested no threat of multicollinearity between the two subscales (all Λs > .606). While the Levene's test did indicate a significant level of heterogeneity in score variances on the N/I subscale ($F(3,125) = 6.11, p = .001$), a further inspection indicated a ratio of 2.47 for the largest to the smallest group variance on this measure. With a ratio of less than 4:1 from the largest to the smallest cell *n*, it can be assumed that *F* would be robust to this minor violation (see Tabachnick Fidell, 2001).

Descriptive statistics for PSD scores by diagnostic group are shown in Table 13. As expected, the MANOVA on these scores indicated a significant multivariate effect for diagnostic group, $V = .38$, $F(6,250) = 9.65, p < .05$.

Table 13. Descriptive statistics for PSD subscales by diagnostic group

Subscale	Diagnostic group	*N*	*M*	*SD*
Narcissism/Impulsivity (N/I)	ADHD	35	0.97	0.33
	Community	42	0.42	0.36
	ADHD+CD	18	1.04	0.50
	CD	34	0.85	0.52
	Total	129	0.77	0.49
Callous/Unemotional (C/U)	ADHD	35	0.62	0.38
	Community	42	0.58	0.48
	ADHD+CD	18	0.96	0.33
	CD	34	0.84	0.44
	Total	129	0.71	0.44

Results of the univariate ANOVAs performed on scores for each of the PSD subscales are shown in Table 14. Using a Bonferroni-adjusted α level of .025, significant univariate effects for diagnostic group were found on both subscales. Furthermore, these effects remained significant at stepdown, regardless of the order in which the variables were entered, $Fs(3,124) \geq 5.17$, $ps \leq .002$. The magnitude of the effect on the N/I subscale was particularly substantial, with diagnostic group accounting for 26.90% of the score variance on this measure.

Table 14. Univariate ANOVAs on PSD subscales by diagnostic group

Source	Subscale	*df*	*MS*	*F*	Partial η^2
Diagnostic group	N/I	3	2.76	15.34*	.27
	C/U	3	0.88	4.86*	.10
Error	N/I	125	0.18		
	C/U	125	0.18		

* Significant at $\alpha = .025$

Tukey post-hoc tests indicated that on the N/I subscale, all three of the clinical groups had significantly higher scores than the community sample ($ps < .025$), but did not differ significantly from one another ($ps \geq .39$). On the C/U subscale, participants in the ADHD+CD group scored significantly higher than those in the community sample ($p = .01$) and marginally higher than those in the ADHD only sample ($p = .03$). Scores for the CD group were also marginally higher than those for the community sample on this measure, although this difference again only approached significance at the .025 level ($p = .05$). All other differences on this measure were not significant ($ps \geq .17$).

A very similar pattern of differences emerged in the matched samples analyses for the PSD. Again, there was a significant multivariate effect for diagnostic group, $V = .59$, $F(6,96) = 6.71$, $p < .05$, with univariate ANOVAs indicating significant group differences on both the N/I and the C/U subscales, $F(3,48) = 9.19$, $p < .025$, partial $\eta^2 = .37$, and $F(3,48) = 5.81$, $p < .025$, partial $\eta^2 = .27$, respectively. Again, both of these effects were significant at stepdown, with $Fs(4,47) \geq 4.58$, $ps < .025$. As in the full sample analysis, all clinical groups scored significantly higher than the community sample on the N/I subscale ($ps \leq .009$), but did not differ significantly from one another ($ps \geq .37$). On the C/U measure, there were again marginal differences between the CD group and the community group ($p = .04$), but in this analysis, ADHD+CDs scored significantly higher than *both* the community *and* the ADHD groups ($ps \leq .02$).

AGGRESSION

Preliminary tests indicated that AQ PHY, VER, and IND scores demonstrated adequate conformity to all assumptions for normality, linearity, and variance homogeneity. Mahalanobis distances and *z*-scores also confirmed the absence of significant outliers on all subscales. Group means and standard deviations for scores on this measure are shown in Table 15. The MANOVA on these scores indicated a significant multivariate effect for diagnostic group, $V = .17$, $F(9,375) = 2.55$, $p < .05$.

Table 15. Descriptive statistics for AQ subscales by diagnostic group

Subscale	Diagnostic group	*N*	*M*	*SD*
Physical Aggression (PHY)	ADHD	35	2.35	1.08
	Community	42	2.19	0.87
	ADHD+CD	18	2.85	0.97
	CD	34	2.99	0.96
	Total	129	2.53	1.02
Verbal Aggression (VER)	ADHD	35	2.67	0.93
	Community	42	2.75	0.76
	ADHD+CD	18	2.87	1.19
	CD	34	2.79	0.84
	Total	129	2.76	0.89
Indirect Aggression (IND)	ADHD	35	2.05	0.68
	Community	42	2.22	0.79
	ADHD+CD	18	2.61	1.15
	CD	34	2.38	0.98
	Total	129	2.27	0.88

Based on a Bonferroni-adjusted α level of .016, univariate ANOVAs (Table 16) indicated a significant difference between the diagnostic groups on the PHY subscale. Post-hoc tests indicated that CD only participants had significantly (p = .003) higher scores than those in the community sample, and marginally higher scores (p = .03) than ADHDs, on this subscale. No other differences approached significance at the .016 level on this scale (all *ps* ≥ .08). Thus, the only clear difference to emerge between groups in terms of aggression was a higher mean score for the CD group over the community group on the PHY subscale.

Table 16. Univariate ANOVAs on the AQ subscales

Source	Subscale	*df*	*MS*	*F*	Partial η^2
Diagnostic group	PHY	3	5.05	5.38*	.11
	VER	3	0.17	0.21	.01
	IND	3	1.44	1.89	.04
Error	PHY	125	0.94		
	VER	125	0.80		
	IND	125	0.76		

*Significant at α = .016

The matched-samples analysis also indicated a significant multivariate effect for diagnostic group, V = .39, F(9,144) = 2.42, p < .05 ANOVAs indicated significant differences between the diagnostic groups only on the PHY subscale, F(3,48) = 8.15, p < .016, partial η^2 = .34. In this case, post-hoc tests indicated significantly higher scores in the

CD group than in *either* the community *or* the ADHD groups (*ps* ≤ .001). Overall, however, the results of the matched-samples analyses were again very similar to those obtained in the full sample analyses.

RELATIONSHIPS BETWEEN LEVELS OF ADHD/CD SYMPTOMATOLOGY, PSYCHOPATHY AND AGGRESSION

The group comparisons on the PSD and the AQ did not offer support for the predictions implied by the fledgling psychopath hypothesis. Confirming this hypothesis relied on demonstrating that ADHD+CD participants outscored those in *both* the ADHD *and* CD only groups on the PSD (and, to a lesser extent, the AQ). Results indicated no significant differences between the ADHD+CD, ADHD, and CD groups on the N/I subscale of the PSD. Further, although ADHD+CDs reported higher scores than ADHDs on the C/U subscale, there was again no significant difference between the ADHD+CD and CD groups on this measure.

As noted previously, however, the variability that exists naturally within the ADHD population can hamper definitive interpretations of diagnostic group comparisons. In this case, data on subtypes were not consistently reported in the background information available for ADHD participants. Further, as indicated, the group comparison tests performed on the SNAP-IV were not entirely consistent with diagnostic classifications. Specifically, the ADHD+CD group did not differ significantly from the CD only group on either of the ADHD indices (IA and H/I). There was also considerable evidence of variability in the severity of symptoms reported *within* these groups, particularly on the H/I subscale. This would have the effect of further reducing the power of the group comparison tests.

For these reasons, a series of multiple regression analyses (MRAs) was conducted to further test the predictions of the fledgling psychopath hypothesis. This analysis also examined relationships between psychopathy and aggression and levels of ADHD/CD symptomatology, but in this case, participants were not divided into diagnostic groups. Instead, scores on the two ADHD subscales of the SNAP-IV (IA and H/I), along with the SNAP-IV CD subscale, were used to provide a direct index of symptom severity in each of these three areas. Thus, ADHD and CD were not operationalized as disorders that were either present or absent within certain groups, but rather as characteristics that were present to a certain level in all study participants.

To determine whether the combination of IA, HI, and CD symptom levels accounted for a significant unique proportion of variance in PSD and AQ scores (i.e., over and above the variance associated with base levels of ADHD/CD symptoms), a new score was created for each participant to represent the three-way IA*H/I*CD interaction. This variable was then orthogonalized against scores for the base IA, H/I, and CD subscales. All four SNAP-IV variables were then entered as predictors in each MRA, with the three individual SNAP-IV indices entered first as a set, followed by the IA*H/I*CD interaction term. Each model, therefore, tested (i) whether scores on the base SNAP-IV indices significantly predicted scores on the PSD and the AQ, and (ii) whether the three-way IA*H/I*CD interaction accounted for a significant proportion of variance in PSD/AQ scores independently of the variance accounted for by base IA, H/I, and CD scores (as predicted by the fledgling psychopath hypothesis). Correlations for all variables in the MRAs are shown in Table 17.

Table 17. Bivariate correlations for measures in the MRA

	IA	H/I	CD	N/I	CU	PHY	VER	IND
IA	--	.05	.02	.46**	.25**	.01	-.07	-.04
H/I		--	.02	.36**	.13	.09	.16	.10
CD			--	.65**	.47**	.20*	.12	.13
N/I				--	.55**	.16	.06	-.01
CU					--	.16	.06	.00
PHY						--	.56**	.48**
VER							--	.37**
IND								--

**Significant at α = .01 (two-tailed); *Significant at α = .05 (two-tailed).

Table 18 presents the outcomes of all five MRAs performed. As indicated, the IA*H/I*CD interaction term made a marginally significant contribution to prediction on the PSD, but only on the N/I subscale. On the AQ, IA*H/I*CD made a significant contribution to prediction only on the VER subscale. All other contributions from this predictor were non-significant.

Table 18. MRA Outcomes

Subscale	Model Statistics						Change Statistics			
	Predictors	βs	R	R^2	R^2_{ADJ}	SE	R^2_{Change}	F_{Change}	df_1	df_2
N/I	IA,H/I,CD	.43,.33,.64	.86	.73	.73	.26	.73	114.84*	3	125
	IA*H/I*CD	.02	.86	.74	.74	.25	.01	5.02$^+$	1	124
CU	IA,H/I,CD	.24,.10,.46	.54	.29	.27	.38	.29	16.83*	3	125
	IA*H/I*CD	-0.02	.54	.29	.27	.38	.00	0.09	1	124
PHY	IA,H/I,CD	.00,.09,.20	.22	.05	.03	1.00	.05	2.11	3	125
	IA*H/I*CD	0.05	.23	.05	.02	1.01	.00	0.32	1	124
VER	IA,H/I,CD	-.08,.16,.12	.21	.04	.02	.88	.04	1.96	3	125
	IA*H/I*CD	0.22	.30	.09	.06	.86	.05	6.51*	1	124
IND	IA,H/I,CD	-.043,.10,.13	.17	.03	.00	.88	.03	1.21	3	125
	IA*H/I*CD	0.12	.20	.04	.01	.88	.01	1.78	1	124

*Significant at α = .025 for N/I and CU; *Significant at α = .016 for PHY, VER, and IND
$^+$Approached significance at α = .025

DISCUSSION

Results of this study indicated that the instruments used generally exhibited sound psychometric properties. Results obtained for the PSD and the AQ were well aligned with those from previous evaluations. Despite this, for both measures, results suggested that in adolescent populations, the proposed subscales may be less distinct than in adult populations. Results obtained for the SNAP-IV were also consistent with the proposed scale structure. In this case, however, the obtained solution indicated a clear separation between the scale components. This result also provides further evidence in support of the view that CD and ADHD should be viewed as separate, though related, disorders (see Gresham et al., 2000).

In general, however, the predictions of the fledgling psychopath hypothesis were not supported. As noted previously, based on this hypothesis, participants in the comorbid ADHD+CD group were expected to exhibit higher levels of psychopathy than *either* the ADHD *or* the CD only group. The group comparisons did indicate higher scores for all three clinical groups than for the community sample on the N/I subscale of the PSD, but there were no significant differences between the three clinical groups on this measure. Thus, there were no significant differences between the ADHD+CD and ADHD/CD only groups on this measure, and, perhaps more surprisingly, no significant differences between the ADHD and CD only groups. This result may reflect the fact that the N/I subscale includes items that relate both to narcissism and to impulsivity. Given the behavioural characteristics which typify adolescents with ADHD and/or CD, it is possible that ADHD adolescents would score higher on impulsivity items (e.g., acts without thinking, does not plan ahead), while adolescents with CD would score higher on those measuring narcissism (e.g., becomes angry when corrected, teases others). Future work on extending the construct of psychopathy to children and adolescents could focus on further differentiating between these two components of the N/I psychopathy dimension.

As noted previously, the presence or absence of C/U traits is generally considered to be the key marker for psychopathy in children and adolescents (e.g., Barry et al., 2000; Frick et al., 2003; Loney et al., 2003; Silverthorn Frick, 1999). In this study, ADHD+CD participants did report higher scores on the C/U subscale than participants in the community sample, and marginally higher scores than ADHDs. However, ADHD+CD participants again did not differ significantly from participants in the CD only group in terms of C/U scores. Thus, results for the C/U subscale indicated only one of the differences that would be required for confirmation of the fledgling psychopath hypothesis.

In terms of aggression, significant differences between groups were apparent only on the physical aggression (PHY) subscale of the AQ. In the full sample analysis, this indicated higher scores for the CD than for the community sample. In the matched samples analysis, there was also a significant difference between the CD and ADHD only groups on this measure. The latter result was not surprising, given that physical aggression is a hallmark of CD (e.g., uses a weapon in fights). More surprising, however, was the failure to find a significant difference between the ADHD+CD group and the non-CD samples. Although the mean score in the former group was similar to that of the CD only group, the statistical power of the comparisons for the ADHD+CD group was lower because of its relatively small sample size. Thus, some degree of caution is warranted in the interpretation of the latter result.

On face value, the absence of any significant differences between the groups on the verbal aggression (VER) subscale of the AQ was also surprising. This is particularly so in light of the diagnostic criteria used in assessing both CD and ADHD. A close examination of the items within the VER subscale, however, suggests that the scale focuses more on what might be considered verbal *assertion* (e.g., telling people who annoy you what you think of them) rather than *aggression*. The construct of verbal aggression would more typically be associated with overtly offensive behaviours such as making threats, swearing, and shouting abuse (DSM-IV, 1994). Thus, it is possible that a clearer pattern of results would be obtained on an instrument that measured more typical or severe forms of verbal aggression.

Overall, therefore, results of the group comparisons did not offer support for the predictions of the fledgling psychopath hypothesis. In general, adolescents with a comorbid ADHD+CD classification did not exhibit higher levels of psychopathy or aggression than those diagnosed with *either* disorder alone. The one exception to this was that ADHD+CDs reported marginally higher scores on the C/U subscale of the PSD than participants with ADHD only. As noted above, however, this difference only approached significance at the Bonferroni-adjusted α level set in the full sample analyses. In the matched-samples analysis, the difference did reach significance, suggesting the possibility of some attenuation due to age variability in the full sample results. The differences between the ADHD+CDs and the CD group did not, however, approach significance in either analysis.

The multiple regression outcomes were, in general, also not consistent with the predictions made. The interaction between inattention, hyperactivity, and conduct disorder symptoms made no unique contribution to predicting CU, PHY, and IND scores. The interaction did contribute uniquely to predicting N/I and VER scores, but as indicated above, these subscales are not considered key markers of psychopathy relative to the characteristics assessed by the C/U and PHY subscales. Overall, therefore, the MRAs also did not support the predictions made on the basis of the fledgling psychopath hypothesis.

It should also be noted here that the results of the group comparisons on the C/U subscale reflect differences between groups *as these are measured by the PSD*. Items in the PSD correspond well with the construct of psychopathy as it is currently defined in children and adolescents. At present, however, accepted definitions of psychopathy in these populations do not require the demonstration of more severe forms of antisocial behaviour. Thus, many children could exhibit the marker symptoms of having a callous/unemotional style (e.g., being unconcerned about schoolwork, failing to keep promises) at one time or another. There is also considerable overlap in the characteristics associated with one of the psychopathy dimensions (narcissism/impulsivity) and the diagnostic criteria for ADHD. For example, items on the N/I subscale of the PSD include characteristics such as, “does not plan ahead”, “acts without thinking”, and “gets bored easily”. These characteristics are also used in the assessment of children and adolescents with ADHD. In light of this, it is not surprising that groups differed significantly on this variable, and that there were strong relationships between ADHD symptoms and scores on the N/I subscale.

Future work is therefore needed to develop a clear picture of the relationship between ADHD, CD, and psychopathy. This work should focus specifically on extending the present findings through the development of instruments that assess alternative dimensions, and perhaps more severe forms, of antisociality in children and adolescents. Longitudinal designs should also be used to examine the developmental trajectories of psychopathy through the lifespan, as well as its most salient precursors.

REFERENCES

Abramowitz, C. S., Kosson, D. S., Seidenberg, M. (2003). The relationship between childhood attention deficit hyperactivity disorder, conduct problems and adult psychopathy. *Personality and Individual Differences, 36,* 1031-1047.

Aiken, L.S., West, S.G. (1991). *Multiple regression: testing and interpreting interactions.* Newbury Park, CA: Sage Publications.

American Psychiatric Association. (1994). *Diagnostic and statistical manual of mental disorders* (4th ed.). Washington, DC: Author.

Barry, C.T., Frick, P.J., DeShazo, T.M., McCoy, M.G., Ellis, M., Loney, B.R. (2000). The importance of callous-unemotional traits for extending the concept of psychopathy in children. *Journal of Abnormal Psychology, 29, 291-498.*

Blair, R.J.R., Colledge, E., Mitchell, D.G.V. (2001). Somatic markers and response reversal: Is there orbitofrontal cortex dysfunction in boys with psychopathic tendencies? *Journal of Abnormal Child Psychology, 29,* 499-511.

Buss, A.H., Warren, W.L. (2000). *The aggression questionnaire.* Los Angeles, CA: Western Psychological Services.

Byrne, B. M. (1989). *A primer of LISREL: Basic applications and programming for confirmatory factor analytic models.* New York: Springer-Verlag.

Caputo, A.A., Frick, P.J., Brodsky, S.L. (1999). Family violence and juvenile sex offending: The potential mediating role of psychopathic traits and negative attitudes towards women. *Criminal Justice and Behaviour, 26,* 338-356.

Cleckley, H. (1976). *The mask of sanity.* St Louis, MO: Mosby.

Forth, A.E., Burke, H.C. (1998). Psychopathy in adolescence: Assessment, violence, and developmental precursors. In D.J. Cooke, A.E. Forth, R.D. Hare (Eds.), *Psychopathy: Theory, research, and implications for society* (pp. 205-229). Netherlands: Kluwer Academic Publishing.

Frick, P., Cornell, A.H., Loney, B., Bodin, S., Dane, H.E., Barry, C. (2003). Callous-unemotional traits and developmental pathways to severe conduct problems. *Developmental Psychology, 39(*2), 246-26.

Frick, P.J. (1998). Callous-unemotional traits and conduct problems: Applying the two-factor model of psychopathy to children. In D.J. Cooke, A.E. Forth, R.D. Hare (eds.), *Psychopathy: Theory, research, and implications for society* (pp. 161-187). Dordrecht, Netherlands: Kluwer Academic Publishing.

Frick, P.J., Hare, R.D. (1996). *The psychopathy screening device.* Toronto: Multi-Health Systems.

Frick, P.J., Bodin, S.D., Barry, C.T. (2000). Psychopathic traits and conduct problems in community and clinic-referred samples of children: Further development of the Psychopathy Screening Device. *Psychological Assessment*, 12, 382-393.

Frick, P.J., O'Brien, B.S., Wootton, J.M., McBurnett, K. (1994). Psychopathy and conduct problems in children. *Journal of Abnormal Psychology*, *103*, 700-707.

Gresham, F. M., Lane, K. L., Lambros, K. (2000). Comorbidity of conduct problems and ADHD: Identification of "Fledgling Psychopaths." *Journal of Emotional and Behavioral Disorders, 8*(2), 83-93.

Hare, R.D. (1991). *The Hare psychopathy checklist-revised.* Toronto, Ontario: Multi-Health Systems.

Hinshaw, S. (1987). Externalising behavior problems and academic underachievement in childhood and adolescence: causal relationships and underlying mechanisms. *Psychological Bulletin, 111*, 127-155.

Jöreskog, K. G., Sörbom, D. (2004). *LISREL 8.72 and PRELIS 2.72.* Chicago: Scientific Software International.

Lahey, B.B., Loeber, R., Quay, H.C., Frick, P.L., Grimm, J. (1992). Oppositional defiant and conduct disorder: Issues to be resolved for DSM-IV. *Journal of the American Academy of Child and Adolescent Psychiatry, 31,* 539-546.

Loney, B.R., Frick, P., Clements, C.B., Ellis, M., Kerlin, K. (2003). Callous-unemotional traits, impulsivity, and emotional processing in adolescents with antisocial behaviour problems. *Journal of Clinical child and Adolescent Psychology, 32*, 66-8.

Lynam, D.R. (1996). Early identification of chronic offenders: Who is the fledgling psychopath? *Psychological Bulletin*, 120, 209-234.

Salekin, R.T., Rogers, R., Ustad, K.L., Sewell, K.W. (1998). Psychopathy and recidivism among female inmates. *Law and Human Behavior, 22,* 109-128.

Saltaris, C. (2002). Psychopathy in juvenile offenders: Can temperament and attachment be considered as robust developmental precursors? *Clinical Psychology Review, 22,* 729-752.

Silverthorn, P., Frick, P.J. (1999). Developmental pathways to antisocial behaviour: The delayed-onset pathway in girls. *Development and Psychopathology*, 11, 101-126.

SPSS International. (2003). *Statistical package for the social sciences version 12.0.1.* Chicago, Illinois: SPSS Inc.

Swanson, J. (1995). *SNAP-IV scale.* Irvine,CA: Child Development Centre University of California.

Tabachnick, B.G., Fidell, L.S. (2001). *Using multivariate statistics (4th ed.).* Boston: Allyn and Bacon.

Tannock, R. (1998). Attention deficit hyperactivity disorder: advances in cognitive, neurobiological, and genetic research. *Journal of Child Psychology and Psychiatry,* 39(1), 65-99.

NOTES ON AUTHORS

Ms Waisam Hoong received a First Class Honours degree from the University of Western Australia for her research into levels of objectivity in children with ADHD. She is currently completing a PhD degree under the supervision of the two other authors.

Professor Stephen Houghton is Professor of Educational Psychology and Special Education at The University of Western Australia and Director of the Centre for Attention Related Disorders. His primary research interests are in the field of childhood developmental disorders. Professor Houghton has published articles in leading international journals such as *The Journal of Abnormal Child Psychology*, the *Journal of Child Neurology*, *Educational Psychology* (USA), and the *Journal of Child Psychology and Psychiatry.*

Dr Elaine Chapman is a lecturer at the Graduate School of Education, The University of Western Australia. Her primary teaching and research interests lie in the areas of educational psychology and quantitative research methods.

In: Attention Deficit Hyperactivity Disorder
Editor: Marvin C. Shriner, pp. 129-143

ISBN: 1-60021 321-9

Chapter V

Behavioural Complications of Attention Deficit Hyperactivity Disorder (ADHD). Justification for Early Intervention

Gerard Hutchinson and Eric Williams
Head, Psychiatry Unit, Faculty of Medical Sciences, University of the West Indies
Medical Sciences Complex, Mount Hope, Champs Fleur, Trinidad

Abstract

Background: Undetected attention deficit hyperactivity disorder (ADHD) can result in a range of behavioural disturbances which create a burden for mental health, social and educational services when it persists into adulthood. Afflicted individuals do not maximize their academic or indeed intellectual potential and are more likely to have mood disorders and substance use related disorders in adulthood. Early recognition and intervention is therefore very important and serves as a preventive strategy to diminish the risk of behavioural dysfunction in adulthood.

Methods: Children referred to the courts for being out of control were assessed for a range of psychopathological symptoms and investigated for the presence of ADHD symptoms. They were then compared with an age and gender matched group of healthy secondary school students. Differences in ADHD symptoms and course were then compared by gender. Statistical analysis was then undertaken using correlation and significance testing. Retrospective analysis was also undertaken on a cohort of adult ADHD patients to determine the trajectory of their lives through adolescence to determine the points at which intervention could have occurred

Results: The children referred to the courts were much more likely to have ADHD symptoms though none of them had been previously diagnosed. These symptoms had contributed to poor academic performance and behavioural symptoms at home. They were also more likely to come from disruptive family backgrounds. The females were more likely to have had sexual experience and they were more likely to have initiated substance use.

A family history of criminal justice system contact also differentiated those with ADHD symptoms. Adults with ADHD underperformed or were excluded from school and initiated substance use and excessive gambling as early signs of adolescent dysfunction.

Discussion/Conclusion: The presence of unrecognized ADHD symptoms does increase the risk of major behavioural problems in early adolescence which are likely to persist into adulthood if they remain untreated. There is some indication that the symptom course may be different in females compared to males. There are associations with a disruptive upbringing suggesting that this may also contribute to the evolution of the disorder or perhaps to its lack of recognition. ADHD is particularly associated with substance use and impulsivity.

Introduction

The clinical syndrome that is Attention Deficit Hyperactivity Disorder (ADHD) was first systematically described in 1902 (Still, 1902), yet remains today an underdiagnosed and therefore undertreated condition that afflicts children and adults (Wender, 1998). Many of the children with this disorder are categorized as having primary behavioural problems such as conduct disorder and therefore little attention is paid to the influence of brain dysfunction that creates developmental problems such as ADHD. This is illustrated by findings among preschoolers which have shown that children with ADHD are likely to be more vocal, more often off task and out of seat and require more adult redirectives to return to task (De Wolfe et al, 1999). They also commit more errors in their work and are unable to sustain visual attention to specific tasks requiring multi skill coordination and therefore took longer to accomplish set tasks. This has implications for teachers who not recognizing the underlying problem may misleadingly target these children as oppositional or conduct disordered with resultant negative outcomes.

There has been a historical debate in the literature that underlines the connection between ADHD and conduct disorder, primarily because hyperactivity is inevitably associated with disruptive behaviour in children. Sergeant (2000) has postulated a three level cognitive energetic model to delineate this process. The first represents dysfunction in lower cognitive processes such as encoding, central processing and response organisation. The second consist of the energetic pool of arousal, activation and effort and the third to the management of executive function. Executive function deficiencies are primarily due to a failure of inhibition but this is shared with oppositional defiant and conduct disordered children. There is some suggestion that ADHD is more closely correlated with neurodevelopmental problems that conduct disordered behaviour which may be more associated with psychosocial difficulties. Distinction between familial influences that are acting biologically and socially is crucial here if one is to establish a means of prediction. However it is very likely that they act synergistically making it impossible to distinguish the relative contributions of heritability and environmental facilitation. The final common pathway however is undoubtedly some form of executive disinhibition (Nigg, 2003).

Attempts to clearly delineate the presence of ADHD from other disorders such as learning disability, autism, schizophrenia, depression, anxiety disorders particularly obsessive compulsive disorder and Tourette's disorders have led to the identification of the frontostriatal system in the brain as being fundamental (Bradshaw and Sheppard, 2000). Factor analysis of rating scales administered by both parents and teachers suggest that the hyperactive child is constantly fidgeting, restless and overactive, fails to finish things and is easily distracted. They also disturb other children. On the other hand the conduct disordered child is more likely to be irritable, touchy, disobedient,lie and be resentful and aggressive (Taylor et al, 1991). It is important that observations are made in a variety of settings but usually home and school are sufficient to make the diagnostic distinction. Other diagnostic entities that need to be distinguished form ADHD include mental retardation, and other developmental disorders both pervasive and specific. Although both ICD-10 and DSM-IV require that the diagnosis be made only when it can be confirmed that the symptoms began before age 6 years, it is sometimes difficult to distinguish between age appropriate overactivity and inattention from the presence of ADHD (American Psychiatric Association, 1994). Frequently this is done in hindsight after problems have arisen in school. However attention dysfunction that falls short of meeting the diagnostic criteria for ADHD is also implicated in a greater risk of substance use in adolescence as well as academic underachievement and problems at school (Merrell and Tymms, 2001; Tapert et al, 2002)

This has important implications for early recognition and treatment. The disorder tends to attenuate as the child grows older frequently disappearing altogether by late adolescence but in a range of approximately 5 - 30% of cases it persists into adulthood leading to a range of familial, educational and occupational problems (Biederman et al, 2000). One of the more interesting findings is the potential of the disorder to evolve into other disorders such as depression, antisocial activities and substance abuse (Barkley et al, 2004). Additionally, if the diagnosis had not been made in childhood, it becomes difficult to retrospectively confirm the presence of the symptoms before age 6 particularly if parents and caregivers are not available. According to DSM-IV (American Psychiatric Association, 1994), associated features would include low frustration tolerance, frequent temper outbursts, bossiness, stubbornness, excessive insistence that requests be met, mood lability, dysphoria, demoralization and rejection by peers. Epidemiological studies also suggest that ADHD is more common in boys than in girls with ratios ranging from 4:1 to 9:1.

Although biological and familial studies have confirmed that central nervous system abnormalities underlie the disorder though as in many psychiatric diagnoses no specific test or measurable neuropsychiatric impairment characterizes the disorder (Dunn and Kronenburger, 2003). Hoiwever there have been many replicated studies implicating the DRD4 and DRD5 receptor genes and the DAT1 transporter gene in the genetics of ADHD increasing the likelihood that the nature of the heritability will be elucidated (Kent, 2004). Similarly a potential genetic endophenotype for schizophrenia has been suggested to be sustained attention deficits (Chen and Faraone, 2000) therby underlining the relationships between neurodevelopmental disorders. The potential overlap of this endophenotype demands that a dimensional approach be undertaken for the classification and severity grading of the attention deficit hyperactivity disorder. The cutoff point must be both culturally and statistically significant for the presence of the disorder and its impact on the individual's life.

The other major evidence for the presence of the disorder is the successful treatment that is possible using psychostimulant medication (Wilens and Spencer, 2000). The success of methylphenidate has undoubtedly invited clinicians to make the diagnosis, making ADHD the most commonly diagnosed psychiatric disorder (Baird et al, 2000). This has contributed to fears regarding the overprescribing of the stimulant methylphenidate in the treatment of the disorder particularly in the United States (Taylor et al, 1991). One of the other controversies that has surrounded the diagnosis of ADHD is the use of psychostimulant treatment and the risk for dependence and future substance abuse. This has been shown to be a fairly negligible risk becoming discernible only when ADHD is definitely comorbid with conduct disorder and where there are independent confounders that contribute to substance dependence (Fischer and Barkley, 2003). As the International Consensus has established, the definitive diagnosis of ADHD should be treated with psychostimulant therapy aided and abetted by appropriate psychosocial interventions. Even when it is comorbid with other disruptive behaviour disorders, pharmacotherapy should be the first option of treatment. There is no rationale to avoid treatment given the high social and economic cost of the consequences arising out of its non treatment.

However the potentially deleterious outcomes that are likely to result from the comorbidity with substance abuse and mood disorders in adults, the search for non stimulant alternatives for treatment show a lot of promise. (Wilens et al, 2001).

These negative outcomes make this condition a major public health problem especially since the persistence of hyperactivity could also be related to the presence of other disorders and to the status of family life. A more adverse psychosocial family environment does contribute to a greater likelihood of persistence of symptoms and may be important in the genesis and recognition of the disorder. This is likely to be confounded by the non compliant behaviour of hyperkinetic children (Biederman et al, 2002). It is also confounded by gender as boys tend to have worse cognitive and interpersonal outcomes, engaging in more antisocial behaviour and having more learning disability than their female counterparts. Girls are however more sensitive to developing both attention and conduct problems when they have been exposed to family violence (Becker and McCloskey, 2002). There is also subtype variation with the combined type leading to more antisocial behaviour, criminal arrests, hostility, paranoia and even attempted suicide than the inattentive type (Murphy et al, 2002). This underlines the intersection of behaviours that occur with ADHD and a range of socially disruptive conditions that could have their origins in many other comorbid or independent disorders. Since both ADHD and disruptive behaviour disorders have been hypothesized to be due to an executive disinhibition which is likely to be familial or at least mediated through familial mechanisms. (Coolidge et al, 2000), identifying parental hyperkinesis should be an important component of assessment. Since ADHD is associated with greater risk of antisocial behaviour, depression and substance use, and these same factors occur more commonly in parents of hyperactive children , this also raises the question of how these various factors interact (Chronis et al, 2003). Parental risk for psychopathology seems directly related to hyperactivity in children as 80% of the risk for ADHD can be attributed to genetic factors (Biederman and Faraone 2002). Maternal nicotine exposure and the experience of psychosocial adversity are also associated. The Rutter index of adversity (Biederman et al, 2002) which include family discord, lower socioeconomic status, criminal and mental health problems in parents and family violence are the main contributors to psychosocial adversity. Perinatal risk and neonatal brain insults may also be implicated but seem to impact more directly on social and learning disability which in turn inccease the risk for ADHD (O'Callaghan and Harvey, 1997).

Delinquent behaviour has become a major problem in the contemporary world. Substance abuse, violence and suicide are now major causes of morbidity and mortality in this age range.and the roots of thee problems must lie in early childhood. The presence of subtle developmental pathologies and provide an appropriate means of intervention that could significantly prevent the occurrence of these problems in later life. Delinquent adolescents if not treated or have their course altered may end up as delinquent adults. This means that identifying the developmental pathways that inform delinquency in adolescence has long term benefits for any society. Retrospective studies that attempt to identify aetiological trends are fraught with bias. This bias is primarily a recal bias that causes mothers and individuals to search more diligently through their past to find potential reasons for the negative situations in which they currently find themselves. In addition, the benefit of current information and experience frequently leads to a re-evaluation of the past. ADHD presents an interesting parallel for the study of pathways to adult maladaptiveness. It is a disorder that begins early in childhood, causes a range of academic and interpersonal dysfunction and if not properly treated can persist into adulthood and there cause a range of maladaptive outcomes that are clearly distinguishable from those it influenced in childhood. Negative long term outcome has been shown to be primarily influenced by severity of symptoms, co-morbidity, suboptimal treatment and learning disability in terms of the disorder itself. In terms of the environment in which it occurs, parental pathology, lower socioeconomic status and family adversity are the crucial factors (Hechtman, 1999).

This study therefore attempts to establish the presence of ADHD in a group of adolescents referred to the probation and criminal justice system because of deviant behaviour and to compare them with age matched non-institutionalised peers. Risk factors associated with ADHD in this group of early adolescents who had been institutionalized because of deviant behaviour would also be identified. To further establish the influence of ADHD on development I would then review the case histories of 4 patients with ADHD and describe how their developmental trajectory had been compromised by this condition. . Missed opportunities for intervention and ways in which the outcomes could have been prevented will also be discussed.

METHODS

The adolescents were identified from the records of two institutions in Trinidad and Tobago which cater for boys and girls referred from the courts for institutional care after they had been reviewed and evaluated by the Probation department. These children would either have been referred by their parents or caregivers because they were incapable of disciplining and/or controlling their behaviour, theschool system because of persistent truancy or disruptive behaviour in school and the criminal justice system after the commission of minor crimes such as shoplifting.

The boys and girls are kept in separate institutions. There are no other facilities catering for this population in the country and therefore allows for a national perspective on the problem of delinquency. The Trinidad and Tobago population is estimated to be 1.3 million and is ethnically mixed , 40 % each of African and East Indian origin respectively and the remaining 20 % a polyglot of European, Chinese, Middle Eastern and Mixed ethnicity (Central Statistical Office 2002).

The entire cohort admitted over two years was identified and they were interviewed on a variety of measures. These included a demographic questionnaire that collected information on age, religion, education, living circumstances, parental occupation, living arrangements, and criminal history. Social and economic status, reasons for referral and admission were also documented. Age matched children attending high schools were recruited as controls.

Information on parental attitudes and experience of caregiving was obtained using the an that explored feelings about parents and any childhood experience of abuse. Educational records and interviews with parents and caregivers corroborated information from the children and established the presence of difficulties in early childhood. Sexual histories incluing age at first sexual intercourse experience and childhood sexual abuse and substance abuse histories were also obtained. The Conners Teacher Rating Scale (Conners, 1969) was administered to the caregivers and room supervisors in the institution who would have observed the children for at least 6 months. The Rosenberg Scale (Rosenberg, 1962) to measure self esteem, the Brief Psychiatric Rating Scale (BPRS) were also utilized to establish psychopathology (Lukoff et al, 1986). These were then completed by a clinical interview obtained from the Diagnostic Interview Schedule for Children (Shaffer et al, 1988) to confirm the presence of ADHD or other psychiatric diagnoses.

Two interviewers conducted the various interviews and the interrater reliability was calculated at Kappa = 0.79 after the interviewers were involved in a pilot interviewing process at a secondary school. The psychiatric interview was undertaken by a trained psychiatrist.

Case histories of 4 patients confirmed with ADHD are also described to document the effects of long term existence without treatment of this disorder and to identify points of missed opportunity and intervention where the deleterious outcomes could have been averted.

RESULTS

A total of 130 institutionalised adolescents were seen (75 girls and 55 boys) and 117 controls 64 girls and 53 boys).

The age range of the entire sample was 11-16 years with a mean of 13.7 (standard deviation 0.8 years) for boys and 13.1 (0.5 years) for girls. The mean ages for the controls was 13.6 for boys and 13.3 for girls. Firstly a brief overview of the children in the institution.

Reasons for Referral

The major reasons for referral and admission to these homes were running away from home and truancy from school (31.3%), stealing (25.7%) and violent confrontations with parents or other adults (19.0%). Girls were more likely to engage in running away and truancy (P = 0.0734) while there was little difference between boys and girls for the other two categories.

Ethnicity

Children of African descent were over represented (69.2%) when compared to the general population, this was very significant (P = 0.00007) There was gender difference in this regard.

Religion

Roman Catholics comprised the majority of the sample (41.5%) compared with other Christian religions (32.4%) and the other non-Christian religions such as Hinduism and Islam.

Education

A significant majority of the children were regarded as school failures having failed the examination that would allow them entry to high school. This amounted to 54% of the sample and compared to the national average at that time of 20% (P = 0.00001).

Most of their behaviour that led to admission to these homes had occurred after their failure of the secondary (high) school entrance examination

Presence of ADHD

32 of the 130 adolescents in the institutions met the criteria for ADHD (24.6%) compared to 5 of the 117 high school children (4.3%) This was significant at a P value of 0.00004.Boys were 5 times more likely to have ADHD (Odds ratio 4.8, 95% confidence interval 2.7-7.3)

Parental Upbringing

There was no significant difference between the two groups in terms of parental upbringing.

One third of both samples was raised by both parents (32% and 35 % respectively). While 37% and 39% were raised by single parents predominantly mothers and the remaining 31% and 26% respectively a combination of stepparents and extended family.

The children with ADHD were more likely to be raised by stepparents or extended family (P = 0.007)

Physical Health

Children with ADHD were more likely to have allergic disorders (P = 0.06)

Thirty percent of the sample had a history of allergic type disorders including asthma, sinusitis, eczema, most with more than one of these disorders. There was no evidence of the prevalence of any other chronic illnesses. For example there were no type 1 diabetes mellitus patients, no known malignancies or children who had been hospitalized for long periods in their past.

Sexual Abuse

Sexual abuse was far more likely to have been experienced by girls (46%) compared to boys (8%). Male relatives either first or second degree were the most likely perpetrators of the abuse in both boys and girls. There was a trend for those with ADHD to have had an experience of sexual abuse P = 0.07

Opinion on Home life

Most of the sample had a positive opinion of home life (67%) however girls were more likely than boys to have a negative opinion of their home experiences, mostly because of the experience of sexual abuse (36% of girls compared to 8% of boys).

Age at First Intercourse

One quarter of the sample admitted to being sexually active and engaged in consensual sexual activity. Twenty percent of the sample had their first consensual sexual encounter between the ages of 11 and 13.

Wage Earning Activity

Twenty percent of the sample had been engaged in full or part time employment prior to admission to the homes. This was entirely a female enterprise and they were variously employed as baby sitters, pavement sales vendors, waitresses, domestic servants and prostitutes. Some held more than one job eg baby sitters during the day and waitresses at night. This did not apply to the secondary school population at all as none of them were engaged in such behaviour. However, none of the females so engaged met the criteria for ADHD.

Socio Economic Status and Housing

There was no differences between those with ADHD and those without with regard to socioeconomic status. Most of the sample was from social class III and IV. Only 28% came from families who owned cars and 20% from families who owned their own homes. Thirty five percent had telephones in their households.

Family History of Criminal Behaviour

Children with ADHD were more likely to have a parent with a criminal history P = 0.00006

Forty three percent of the sample had first or second degree relatives who had been convicted of criminal offences in the past. Offences ranged from possession of drugs to murder. This was more likely to be true for boys (48%) than for girls (38%).

Family History of Substance Abuse

Children with ADHD were also ore likely to have a parent with a history of substance abuse P = 0.002

Thirty five percent had a relative with a substance abuse problem. Most of these were cannabis and/or cocaine.

Co-Morbidity

Co-morbidity with other psychiatric disorders occurred in 30% of those with ADHD including depression and substance abuse compared with 12 % in those without ADHD (P = 0.008). Overactivity and inattention were the dimensions most represented when compared with impulsivity.

Low self esteem was seen in 46% of the total sample but significantly was found in 86% of the children with ADHD Ccompared to 26% in those without (P =0.0006). Only 2 children had psychotic symptoms, both of whom were diagnosed with bipolar disorder. There was general concurrence between the caregivers at the institutions and the parents with regard to the children found to have ADHD.

Regression Analysis

The factors which were independently associated with the presence of ADHD were a family history of criminal behaviour or substance abuse and the presence of another psychiatric disorder in the child

Case Histories

Case 1 is a 22 year old man referred because of excessive gambling and substance abuse who had exhibited symptoms of overactivity and impulsivity. He had been referred for evaluation at several stages in his school career as he was thought to be underachieving.

However this remained limited to visual and intellectual testing.

On examination, he fulfilled criteria for ADHD including predominantly symptoms of hyperactivity-impulsivity. He had begun drinking heavily at age 17 as he found that alcohol helped him to temper his outbursts but it too had grown out of control and he was now drinking daily. In the previous 2 years, he had begun gambling in an attempt to find an outlet for his extra energy and seemed intent on destroying himself. His parents had broken up at an early point in the marriage and he suspected his father of also having a problem with alcohol though he did not think that he had ADHD.

Case 2 is a 19 year old young lady who lived in a home with 6 other siblings but had been expelled from school for fighting after several reports that she was disruptive and inattentive from her teachers. This was at age 14 and culminated a tumultuous school career that arose out of many instances of fighting, leaving classes and seemingly always distracted. Her mother reported at home the same occurred with constant fidgeting and interfering with household items while having difficulty establishing relationships with siblings. There was no substance abuse here.

Case 3 was a young 22 year old lady referred by her Employee Assistance Programme (EAP) because of distractibility at work, always telling jokes and not completing her assignments because of these unnecessary distractions.. She exhibited similar symptoms since early childhood and was described as a capable but distracted child who was not fulfilling her potential in her school reports. She had no family history of ADHD and no history of substance abuse.

Case 4 is a 35 year old man referred by a substance abuse rehabiliotation centre where his fidgeting and inability to function effectively in groups because of his inadvertent answering of questions and inability to not interrupt others when they were speaking alerted the psychologist that this might be a case of ADHD. This turned out to be true as he too had underperformed at school and was suspended several times for fighting and stealing things though he admitted that he was seeking excitement and always returned what he stole. He felt unable to control his impulses and felt as he was driven by a motor. He had worked in a variety of jobs and invariably was fired for his inability to finish assigned tasks effectively. He had no known family history of substance abuse or ADHD.

Discussion

These findings underline the importance of early recognition and aggressive treatment of ADHD. The presence of ADHD can profoundly affect the families of the children affected as well as their general health and education , and contribute to major societal problems. While the absolute number of ADHD cases identified here among these children apprehended for deviant behaviour ((32) are not great, they represent a significant minority whose problems may have been effectively solved had their ADHD been treated. The appropriate management of diagnosed ADHD is now universally acknowledged to be successful and efficacious and combines pharmacotherapy and behaviour and family therapy. Pharmacotherapy consists of stimulants and antidepressants although some antihypertensives eg clonidine have also been reported to be effective (Kutcher et al, 2004). The overrepresentation of adolescents with deviant behaviour compared to a school attending population suggests that assessment in schools with behavioural problems may identify underlying ADHD.

The association with allergies is interesting as some studies have shown that children with atopic disorders are more likely to have psychopathology when compared with their peers (Mrazek, 2003). However it is unclear whether this is due to the burden of a chronic and irritating illness than to a real biological association between atopy and psychopathology. For ADHD, the evidence is mixed (Gaitens et al, 1998) but there does seem to be some kind of relationship as evidenced by the findings of this study. This offers another means of prevention and early recognition. Routine screening at paediatric clinics would be a means to identify children with ADHD in particular and other psychiatric disorders in general among this population. Children who attend these clinics with non specific problems should also be identified.

Another route of prevention would be accident and emergency services since children with ADHD are more likely to be involved in accidents and physical injury (King et al, 2003). This arises out of the impulsive behaviour central to the ADHD behaviour spectrum. This may also be related to the high rates of co morbidity with diagnoses such as childhood depression which may also lead to self destructive behaviour. There is an increased rate of other psychiatric disorders in children and adults with ADHD so there should always be a high index of suspicion particularly when seeing patients with mood disorders and substance abuse (Burd et al, 2003). Treatment of the ADHD may prove to be more cost effective in the long term management of the individual. ADHD pathology should always be considered when children and adolescents are being evaluated.

Family history is perhaps the greatest mechanism of establishing those children at risk. Since it is unlikely that parents would have been diagnosed with the disorder even if they had it, the associated disorders of substance abuse and depression and perhaps bipolar disorder must be considered as high risk for having children with ADHD. In addition, criminal behaviour and the absence of supervisory parenting would increase the vulnerability for children exposed to this to have the resilience to prevent the development of ADHD. It has been shown that parental substance abuse increases the risk of adolescent substance use in children with ADHD independent of the genetic risk (Biederman et al, 2000)

The poor educational attainment of the institutionalized children is also a sign that in addition to ADHD they are more likely to have other developmental academic problems which inhibited their ability to perform well in school and increased the likelihood of becoming involved in deviant behaviour. Since attention deficits can begin having negative effects in early childhood, it is likely that educational progress from very early in life is stunted and perhaps labeled as oppositional or conduct disordered behaviour (DeWolfe et al, 1999). This has obvious deleterious consequences for long term interaction with the educational system (Daley, 2004).

The lack of association with low socioeconomic status suggests that this may be a proxy for environments where there might be more severe parental discord or family disruption leading to a chaotic upbringing. This also underlines the powerful contribution of an inherent biological vulnerability. In affecting families, however it may lead to a recurring cycle of under-optimisation of potential to fulfill intellectual and social potential. The problems with education are complex because if there are no mechanisms to address educational failure these children become long term casualties of the social system and are more likely to be excluded from social functioning. This in turn increases their risk of antisocial behaviour and further isolation and stigmatization leading to an unending cycle of deviance and likely long term criminal histories particularly in boys. There has been some speculation about the falling educational achievement of boys compared to girls in general and this is borne out here though it may be that this is being mediated by a greater risk of ADHD in boys. The association of this disorder with lowered self esteem may be germane to this discussion and the negative impact it could have not just on life trajectory but on perception of possibilities and therefore setting of goals and realistic planning to achieve them (Daley, 2004). The variability of the clinical syndrome of ADHD could also contribute to this (Burd et al, 2003). It has been suggested that ADHD Combined type is more likely to be associated with aggressive behaviour than ADHD Inattentive type which is more likely to be associated with social passivity and deficits in social knowledge leading to low estimation of social worth (Maedgen and Carlson, 2000).

A major question that needs to be resolved is whether the disability evident in adults who have had childhood ADHD is due to the persistence of the disease or to the disruptions caused in childhood. Certainly the problems associated with a lack of completing one's education successfully would be a factor in future occupational dissatisfaction for example. Similarly as evidenced by these children surveyed in this study, becoming institutionalised is likely at this early age can result in an increasing risk of further antisocial behaviour. However one longitudinal study (Mannuzza and Klein, 2000) has shown that it is the maintenance of the ADHD symptoms that is responsible for substance abuse and antisocial behaviour in late teenage and early adult life. There may also be shared heritability between certain learning disabilities and a range of psychopathological conditions such as anxiety and mood disorders. Addiction behaviour and ADHD may share important connection in terms of biological markers such as dopamine reward systems in the brain and clinical correlates. This means that children of substance abusers as we have found here would be more likely to have ADHD though it would be difficult to control for the confounding effect of poor parenting in such a situation.

Maintenance of ADHD symptoms in adulthood may therefore be facilitated by the presence of comorbid disorders and thereby greatly increasing the risk of relationship, academic and occupational dysfunction (Trollor, 1999). The role of impulsivity in sexual functioning for example needs to be addressed. Many of these children had been sexually abused, does ADHD increase the risk of that occurring or does sexual abuse increase the risk of mild inattention or hyperactivity symptoms developing into ADHD? There is little literature on this subject. However impaired judgment and impulsivity could lead to injudicious sexual choices and therefore a greater risk of sexually transmitted diseases including HIV/AIDS and perhaps more significantly maladaptive partner choices. These in turn would result in problem parenting and a perpetuation of the cycle of deviance and underachievement. It would also be the source of great psychoemotional distress and unhappiness.

The persistence of the disease into adulthood and a range of presentations underline s the importance of early diagnosis and treatment. The evolution into acts such as gambling, substance use and even sexual overactivity have not been sufficiently explored. The risk for mood disorders and substance abuse have been addressed but not how to ensure that clinicians are made aware of the possible existence of underlying ADHD as the main predisposition to these other conditions that are quite prevalent in their own right.

Treatment across the life course is now extremely effective and while there remain uncertainties about the ideal duration of treatment, clinical judgment should serve as the best guide.

References

American Psychiatric Association (1994) Diagnostic and Statistical Manual of Mental Disorders. *DSM-IV™* American Psychiatric Press, Washington.

Baird J, Stevenson JC and Williams DC (2000) The evolution of ADHD: a disorder of communication? *Quarterly Review of Biology* 75 (1), 17-35

Barkley RA, Fischer M., Smallish L and Fletcher K (2004) Young adult follow up of hyperactive children: antisocial activities and drug use. *Journal of Child Psychiology and Psychiatry* 45 (2), 195-211.

Becker KB and McCloskey LA (2002) Attention and conduct problems in children exposed to family violence. *American Journal of Orthopsychiatry* 72 (1), 83-91.

Biederman J, Faraone SV and Montuceaux MC (2002) Differential effect of environmental adversity gy gender. Rutter's index of adversity in a group of boys and girls with and without ADHD. *American Journal of Psychiatry* 159 (9), 1556-1562.

Biederman J and Faraone SV (2002) Current concepts in the neurobiology of ADHD. *Journal of Attention Disorder* 6 (suppl 1), S7-12

Biederman J, Mick E and Faraone S. (2000) Age dependent decline of symptoms of attention deficit hyperactivity disorder: impact of remission definition and symptom type. *American Journal of Psychiatry* 157(5), 816-818.

Biederman J, Faraone SV, Monuteaux MC and Feighner JA (2000) Patterns of alcohol and drug use in adolescents can be predicted by parental substance use disorders. *Pediatrics* 106 (4), 792-797.

Bradshaw JL and Sheppard DM (2000) The neurodevelopmental frontostriatal disorders: evolutionary adaptiveness and anomalous lateralization. *Brain and Language* 73 (2), 297-320.

Burd L, Klug MG, Coumbe MJ and Kerbeshian J (2003) The attention deficit hyperactivity disorder paradox : 2.Phenotypic variability in prevalence and cost of comorbidity. *Journal of Child Neurology,* 18 (9), 653-660.

Central Statistical Office (2002) *Prelimanry Report on Population of Trinidad and Tobago.* The 2000 Census. Central Staistical Office, Ministry of Planning and Development, Port of Spain, Trinidad and Tobago.

Chen WJ and Faraone SV (2000) Sustained attention deficits as markers of genetic susceptibility to schizophrenia. *American Journal of Medical Genetics* 97 (1), 52-57.

Chronis AM, Lahey BB, Pelham WE, Kipp HL, Baumann BL and Lee SS (2003) Psychopathology and substance abuse in parents of young children with ADHD. *Journal of American Academy of Child and Adolescent Psychiatry* 42 (12), 1424-1432.

Conners CK (1969) A teacher rating scale for use in drug studies with children. American *Journal of Psychiatry*, 126, 884-888.

Coolidge FL, Thede LL and Young SE (2000) Heritability and the comorbidity of attention deficit hyperactivity disorder with behavioural disorders and executive function deficits: a preliminary investigation. *Developmental Neuropsychology* 17 (3), 273-287.

Daley KC (2004) Update on attention deficit hyperactivity disorder. *Current Opinion Pediatrics* 16 (2), 217-226.

De Wolfe NA, Byrne JM and Bawden HN (1999) *Early clinical assessment of attention Clinical Neuropsychology* 13 (4), 458-473.

Dunn DW and Kronenburger WG (2003) Attention deficit hyperactivity disorder in children and adolescents. *Neurology Clinics* 21 (4), 933-940.

Fischer M and Barkley RA (2003) Childhood stimulant treatment and risk for later substance abuse. *Journal of Clinical Psychiatry* 64 (suppl 11), 19-23.

Gaitens T, Kaplan BJ and Freigang B. (1998) *Absence of an association between Ig-E mediated atopic responsiveness and attention deficit hyperactivity disorder symptomatology*. 39 (3), 427-431.

Hechtman L (1999) Predictors of long term outcome of children with ADHD. *Pediatric Clinics of North America 46*)5), 1039-1052.

Kent L (2004) Recent advances in the genetics of attention deficit hyperactivity disorder *Current Psychiatry Reports 6* (2), 143-148.

Kutcher S., Aman M, Brooks SJ, Buitelaar J, van Daalen E, Fegert J, Findling RI, Fisman S, Greenhill LL, Huss M, Kusumaker V, Pine D, Taylor E and Tyano S. (2004) International consensus statement on ADHD and disruptive behaviour disorders (DBD): clinical implications and treatment practice suggestions. *European Neuropsyhopharmacology* 14 (1), 11-28.

Lukoff D, Liberman RP and Neuschterlein KH (1986) Symptom monitoring in the rehabilitation of schizophrenia patients. *Schizophrenia Bulletin,* 12 (4), 578-602

Maedgen JW and Carlson CL (2000) Social functioning and emotional regulation in the sttention deficit hyperactivity subtypes. *Journal of Clinical Child Psychology* 29 (1), 30-42.

Mannuzza S and Klein RG (2000) Long term prognosis in ADHD. Child and Adolescent *Psychiatric Clinics of North America* 9 (3), 711-726.

Merrell C and Tymms PB (2001) Inattention, hyperactivity and impulsiveness. Impact on academic achievement and progress. *British Journal of Educational psychology* 71 (1), 43-56.

Mrazek DA. (2003) Asthma and psychopathology. *Child and Adolescent Psychiatric Clinics of North America* 12 (3), 459-471.

Murphy KR, Barkley RA and Bush T (2002) Young adults with an attention deficit hyperactivity disorder: subtype differences in comorbidity, educational and clinical history. *Journal of Nervous and Mental Disease* 190 (3), 147-157.

Nigg JT (2003) Response disinhibition and disruptive behaviour: toward a multiprocess conception of etiologic heterogeneity for ADHD. *Annals of the New York Academy of Sciences* 1008, 170-182.

O'Callaghan MJ and Harvey JM (1997) Biological predictors and co-morbidity of ADHD in extremely low birthweight infants at school. Journal of Pediatrics and Child Health 33 (6), 491-496.

Rosenberg M (1962) The association between self esteem and anxiety. *Journal of Psychiatric Research* 1, 135-152.

Sergeant J (2000) The cognitive energetic model: an empirical approach to attention deficit hyperactivity disorder. *Neuroscience and Biobehavioural Review* 24 (1), 7-12.

Shaffer D, Schwab-Stone M, Fisher P, Davies M, Piacentini J and Gioia P (1986) A revised version of the Diagnostic Interview Schedule for Children (DISC-R) . Results of a field rial and proposals for a new instrument. Rockville MD: Epidemiology and Psychopathology Research Branch, *National Institute of Mental Health, Washington*, DC

Still FG (1902) Some abnormal physical conditions in childhood. *Lancet I*, 1008.

Tapert SF, Baratta MV, Abrantes AM and Brum SA (2002) Attention dysfunction presicts substance involvement in community youths *Journal of the American Academy of Child and Adolescent Psychiatry* 41 (6), 680-686.

Taylor E., Sandberg S., Thorley G. and Giles S (1991) *The Epidemiology of Childhood Hyperactivity. Maudsley Monograph* 33, Institute of Psychiatry, Oxford University Press, Oxford.

Trollor JN (1999) ADHD in adults: conceptual and clinical issues. *Medical Journal of Australia* 171 (8), 421-425.

Wender PH (1998) ADHD in adults. Psychiatric Clinics of North America 21 (4), 761-774.

Wilens TE and Spencer TJ (2000) The stimulants revisited. *Child Psychiatric Clinics of North America* 9 , 573-603.

Wilens TE, Spencer TJ, Biederman J, Girard K, Doyle R, Prince J, Polisner D, Solhikah R, Corneau S, Monuteaux MC and Parekh A. (2001) A controlled clinical trial of bupropion for attention deficit hyperactivity disorder in adults. *American Journal of Psychiatry* , 158 (2), 282-288.

INDEX

A

D

E

F

G

H

I

J

K

L

M

N

O

P

Q

R

S

W

Y